John Herbert Sangster

Natural Philosophy

Volume 2

John Herbert Sangster

Natural Philosophy
Volume 2

ISBN/EAN: 9783337080532

Printed in Europe, USA, Canada, Australia, Japan

Cover: Foto ©Thomas Meinert / pixelio.de

More available books at **www.hansebooks.com**

LOVELL'S SERIES OF SCHOOL BOOKS.

NATURAL PHILOSOPHY,

PART II,

BEING A

HAND-BOOK OF CHEMICAL PHYSICS;

OR,

The Physics of Heat, Light, and Electricity.

BY

JOHN HERBERT SANGSTER, M.A.,

MATHEMATICAL MASTER AND LECTURER IN CHEMISTRY AND NATURAL
PHILOSOPHY IN THE NORMAL SCHOOL FOR UPPER CANADA.

Montreal:
PRINTED AND PUBLISHED BY JOHN LOVELL,
AND SOLD BY ROBERT MILLER.

Toronto:
ADAM MILLER, 62 KING STREET EAST.

1864

Entered, according to the Act of the Provincial Parliament, in the year one thousand eight hundred and sixty-one, by JOHN LOVELL, in the Office of the Registrar of the Province of Canada.

PREFACE.

The design of the Author in preparing the following pages was to furnish the student with a brief yet comprehensive *resumé* of all that is important in the departments of natural science of which it treats. He believes that the student of chemistry will find included all that is necessary or desirable as an introduction to that important branch of knowledge, without being so diffuse as to extend to several hundred pages. He has aimed throughout at being as clear and as concise as possible in his definitions, explanations, and statements; and, on that account, he feels confident that teachers who employ his little work as a text-book in their schools will find their pupils master the matter with much more ease than by the use of, it may be, an equally comprehensive but less condensed treatise. Whenever the nature of the subject has permitted the use of problems to illustrate and enforce particular principles, they have been introduced, so that the plan adopted in Part I. has been steadily kept in view in the preparation of the present book. It is believed that the entire work, including Parts I. and II., is calculated to impart a much more complete and practical knowledge of Natural Philosophy than the text-books on that science commonly met with in our schools; however that may be, the Author submits it to the kind consideration of his fellow-teachers, with the hope that it may be found to supply, in a measure at least, the want of a reliable text-book on the subject in our Canadian series of school-books.

The Author avails himself of this opportunity of returning his thanks to Professor Kingston, of the Toronto Observatory, for valuable information furnished him by that gentleman with regard to the declination of the magnetic needle in Canada.

TORONTO, October, 1861.

CONTENTS.

	PAGE
Heat, Definitions of	5
" Theories as regards	6
" Sources of	7
" Transferrence of	8
" Conduction of	9
" Convection of	10
" Radiation of	11
" Reflection of	12
" Absorption of	14
" Transmission of	14
Theory of Exchanges of Heat	15
Expansion of Gases	17
Air Thermometer	17
Differential Thermometer	18
Expansion of Liquids	18
Mercurial Thermometer	19
Reduction of Thermometric Scales	21
Intensity and Quantity of Heat	22
Expansion of Solids	23
Breguet's Thermometer	24
Pyrometers	25
Exceptions to Laws of Expansion	26
Specific Heat	28
Calorimeter	30
Problems on Specific Heat	31
Specific Heat of Elementary Atoms	33
Melting Points	35
Latent Heat	37
Freezing Mixtures	38

CONTENTS.

	PAGE
Boiling Points	40
Nature of Vapours	42
Elastic Force of Vapours and Gases	44
Ebullition, Theory of Boiling	46
Elevation of Boiling Points	46
Depression of Boiling Points	47
High Pressure Steam	50
Elastic Force of Steam	51
Latent Heat of Steam	53
Spontaneous Evaporation	54
The Cryophorus	55
Hygrometers	56
Spheroidal State	58
Sun and Stars as Sources of Heat	61
The Earth as a Source of Heat	62
Light, Theories as regards	64
" Definitions of	65
Photometry	67
Decomposition of Light	68
Newton's Spectrum	69
Magnitude of Colored Spaces	70
Brewster's Spectrum	72
Absorption of Light	74
Natural Coloration of Bodies	76
Complementary Colors	77
Theory of Transverse Vibrations	78
Interference of Light	79
Colors of Thin Films	81
" Grooved Surfaces	85
Heat as a Source of Light	85
Chemical Action as a source of light	87
Phosphorescence as a source of light	89
Fluorescence	90
Catoptrics, Definitions of	91
Reflection from Plane Mirrors	92
" Concave "	93
" Convex "	94
Problems	95

CONTENTS.

	PAGE
Formation of Images by Mirrors	98
Problems on Formation of Images	104
Dioptrics, Definitions of	105
Laws of Refraction	106
Indices of Refraction	106
Total Reflection	107
Lenses	108
Properties of Lenses	109
Rules for finding Focal Lengths of Lenses	111
Problems on Focal Lengths of Lenses	113
Formation of Images by Lenses	115
Magnifying Power of Lenses	116
Spherical Aberration	118
Chromatic Aberration	120
The Microscope	122
Problems on the Microscope	125
The Telescope	126
The Magic Lantern	129
The Camera Obscura	131
The Eye and Vision	131
Long and Short Sight	136
Color Blindness	138
Compound Eyes	138
Optical Phenomena of the Atmosphere	139
Polarization and Double Refraction	142
Electricity, Definitions of	146
" History of	147
" Conductors of	149
Electrics and non-Electrics	149
Insulation of Bodies	150
Sources of Electricity	150
Electroscopes	151
Electrometers	151
Theories of Electricity	153
Negative and Positive Fluids	153
Distribution of Free Electricity	155
Intensity, Tension and Quantity	156
Induction	156

CONTENTS.

	PAGE
Laws of Variation in Intensity	157
Electrical Machine	158
" " Theory of	159
Electrophorus	161
" Theory of	162
Leyden Jar	162
" Theory of	163
Varieties of Discharge	163
Effects of Discharge	164
Illustrative Experiments	165
Atmospheric Electricity	166
Lightning Rods	168
Dynamical Electricity	169
" " History of	172
Voltaic Piles	173
Voltaic Batteries	174
Ohm's Formulæ of Resistance	181
Effects of Voltaic Current	187
Chemistry of Voltaic Current	190
Electrolysis of Bodies	191
Faraday's Laws of Definite Action	192
Electro-Chemical Theory	193
Electrotype Process	193
Theories of Voltaism	194
Magnetism and Magnets	195
Properties of a Magnet	197
Dia-Magnetism	200
Formation of Magnets	201
Terrestrial Magnetism	204
Declination of Needle	205
Inclination of Needle	206
Theories of Terrestrial Magnetism	207
Electro-Magnetism	209
Electric Telegraph	212
Magneto-Electricity	215
Thermo-Electricity	217
Animal Electricity	217
Miscellaneous Problems	218

CHEMICAL PHYSICS.

HEAT.

LECTURE I.

DEFINITIONS, THEORIES, SOURCES, CONDUCTION, CONVECTION.

DEFINITIONS.

1. Every body contains more or less of that mysterious agent to which the name *heat* or *caloric* has been applied.

2. When any substance possesses heat of greater intensity than the human body, it is, in common language, said to be hot or warm; when less, it is said to be cold.

3. Cold is merely the absence or abstraction of heat.

When we touch a body not containing heat of as great intensity as the hand, caloric is withdrawn from the latter and a sensation of cold is produced. Cold is therefore only a negative property; and it is necessary to remember that, since all bodies contain a greater or less amount of heat, *heat* and *cold* are simply relative terms, being analogous to the terms *positive* and *negative* in electricity.

4. It is customary with some writers to apply the term *heat* to the *sensation* experienced by touching a hot body, and the term *caloric* to the *agent* or *cause* which produces that sensation. In practice this distinction is not very rigidly observed, and in the following pages we shall use the terms indiscriminately.

5. We commonly speak of a portion of heat as a something that is capable of being *added, subtracted, multiplied, divided, conducted, conveyed, radiated, reflected, absorbed, transmitted,* &c.; but it must be distinctly borne in mind that, as the nature of caloric is a matter of pure hypothesis, these terms must be received with extreme caution, as merely convenient modes of describing facts, and not as explanations of those facts.

THEORIES AS TO THE NATURE OF HEAT.

6. Two theories have been advanced by philosophers for the explanation of thermal phenomena, and are known as

1st. The Corpuscular Theory, which regards heat as being a *fluid;* and,

2nd. The Wave Theory, which regards heat as being merely a *motion.*

7. According to the *corpuscular theory*, heat or caloric may be defined to be a highly elastic imponderable fluid of great tenuity, and of which the particles are possessed of indefinite self-repulsive powers. This fluid is supposed to pervade all space not actually occupied by material atoms, and to enter into the composition of different bodies in different proportions, thereby determining the degree of their fluidity, solidity, &c.

8. The *wave theory* assumes that every particle of every body in the universe is in a state of perpetual vibration, and that these vibrations, varying in extent and velocity, constitute or produce heat. It further assumes that this vibratory or oscillatory motion among the atoms of matter, has a constant tendency to equalize itself by communication from atom to atom, and from body to body, by means of waves or undulations propagated through the ether which is supposed to fill all space not actually filled with material atoms.

NOTE.—Many of the phenomena of heat are equally well explained by either of these hypotheses; others are rendered more intelligible by one than by the other, and some few seem to require a union of both suppositions for their satisfactory comprehension. The wave theory is adopted by many philosophers at the present day on account of the striking analogy of heat to light; the rays of heat, like those of light, being capable of reflection, refraction, absorption, polarization, &c.

SOURCES.

9. The principal sources of heat are :
 1st. The Sun and the Earth.
 2nd. Chemical Action.
 3rd. Friction.
 4th. Compression or Percussion.
 5th. Electricity.

10. Chemical action, including as it does all cases of combustion, is, after the sun and the earth, the most important source of heat.

Thus, every one is familiar with the fact that a large amount of heat is evolved during the burning of wood, coal, spirits, &c. When water is mixed with sulphuric acid in a glass vessel, the temperature of the mixture rises almost to the boiling point of water. So also when water is thrown upon quicklime, so much heat is evolved that it sometimes ignites wood.

11. Friction is a very important source of heat.

Thus, Rumford found that in boring a brass cannon $8\frac{1}{4}$ inches in diameter, the borer making 32 revolutions per minute under a pressure of 10,000 lbs., sufficient heat was generated to boil $18\frac{1}{2}$ lbs. of water in $2\frac{1}{2}$ hours.

As other examples of the development of heat by friction, we may mention the fact that the ungreased axles of waggons, railway cars, &c., sometimes take fire spontaneously; the custom of savages igniting wood by friction; the fact that in grinding steel swords, knives, axes, &c., small portions of the metal become incandescent, i. e. red hot.

12. The evolution of heat by compression seems to depend on its diminishing the bulk of the body; for, as a general rule, whenever a body is decreased in size, heat is evolved.

According to the corpuscular theory, this is easily accounted for. Thus all bodies are more or less porous, and the insensible heat they contain is condensed in their interstices. Now when a body is compressed, its pores are diminished in capacity, and, no longer capable of containing so much heat, a portion is pressed out and becomes sensible; just as when we take a wet sponge in the hand and compress it, a part of the contained water is expelled.

This fact is well explained by the action of the coining-press. Thus Bertholet placed a piece of copper in a press, and found that the evolution of heat was greatest at the first stroke, and diminished at each succeeding one; the temperature being elevated at each stroke as follows:

1st stroke.............. 17.8° Fahr.
2nd stroke.............. 7.5°   "
3rd stroke.............. 1.9°   "

We have additional examples of the production of heat by compression in the fact that a blacksmith can render a piece of soft iron red hot by rapidly hammering it; and a piece of German tinder can be ignited by strongly and suddenly compressing some air contained in a cylinder.

13. The heat produced by electricity, as for example in the galvanic battery, is among the most intense that can be obtained by artificial means, and is capable of melting many of the most refractory substances known.

TRANSFERENCE.

14. When a red-hot ball or other ignited mass is placed in the open air, it rapidly loses its heat, and its temperature sinks until it reaches that of the surrounding bodies. The heat thus lost is transferred by several modes:

1st. A part is carried away by the metallic support or other body on which the ignited mass rests. This process is called *conduction*.

2nd. A part is conveyed away by certain motions set up in the air. This is known as *convection*.

3rd. A part is emitted from the surface of the ignited mass in the form of rays, which pass in straight lines and with the velocity of light through a vacuum, and through air and certain other transparent media. This process is termed *radiation*.

Hence heat is transferred in three ways:

    1st. By Conduction;
    2nd. By Convection; and
    3rd. By Radiation.

NOTE.—The term *conduction* is objectionable, as it implies that the particles of a body are in contact, which we know to be impossible. Hence Conduction is properly called *Interstitial Radiation*, or radiation from particle to particle across the inter-molecular spaces.

CONDUCTION.

15. Different bodies possess the power of conducting heat in very different degrees. Those which, like the metals, readily convey it, are, in common language, called *conductors*, while those along which it passes but imperfectly are termed *non-conductors*.

It must be remembered, however, that the terms *conductor and non-conductor* are merely relative terms. In point of fact, all substances conduct heat, but some much more perfectly than others, and hence there is no body that is absolutely a non-conductor.

The following table given by Despretz, shows the relative conducting powers of different bodies, expressing that of gold as 1000:

TABLE OF CONDUCTING POWERS.

Gold...........	1000	Tin............	304
Silver..........	973	Lead...........	180
Copper.........	898	Marble.........	24
Iron............	374	Porcelain.......	14
Zinc............	363	Clay............	11

16. Liquids and gases are very imperfect conductors, and when they become warmed it is generally by the convection rather than by the conduction of heat.

This may be clearly illustrated by holding a test-tube nearly filled with water so that the flame of a spirit-lamp may be directed against the upper part, when it will be found that the upper portion of the water may be made to boil without elevating the temperature of that in the lower part of the tube to any appreciable extent.

17. The advantage of using light porous fabrics such as woollens, silk, cotton, fur, &c., for clothing, is referable to the fact that these hold entangled in their meshes a portion o atmospheric air, which, like all other gases, is a very imperfect conductor.

The finer the fabric of the cloth, the more perfectly does it hold he air imprisoned among its fibres, and hence the warmer it is as an article of clothing. The down of the eider-duck is almost unrivalled in this respect.

In accordance with this fact, it is found that if the fibres are pressed into close contact, the non-conducting power of the cloth is very much impaired.

From the fact that air is an excellent non-conductor, arises the use of double windows for preserving the heat in apartments; the stratum of air between the windows offering an almost impassable barrier to the escape of the heat contained in the room. Hence also ice-houses are constructed with double walls, and the surface of the ice covered with saw-dust, woollen cloths, straw, &c., in order to preserve it. It is also partly on accoun of the air contained within its pores, and partly from the fact that it is itself a very imperfect conductor, that snow acts as a protective covering to the earth, preventing its temperature from sinking as low as it would do otherwise.

CONVECTION.

18. When a liquid or a gas is warmed, the process is carried on principally by convection, i.e. by the particles which come in contact with the source of heat *flying off and carrying with them* a certain amount of caloric, which they distribute among the cooler overlying portions.

Fig. 1.

It follows that when a liquid or a gas is heated from below, currents are produced; as may be beautifully shown by placing a lighted lamp under a flask containing water, with which is mixed some fine insoluble powder, as pulverized amber. The small fragments of amber will be seen to rise in the centre, gradually flow off towards the sides, and then fall again towards the bottom.

NOTE.—An important inference from this fact is that in a room which has to be warmed by a fire-place or a stove, the grate or the stove must be placed at or near the floor.

LECTURE II.

RADIATION, ABSORPTION, TRANSMISSION, THEORY OF EXCHANGES OF HEAT.

RADIATION.

19. Heat is emitted from the surface of a hot body equally in all directions, and always in straight lines.

20. The intensity of radiant heat varies inversely as the square of the distance from its source.

*Thus, if a certain amount of heat fall upon a given surface at the distance of one foot from the ignited mass, at the distance of two feet only *one-fourth* as much, and at the distance of three feet only *one-ninth* as much, will impinge upon it.

21. The rapidity of the radiation of heat from hot bodies is influenced in a remarkable manner by the nature and condition of their surfaces.

Thus, it has been found that—
1st. Bright and polished surfaces radiate heat very slowly.
2nd. Metals equally polished radiate heat with equal rapidity.
3rd. The radiating power of a metal is increased by roughening its surface or by coating it with lampblack, or tightly covering it with linen, &c.
4th. The radiating power of a body does not depend altogether on the degree of polish, since glass equally polished with metallic surfaces radiates heat much more rapidly.
5th. The radiating power of a surface is not affected by its color; hence no particular color is better adapted than another for winter clothing.

NOTE.—The absorbing power of bodies for heat depends closely on their color.

22. In order to observe the radiating power of unlike surfaces, Rumford obtained two similar brass cylinders, both highly polished, and, having surrounded one with a tight covering of linen, filled them both with boiling water. He then found that the water in the uncovered cylinder cooled 10° F.

in 55 minutes, while that in the other cooled 10° F. in 36½ minutes; or, in other words, the water in the naked vessel required half as long again to cool through a given number of degrees as that in the covered one.

23. Sir John Leslie investigated the radiating power of different surfaces by placing hot water in square tin canisters coated with various substances. Presenting these surfaces in succession to a parabolic reflector, he concentrated the radiated heat upon a differential thermometer, and then compared the results.

The following table expresses the relative radiating powers of the various substances with which the canister was coated,—that of lampblack being represented by 100:

TABLE OF RADIATING POWERS.

Lampblack	100	Plumbago	75
Water (by estimate)	100	Tarnished lead	45
Writing paper	98	Polished lead	19
Sealing-wax	95	Polished iron	15
Crown-glass	90	Other metals polished	12

It hence appears that lampblack radiates *five times* as much heat as polished lead, nearly *seven times* as much as polished iron, and about *eight and a half times* as much as polished gold, silver, tin, brass, &c.

This explains why it is more advantageous to use bright metallic tea-pots than those made of porcelain,—the former keeping the beverage hot much longer than the latter; also the use of bright metallic covers for dishes at table, &c.

24. When radiant heat falls on a surface, any one of three things may occur:

    1st. It may be reflected;
    2nd. It may be absorbed; or,
    3rd. It may be transmitted.

NOTE.—It may be partly reflected and partly absorbed, partly absorbed and partly transmitted, or partly reflected and partly transmitted.

REFLECTION.

25. The rays of heat, like those of light, may be collected in a focus. Thus if a heated body, as a hot ball of iron (C), be

placed in the focus of a concave parabolic reflector (A), the diverging rays that fall upon the reflector become parallel in

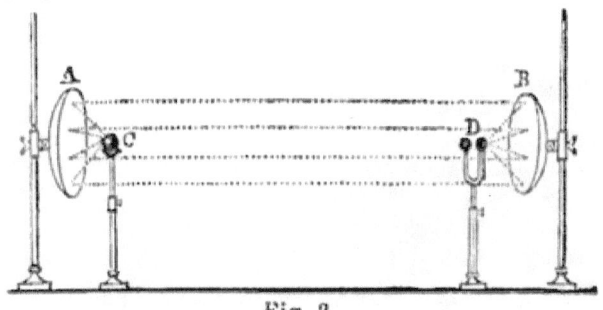

Fig. 2.

direction; and if these parallel rays be made to impinge upon a second concave parabolic reflector (B), they become convergent and are reflected to a focus (D). If a screen be interposed between the mirrors and some phosphorous be placed at D, upon withdrawing the screen the phosphorous instantly ignites.

NOTE.—If a snowball and a thermometer be made to occupy the foci of a pair of reflectors, the snowball begins to melt and the mercury in the thermometer falls. This was formerly explained by saying that the ball of snow radiates its cold to the thermometer; but as cold is merely a negative property, this is evidently impossible. In point of fact, the thermometer, which in this case is the hotter body, radiates heat to the ball of snow, and hence the melting of the latter and the fall of the mercury in the former.

26. There is an intimate connection between the radiating powers of different surfaces and their capabilities for reflecting or absorbing heat. Thus those surfaces—as lampblack, glass, &c.,—which radiate freely, also absorb a large part of the heat which falls upon them; while those that radiate and absorb but feebly,—as, for instance, the bright metals,—are excellent reflectors.

A polished metallic reflector remains perfectly cold although it collects a large amount of heat in its focus, while a glass reflector absorbs so much of the heat as to become itself hot.

27. The reflecting powers of different surfaces have been determined by Buff to be as follows:—Of 100 rays incident at an angle of 60 from the perpendicular, there were reflected—

ABSORPTION—TRANSMISSION.

TABLE OF REFLECTING POWERS.

By polished gold	76
" " silver or brass	62
" brass, not polished	52
" polished brass, varnished	41
" looking-glass	20
" glass-plate blackened on back	12
" metal-plate blackened	6

ABSORPTION.

28. Color influences to a very great degree the absorbent power of a surface for rays of heat when accompanied by rays of light. Thus with the rays of heat emitted by the sun or by any incandescent mass, the darker the color the more rapid the absorption; and hence the reason that dark-colored clothes are preferable for winter and light-colored for summer use.

TRANSMISSION.

29. Those substances that possess the power of transmitting heat through them as glass transmits light, are termed *diathermanous* or *transcalescent*.

30. The heat of the sun passes through any transparent body without loss; but only a portion of the heat from terrestrial sources is permitted to pass, and the amount transmitted increases as the temperature of the radiant body rises. Thus when the temperature of the radiant body was 180° F., $\frac{1}{10}$th of all the rays emitted passed through a screen of glass; when the temperature of the radiant body was 360° F., $\frac{1}{10}$ was transmitted; and when the temperature was 960° F., $\frac{1}{2}$th was transmitted.

31. Rays of heat which have passed through one plate, are less liable to absorption in passing through a second.

Thus Melloni found that out of 1000 colorific rays from an oil flame, 451 were intercepted in passing through four glass plates of equal thickness; and of these 451 rays—

381 were intercepted by the first plate.
43 " " second plate.
18 " " third plate.
9 " " fourth plate.

32. All transparent bodies are not equally transcalescent,—and indeed some good diathermanous bodies are opaque, or even black.

Thus Melloni placed plates one tenth of an inch in thickness before the flame of an Argand burner, and found that of 100 incident rays, there were transmitted by—

TABLE OF TRANSCALESCENCY.

Rock-salt.................................	92 rays.
Glass, rock crystal, and Iceland spar........	57 "
Emerald..................................	29 "
Fluor spar and citric acid..................	15 "
Rochelle salt and alum....................	12 "
Sulphate of copper........................	0 "

33. Rock-salt is the most perfectly diathermanous body known. Not only does it transmit the largest amount of the heat emanating from a body of given temperature, but it is the only substance that is equally transcalescent to heat of all intensities; a piece of rock-salt transmitting 92 per cent. of the incident rays of heat, whether they be radiated from the hand or from an incandescent body.

NOTE.—Lenses and prisms of rock-salt are as invaluable in experiments upon the transmission of heat, as those of glass are in researches into the nature of light.

THEORY OF EXCHANGES OF HEAT.

34. When several bodies of different temperatures are placed near one another, their temperatures gradually approximate until finally an equilibrium is attained. In order satisfactorily to explain this phenomenon, it has been supposed that bodies *exchange* heat at all times, no matter how different their temperatures may be. This hypothesis is known as the *theory of exchanges of heat*, and may be thus enunciated:

All bodies, no matter what their temperature, are radiating heat at all times, and the rate of radiation depends upon the temperature; increasing as the temperature rises, and decreasing as it falls.

Thus, if a red-hot cannon-ball and a mass of ice be placed near one another, they exchange heat,—the cannon-ball giving more and receiving less, and the ice giving less and receiving more; and this process of exchanging heat goes on even after an equilibrium of temperature has been attained, the only difference being that each body then gives as much heat as it receives.

LECTURE III.

EXPANSION OF GASES AND LIQUIDS, THERMOMETERS, THERMOMETRIC SCALES.

EXPANSION.

35. All bodies expand under the influence of an increasing temperature, and contract again as their temperature falls.

Thus the magnitude of all bodies is dependent on their temperature. A measure that is exactly a yard long in winter, is more than a yard long in summer; a vessel that will exactly hold a gallon in summer, will hold less than a gallon in winter; and the dimensions of all objects are subject to daily and hourly change.

This affords an explanation of the irregularity in the movements of our time-pieces. The longer the pendulum of the clock, or the greater the diameter of the balance-wheel of the watch becomes, the more slowly does it perform its oscillations; while if the pendulum be shortened or the balance-wheel lessened in diameter, the more rapidly does it move. But the pendulum and the balance-wheel are constantly varying in their dimensions, owing to increase and decrease of the temperature, and therefore the clock or the watch whose motions they govern does not keep exact time.

Hence arises the use of *compensation pendulums* for clocks, and *compensation balance-wheels* for watches.

36. Of the three forms of matter, gases expand most and solids least under the same increment of temperature.

Thus, heated from the freezing point to the boiling point of water—

EXPANSION OF GASES.

1000 cubic inches of Iron	become	1004
1000 " of Water	"	1045
1000 " of Atmospheric Air	"	1365

NOTE.—Since the attraction of cohesion acts most powerfully in solids and least powerfully in gases, and cohesion and caloric are antagonistic forces, it follows necessarily that the same increment of heat will produce a greater degree of expansion in a gas or liquid than in a solid.

EXPANSION OF GASES.

37. FIRST LAW.—*All permanently elastic gases, as atmospheric air, expand equally for the same increment of temperature, and the amount of this expansion is equal to $\frac{1}{491}$ of their volume at $32°$ Fahr. for every additional degree of Fahrenheit's thermometer.*

NOTE.—The fraction $\frac{1}{491}$ is called the coefficient of expansion of gases.

Thus 491 volumes of a gas at $32°$ Fahr. become

492	"	" " at $33°$	"
493	"	" " at $34°$	"
500	"	" " at $41°$	"
490	"	" " at $31°$	"
459	"	" " at $0°$	" &c.

38. SECOND LAW.—*The same gas expands with uniformity as its temperature rises.*

Thus 10 degrees of heat produce the same amount of expansion, whether applied to a portion of gas having a very high or a very low temperature.

39. The Air-Thermometer (called also Sanctorio's thermometer) consists of a tube of glass open at one end and Fig. 3. terminating in a large bulb at the other. The open end passes through a cork and dips beneath the surface of some colored water contained in a bottle. The bulb and upper part of the tube contain air; the lower part of the tube, to which a graduated scale is attached, is filled with a portion of the colored liquid contained in the bottle. When warmth is applied to the bulb, the air expands and forces down the column of colored liquid; so when cold is applied to the bulb, the contained air contracts, and the colored liquid rises into the tube, owing to the pressure of the atmosphere upon the surface of the water in the bottle. The movements of the column of colored water, either way, are measured by the attached graduated scale.

NOTE.—It is necessary to cut away part of the cork, so as to allow a free communication between the inside and the outside of the bottle; otherwise the air in the upper part of the bottle would expand, and by its elasticity counterbalance the downward pressure of the air in the bottle.

The indications of the air-thermometer are not to be relied on, as the movements of the column of colored liquid are as much influenced by atmospheric pressure as by temperature. This is at once shown by placing the air-thermometer in the receiver of an air-pump: directly we begin to exhaust the air, the column of colored liquid begins to descend, owing to the elastic force of the air in the bulb.

40. The Differential Thermometer (invented by Sir John Leslie) consists of a tube bent twice at right angles and terminating in a bulb at each end. The bulbs both contain air, and the tube is filled with sulphuric acid colored with indigo. It is called the *differential* thermometer because it indicates the difference of temperature of the air in the two bulbs. The principle on which it acts will be seen from the following facts:

Fig. 4

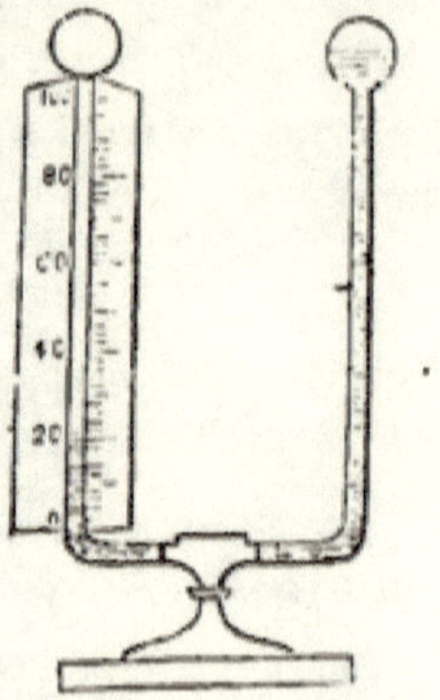

1. If both bulbs be subjected to the same degree of heat, the air in each expands or tends to expand equally, and consequently the column of liquid will not move at all.
2. If both bulbs be subjected to the same degree of cold, the air in each contracts or tends to contract equally, and consequently the colored fluid moves neither one way nor the other.
3. If one bulb be subjected to a greater degree of heat than the other, the air in that bulb expands and the fluid moves towards the other.
4. If one bulb be subjected to a greater degree of cold than the other, the air in that bulb contracts and the colored liquid moves toward it.

EXPANSION OF LIQUIDS.

41. FIRST LAW.—*All liquids do not expand equally for the same increment of temperature.*

EXPANSION OF LIQUIDS. 19

Thus, when heated from the freezing-point to the boiling-point of water,

Alcohol expands $\frac{1}{9}$, or, in other words, 9 measures become 10
Fixed oils " $\frac{1}{12}$, " 12 " 13
Water " $\frac{1}{22.75}$, " $22\frac{3}{4}$ " $23\frac{3}{4}$
Mercury " $\frac{1}{55.5}$ " $55\frac{1}{2}$ " $56\frac{1}{2}$

NOTE.—From this it appears that by the same increment of heat, alcohol or spirits of wine is about six times as expansible as mercury. In the middle of summer, alcohol will measure 5 per cent. and oil nearly 4 per cent. more than in the depth of winter.

42. SECOND LAW.—*Liquids are progressively more expansible at high than at low temperatures.*

Thus, mercury, which of all liquids is the least irregular in its expansions, increases, when heated through successive increments of 180° F., as follows:—

Heated from   0° to 180°   1 volume in $55\frac{1}{2}$
"   180° to 360° 1   "   in $54\frac{1}{2}$
"   360° to 540° 1   "   in 53

43. The Thermometer is an instrument used for measuring the intensity of heat.

44. The liquids usually selected for thermometric purposes are *mercury* and *alcohol*; the former being better adapted for measuring high, and the latter for low degrees of temperature.

NOTE.—Mercury boils at 662° Fahr., and freezes at 40° below zero; Alcohol boils at 170° Fahr., but no degree of cold has yet frozen absolute alcohol. It follows that a Mercury Thermometer will act up to about 600° and down to 35° F., and an Alcohol Thermometer will act up to 150° Fahr., and down to — 150° or — 200°, with tolerable regularity.

45. Mercury is better adapted for a thermometer, than any other liquid, from the following considerations:—

    1st. It can always be obtained in a state of purity.
    2nd. It expands more regularly than other liquids.
    3rd. It measures a greater range of temperature.
    4th. It does not soil or adhere to the tube.
    5th. It is very sensitive, being readily affected by a small increment of heat.

NOTE.—The mercury is purified by subliming it, and afterwards boiling it to deprive it of air.

EXPANSION OF LIQUIDS.

46. The Mercurial Thermometer consists of a capillary glass tube, 10 or 12 inches in length, and of equal bore throughout. The lower end of the tube terminates in a thin bulb of moderate size. The bulb and part of the tube are filled with mercury. The air is expelled from the rest of the tube by expanding the mercury in the bulb until it rises to the top of the tube, and at that moment directing the flame of a blow-pipe against the open end of the tube and thus hermetically sealing it. As the quicksilver in the thermometer cools, it recedes from the top of the tube and leaves a vacuum above it.

In order to graduate the thermometer, it is attached to a flat piece of wood or ivory and placed in melting ice, when the height of the mercury in the tube is carefully marked. The instrument is next plunged into boiling water and the height of the quicksilver again carefully marked. At the former of these points the number 32 is placed and at the latter 212, to indicate respectively the melting point of ice and the boiling point of water. The space between these two points is carefully divided into 180 equal parts or degrees, and similar equal divisions are continued above the boiling point and below the freezing point.

NOTE.—Mercury expands 20 times as much as glass and therefore it is that it rises and falls in the thermometer tube with every change of temperature. Thick glass bulbs do not make as sensitive thermometers as thin bulbs, but the latter are apt to collapse after long use or by sudden exposure to very high or very low temperatures. The greater the bulb and the smaller the diameter of the tube, the longer the degrees or divisions of the scale.

47. Three different thermometric scales have been adopted by the chemists of different countries. In all the fixed points are the same, viz., the melting point of ice and the boiling point of water, but the divisions on the scales are different, being as follows:—

In Fahrenheit's scale the melting point of ice = 32°; boiling point of water = 212°.

In the Centigrade scale the melting point of ice = 0°; boiling point of water = 100°.

In Reaumur's scale the melting point of ice = 0°; boiling point of water = 80°.

EXPANSION OF LIQUIDS.

That is, in Fahrenheit, scale 0° or zero is placed 32° below the melting-point of ice, and the space between the melting point of ice and the boiling-point of water is divided into 180 equal parts. In the Centigrade scale and the scale of Reaumur, zero corresponds to the melting-point of ice, and the space between it and the boiling-point of water is divided in the former into 100 and in the latter into 80 equal parts.

REDUCTION FROM ONE SCALE TO ANOTHER.

I. To reduce Centigrade degrees to degrees of Fahr.

RULE. *Multiply by 9, divide the result by 5 and add 32.*

EXAMPLE.—$100° C. = 212° F.$ Thus $100 \times 9 = 900 \div 5 = 180 + 32 = 212$.
Reason. $100° C. = 180° F.$ or $5° C. = 9° F. \therefore 1° C. = \frac{9}{5}° F.$, and since $0° C.$ corresponds to $32° F.$, we add $32°$.

II. To reduce degrees of Fahrenheit to Centigrade degrees.

RULE. *Subtract 32, multiply the remainder by 5 and divide the product by 9.*

EXAMPLE.—$212° F. = 100° C.$ Thus $212 - 32 = 180 \times 5 = 900 \div 9 = 100$.
Reason. Similar to that in 1.

III. To convert degrees of Reaumur into degrees of Fahr.

RULE. *Multiply by 9, divide the product by 4 and add 32.*

EXAMPLE.—$80° R. = 212° F.$ Thus $80 \times 9 = 720 \div 4 = 180 + 32 = 212$.
Reason. $80° R. = 180° F. \therefore 4° R. = 9° F.$ or $1° R. = \frac{9}{4}° F.$, and we add $32°$ because $0° R.$ corresponds to $32° F.$

'V. To convert degrees of Fahr. into degrees of Reaumur.

RULE. *Subtract 32, multiply the remainder by 4 and divide the result by 9.*

EXAMPLE.—$212° F. = 80° R.$ Thus $212 - 32 = 180 \times 4 = 720 \div 9 = 80$.
Reason. Analogous to that in 111.

V. To reduce degrees of Centigrade to degrees of Reaumur.

RULE. *Multiply by 4, and divide the product by 5.*

EXAMPLE.—$100° C. = 80° R.$ Thus $100 \times 4 = 400 \div 5 = 80$.
Reason. $100° C. = 80° R.$, or $5° C. = 4° R. \therefore 1° C. = \frac{4}{5}° R.$

VI. To reduce degrees of Reaumur to degrees of Centigrade.

RULE. *Multiply by 5, and divide the product by 4.*

EXAMPLE.—$80° R. = 100° C.$ Thus $80 \times 5 = 400 \div 4 = 100$.
Reason. $80° R. = 100° C.$, or $4° R. = 5° C. \therefore 1° R. = \frac{5}{4}° C.$

EXPANSION OF LIQUIDS.

EXERCISE.

1. 219° F.	=	103.8° C.	=	83.1° R.
2. 117° F.	=	47.2° C.	=	37.7° R.
3. 26° F.	=	−3.3° C.	=	−2.6° R.
4. 9° F.	=	−10.2° R.	=	−12.7° C.
5. −4° F.	=	−16° R.	=	−20° C.
6. −23° F.	=	−24.4° R.	=	−30.5° C.
7. 73° C.	=	163.4° F.	=	58.4° R.
8. 49.6° C.	=	121.2° F.	=	39.6° R.
9. 93.2° C.	=	199.7° F.	=	74.5° R.
10. 217° C.	=	173.6° R.	=	422.6° F.
11. −143° C.	=	−34.4° R.	=	−45.4° F.
12. −10.9° C.	=	−32.7° R.	=	−41.6° F.
13. 19.7° R.	=	76.3° F.	=	24.6° C.
14. −23.4° R.	=	−20.6° F.	=	−29.2° C.
15. 267.8° R.	=	693.3° F.	=	367.3° C.
16. −16.9° R.	=	−21.1° C.	=	−6° F.
17. 27.4° R.	=	34.2° C.	=	93.6° F.
18. 392° R.	=	111.1° C.	=	232° F.

48. A thermometer does not measure the quantity of heat present in a body, but merely its intensity.

Thus, if from a barrel of water of any temperature we fill a glass and then place a thermometer in each, the mercury will stand at the same height in each thermometer, although there is obviously much more heat in the barrel of water than in the glass full.

49. Although we can say that one body is hotter or colder than another, we cannot say that one body is *twice* as hot or *twice* as cold as another. This arises from the fact that we do not know the true zero points of bodies, or in other words we do not know what is the least bulk into which a given body is capable of being condensed by cold. Now to say that one body is twice as hot as another, is, in reality, to say that " this body exceeds its minimum bulk by twice as much as that body exceeds its minimum bulk."

---

* When the given number of degrees F. is below 32°, find the number of degrees below 32 and multiply that number by $\frac{5}{9}$ to reduce to Centigrade, and by $\frac{4}{9}$ to reduce to Reaumur.

† When the given number of degrees C. or R. is —, i. e. below zero, multiply by $\frac{9}{5}$ or $\frac{9}{4}$ and *subtract* 32 to reduce to F.

NOTE.—When we say that the temperature of one body is 120° and that of another body 60°, it may, at first sight, appear that the former must be twice as hot as the latter; but it must be borne in mind that the numbers 120° and 60° are merely reckoned from an arbitrary zero-point, adopted because the real zero-point is unknown.

LECTURE IV.

EXPANSION OF SOLIDS, PYROMETERS, EXCEPTIONS TO GENERAL LAW OF EXPANSION.

EXPANSION OF SOLIDS.

50. FIRST LAW.—*All solids do not expand equally under the same incrément of temperature.*

Thus when heated from the melting-point of ice to the boiling-point of water, the linear expansion of rods of different substances is shewn in the following—

TABLE OF EXPANSION.

Zinc expands	1 part in		323	Pure Gold expands	1 part in		682
Lead	"	1	"	"	351	Iron wire	"	1	"	"	812
Tin	"	1	"	"	516	Palladium	"	1	"	"	1000
Silver	"	1	"	"	524	Glass	"	1	"	"	1142
Copper	"	1	"	"	581	Platinum	"	1	"	"	1167
Brass	"	1	"	"	584	Black Marble "	1	"	"	2833

NOTE.—The increment in bulk is about three times as great as the linear increment. Thus the linear increment of Lead is $\frac{1}{351}$, the solid increment is $\frac{3}{351}$ or $\frac{1}{117}$; that is, lead increases in *bulk* 1 part in 117 when heated from 32° F. to 212° F.

51. SECOND LAW.—*The same solid is progressively more expansible at high than at low temperatures.*

NOTE.—Platinum is the most uniform in its expansion.

EXPANSION OF SOLIDS.

52. A compound bar made by soldering two thin plates of brass and iron, or of copper and platinum, illustrates very clearly the unequal expansion of these metals. When heat is applied to the bar, the metals both expand, but the copper much more than the platinum; and the result is that the bar becomes curved, so that the platinum is on the inside of the curve. When the bar is subjected to great cold, the reverse takes place; for then the copper contracts more than the platinum, and the latter occupies the outside of the curve.

Fig. 5.

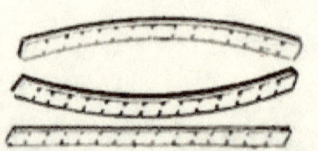

NOTE.—By careful attention to the different degrees of expansibility of metals, a compound bar may be so constructed that its ends shall be the same distance apart, no matter how much its temperature may vary. This is the principle upon which the gridiron pendulum and the balance-wheels of chronometers are constructed.

53. The same principle has been beautifully applied to the construction of a thermometer from solid materials by Breguet. This consists of a thin ribbon of silver soldered to a similar slip of platinum, and the compound slip of metal coiled into a helix or spiral. The upper part of the spiral is fixed to a support, and the lower end terminates in an index 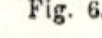 which plays over a graduated circle, as exhibited in the figure. Silver is twice as expansible as platinum. When, therefore, the instrument is subjected to an increasing temperature, the unequal expansion of the two metals causes the helix to coil more closely. Similarly, when it is subjected to a decreasing temperature, the unequal contraction of the slips causes the helix to uncoil; and in either case the movement is measured by the number of degrees through which the index passes.

Fig. 6.

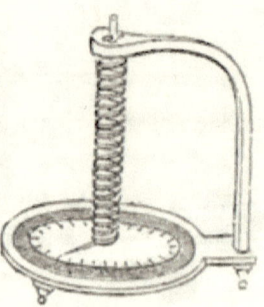

NOTE.—When the metallic ribbons are very thin, Breguet's thermometer is one of the most delicate and sensitive instruments we possess; the slightest variation of temperature being measured with precision and rapidity.

54. When hot water is suddenly poured upon a thick plate of glass, or when the flame of a lamp is directed against it, one surface becomes hot and expands before the heat penetrates to the other surface of the plate. As in the case of the compound bar of metal (Art. 52), we have here unequal expansion, and the plate tends to curve with the heated and expanded surface on the outside, but, owing to its inflexibility, it is broken. When cold is applied to a heated plate of glass, it breaks from the opposite cause, i. e, owing to the unequal contraction of the two surfaces.

PYROMETERS.

55. Pyrometers, or *fire-measurers*, are instruments used for determining very high degrees of heat. The best is that of Daniell.

56. Daniell's Pyrometer consists of a tube of plumbago containing a rod of platinum. The tube is closed at one end, and, as the rod of platinum expands, it pushes forward a tightly fitting plug or wedge at the other or open end. The extent of the displacement of the wedge measures the amount of expansion which the platinum has undergone.

57. The air pyrometer of Pouillet consists of a hollow platinum sphere fitted with an escape-tube. When this instrument is subjected to an increase of temperature, a part of the contained air is expelled; and the greater the intensity of the heat, the greater the amount of air driven out. The expelled air is received over water, and the temperature to which the platinum vessel was subjected is thus measured. This pyrometer is very accurate and reliable.

58. Another mode of measuring high temperatures is that of Wilson. This consists in placing a given weight of platinum in a furnace the heat of which is to be measured, and, when it has attained the temperature of the furnace, plunging it in a given weight of water of known temperature. The intensity of the heat to which the platinum was subjected, is estimated by the number of degrees through which it raises the temperature of the water.

Thus, suppose that the platinum weighs 1 lb., and that it is plunged in 1 lb. of water at the temperature of 60°, and suppose the temperature of the water to rise to 110°, then the increase of temperature of the water is equal to 50°; and to convert this into degrees of Fahrenheit we multiply by 31, because the heat that raises a given weight of water through 1 degree would raise an equal weight of platinum through 31 degrees. Then $50° \times 31 = 1550°$ = temperature of the furnace.

Again if the 1 lb. of platinum raise the temperature of 3 lbs. of water 40°, then $40° \times 3 = 120°$ = degrees through which the 1 lb. of platinum would have raised 1 lb. of water. And $120° \times 31 = 3720°$ = temperature of the furnace.

EXCEPTIONS TO GENERAL LAW OF EXPANSION.

59. Certain bodies form remarkable exceptions to the general law that all bodies expand when subjected to an increasing, and contract when subjected to a decreasing, temperature. These exceptions are—

    1st. Type-metal.
    2nd. Rose's Fusible Metal.
    3rd. Water.

NOTE.—When clay is exposed to very high temperatures, it contracts, and thus appears to be an exception to the general law. In reality, however, the contraction of the clay is due to the dissipation of the water it contains; and although the clay itself expands, the amount of this expansion is more than counterbalanced by the diminution of bulk caused by the loss of the water it originally contained.

60. Type-metal, which is an alloy of lead and antimony, expands as it passes from the fluid to the solid state. This property causes it to fill the sharp indentations of the mould, and thus enables us to cast many hundreds of type in the same mould, whereas otherwise we should have to shape and cut each separately. Iron and some other metals possess the same property.

61. Rose's fusible metal is an alloy of—

    2 parts by weight of bismuth.
    1 "   "   " lead.
    1 "   "   " tin.

This compound expands regularly like other bodies up to 111°. It then rapidly contracts up to 156°, when it attains its

EXCEPTIONS TO LAW OF EXPANSION. 27

point of maximum density and is less in bulk than at 32°. From 156° it again regularly expands until it melts at 201°. In cooling it goes through a similar series of changes.

NOTE.—The sudden expansion which type-metal, iron, and other metals undergo when passing into the solid form, is accounted for by these bodies becoming crystallized and the crystals arranging themselves in angles across one another. This increase is analogous to the *sudden* expansion of water in freezing. Rose's fusible metal is a chemical compound of such a nature that we should almost expect it to be irregular in its expansion. Water is therefore the only well-marked exception to the general law.

62. When boiling water is allowed to cool, it regularly contracts until its temperature is about 39° or 40°, at which point it has attained its maximum density. When cooled below this point, instead of contracting, it expands. This fact was very beau-

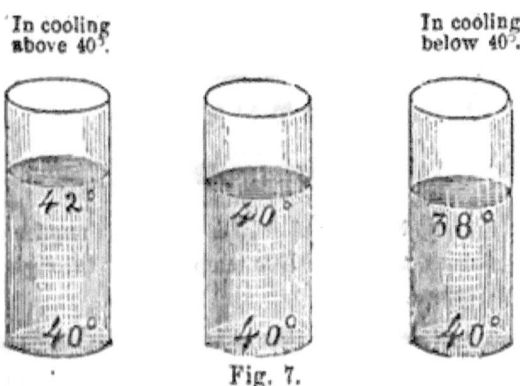

Fig. 7.

tifully illustrated by the experiment of Dr. Hope, who carried into a very cold room a jar containing water of the temperature of 50° F., and having immersed in the water two delicate thermometers, one at the bottom and one near the surface. As the water cooled, the upper thermometer indicated a temperature higher than the lower till the temperature descended to 40°. In other words, as the surface-water cooled, it became specifically heavier and sunk. When the lower thermometer had attained the temperature of 40°, it remained stationary until the upper reached the same point. As the cooling still continued, the lower thermometer remained steadily at 40°, while the upper thermometer still continued to fall; or, in other words the water became specifically lighter as it became cooled below 40° F., and therefore continued at the surface.

NOTE.—The point of maximum density of water has been ascertained to be accurately 39.2° F.

63. The fact that water has a point of maximum density influences to a remarkable extent the duration of the seasons. If water followed the same law as other bodies, the upper layers in our lakes, rivers, ponds, &c., as they cooled, would sink until the whole reached the freezing-point, when it would become solid from the bottom upward. The result would be that our rivers, lakes and ponds would be converted into solid masses of ice, and the heat of summer would not, in what are now the temperate zones, be sufficient to melt them. In point of fact, however, the upper surface alone freezes; and the ice thus formed, being a very imperfect conductor of heat, protects the underlying mass of water from the cold of the atmosphere

LECTURE V.

SPECIFIC HEAT.

64. Different bodies of equal weights require different amounts of heat to raise their temperatures through the same number of degrees.

Thus if two bottles of the same size, shape, &c., be so placed before a fire that they shall receive equal amounts of heat from the fire, and one of the bottles be filled with water and the other with quicksilver, it will be found that the temperature of the latter will be elevated in a given time twice as much as that of the former. If equal weights instead of equal volumes be used, the same amount of heat raises the temperature of the mercury 30 times as much as that of the water. Hence all bodies are said to have different *capacities for heat;* thus water is said to have twice the capacity for heat that mercury has, bulk for bulk, or 30 times the capacity, weight for weight.

65. *If the heat required to raise a given weight of water through a given number of de bsfgerun aefsroeoebmɹepr tmented by 1000, then the heat required to raise an equal weight of any other body through the me esgeerepdr ertauees of temperature is termed its* SPECIFIC HEAT.

SPECIFIC HEAT. 29

66. The following table by Regnault gives the specific heat of various bodies, that of water being 1000:

TABLE OF SPECIFIC HEATS.

Water	1000	Tin	56
Sulphur	203	Iodine	54
Glass	198	Antimony	51
Iron	114	Mercury	33
Nickel	109	Gold	32
Zinc	95	Platinum	32
Copper	95	Lead	31
Silver	57	Bismuth	31

Note.—From this table it appears that the capacity of water for heat is 5 times as great as that of sulphur or glass, 9 times as great as that of iron or nickel, 10 times as great as that of copper or zinc, 18 times as great as that of silver, tin, or iodine, 30 times as great as that of mercury, and 31 or 32 times as great as that of gold, platinum, lead, or bismuth.

67. The capacities of different bodies for heat may be determined in four ways:

    1st. By the method of *warming*.
    2nd. By the method of *cooling*.
    3rd. By the method of *melting*.
    4th. By the method of *mixture*.

68. The method by warming consists in exposing equal weights of different bodies to the same source of heat, and observing to what height their several temperatures rise in a given time.

Thus if iron, silver, platinum, and water be exposed to the same source of heat, it will be found that the temperature of the iron rises 9 times, that of the silver 18 times, and that of the platinum 31 times as rapidly as that of the water. Hence, as they all absorb an equal amount of heat, the capacity of water for heat is 9 times that of iron, 18 times that of silver, and 31 times that of platinum. So also the capacity of iron is twice that of silver and 3½ times that of platinum.

69. The method by cooling, known also as the method of Dulong and Petit, gives very exact results, but in practice requires several important precautions, such as cooling the bodies in vacuo, &c. It consists essentially in placing several bodies heated to the same temperature in similar circumstances

and observing the rapidity with which they cool. Those bodies which, like mercury, have a low capacity for heat and therefore contain but little of it, require far less time to cool through a given number of degrees than those which, like water, have a great capacity for heat.

70. The method by melting involves the use of the Calorimeter, and is frequently spoken of as Calorimetry.

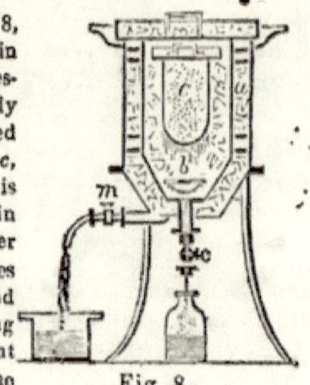

Fig. 8.

The Calorimeter, of Lavoisier, Fig. 8, consists of three tin vessels, one within the other. The space between the vessels is filled with crushed ice. The body whose specific heat is to be determined is introduced into the inner vessel, c, and the amount of heat it contains is determined by the amount of the ice in the vessel b that it melts. The water obtained from the melting ice in b passes through the tube e and is collected and carefully measured. The object of having ice in the outer vessel, a, is to prevent the external air from melting any of the ice in the middle vessel.

Another form of the Calorimeter consists simply of two blocks of ice fitting accurately one over the other, and the lower one containing a cavity into which the heated mass is placed.

71. To calculate the specific heat of bodies by the Calorimeter, we proceed as follows:

Let w = the weight in lbs. of the body introduced into the Calorimeter,
    t = its temperature in degrees of Fahrenheit,
    w' = the weight in lbs. of the ice melted,
    s = the specific heat of the body under experiment,

Then $\dfrac{w'}{t-32}$ = the lbs. of ice dissolved by the heat that would raise the temperature of the body in the Calorimeter 1°.

$\dfrac{w'}{w \times (t-32)}$ = the lbs. of ice dissolved by the heat that would raise the temperature of 1 lb. of the given body 1°.

Then since the latent heat or caloric of fluidity of water is 142°, we have
$$s = \frac{w' \times 142 \times 1000}{w \times (t-32)}$$

INTERPRETATION.—*Multiply the weight, in lbs., of ice dissolved, by 142, and this by 1000, and divide the product by the weight of the given body, in lbs., multiplied by the degrees of temperature it loses.*

SPECIFIC HEAT. 31

EXAMPLE 1.—If 5 lbs. of charcoal of the temperature of 752° F. dissolve 6.75 lbs. of ice, what is the specific heat of the charcoal?

$$s = \frac{w' \times 142 \times 1000}{w \times (t-32)} = \frac{6.75 \times 142 \times 1000}{5 \times (752-32)} = \frac{6.75 \times 142 \times 1000}{5 \times 720} = 266.25 \; Ans.$$

EXAMPLE 2.—If 3 lbs. of platinum at the temperature of 932° F. dissolve ·6 of a lb. of ice, what is the specific heat of the platinum?

$$s = \frac{w \times 142 \times 1000}{w \times (t-32)} = \frac{\cdot 6 \times 142 \times 1000}{3 \times (932-32)} = \frac{\cdot 6 \times 142 \times 1000}{3 \times 900} = 31.5 \; Ans.$$

EXERCISE.

3. If 4 lbs. of water at the temperature of 245° F. dissolve 6 lbs. of ice, what is the specific heat of the water? *Ans.* 1000.

4. If 11 lbs. of mercury at the temperature of 572° dissolve 1.4 lbs. of ice, what is the specific heat of the mercury? *Ans.* 33·4.

5. If 6 lbs. of sulphur at the temperature of 332° F. melt 2.57 lbs. of ice, what is the specific heat of the sulphur? *Ans.* 202·7.

6. If .5 of a lb. of arsenic at the temperature of 382° F. melts .0998 of a lb. of ice, what is the specific heat of the arsenic? *Ans.* 80·9.

---

72. The method by mixture consists in placing in a given quantity of water of known temperature, a known weight of any body of an ascertained higher temperature, and when the two bodies have attained an equilibrium, comparing the loss of temperature of the given body with the gain of temperature of the other.

Thus if 1 lb. of water at 100° F. be mixed with 1 lb. at 50° F., the resulting temperature will be the mean between 100° and 50°, i.e. $\frac{100° + 50°}{2} = 75°$; but if a pound of mercury at 100° be mixed with a pound of water at 50°, the resulting temperature will not be 75°, but only about 51.6°, that is, the 43.4° lost by the mercury only raises the temperature of an equal weight of water through 1.6°, or, in other words, mercury has only $\frac{1}{30}$th the capacity for heat that water has.

73. To ascertain the specific heat of any body by the method of mixture,—that of water being represented by 1000,—we proceed as follows:

Let w = the weight in lbs. of the body whose specific heat is to be determined.

t = its temperature in degrees F.

w' = the weight in lbs. of the water.

t' = its temperature.

T = the common temperature after an equilibrium has been attained.

Then $T - t'$ = gain of temperature of the w' lbs. of water.

$t - T$ = the loss of the temperature of the w lbs. of the other body.

s = specific heat of the body.

SPECIFIC HEAT.

Then the heat gained by the water will be its *specific heat* $\times w'$ $\times (T - t')$, and the heat lost by the other body will be its *specific heat* $\times w \times (t - T)$; or, since the specific heat of water is represented by 1000 and that of the other body by s, and since the heat gained by the water is just that lost by the other body, we have—

$s \times w \times (t - T) = 1000 \times w' \times (T - t')$, and therefore

$$s = \frac{w' \times (T - t') \times 1000}{w \times (t - T)}.$$

INTERPRETATION.—*Multiply together the weight of the water in lbs., its gain in temperature, and* 1000, *and divide the product by the weight of the given body in lbs. multiplied by its loss of temperature.*

NOTE.—If equal weights of water and of the other body are used, the rule becomes—

$$s = \frac{(T - t') \times 1000}{(t - T)}.$$

EXAMPLE 1.—If 1 lb. of copper at 300° F. be plunged into 1 lb. of water at 50° and the resulting temperature be 72°, what is the specific heat of the copper?

Here, since the weights are equal, we have

$$s = \frac{(T - t') \times 1000}{t - T} = \frac{(72 - 50) \times 1000}{300 - 72} = \frac{22 \times 1000}{228} = 96.4 \; Ans.$$

EXAMPLE 2.—If 3 lbs. of platinum at 714° F. be plunged into 7.2 lbs. of water at 65° and the resulting temperature be 73.5°, what is the specific heat of the platinum?

$$\text{Here } s = \frac{w' \times (T - t') \times 1000}{w \times (t - T)} = \frac{7.2 \times (73.5 - 65) \times 1000}{3 \times (714 - 73.5)}$$
$$= \frac{7.2 \times 8.5 \times 1000}{3 \times 640.5} = 31.8. \; Ans.$$

EXERCISE.

3. If 1 lb. of zinc at the temperature of 490° F. be plunged in 1 lb. of water at the temperature of 58° and the resulting temperature is 95.4°, what is the specific heat of the zinc?   *Ans.* 94.6.

4. If 5 lbs. of silver at the temperature of 809° F. be plunged into 9.5 lbs. of water at the temperature of 62°, the resulting temperature is 83.8°; what is the capacity of the silver for heat?   *Ans.* 57.7.

5. If 5 lbs. of cobalt at the temperature of 481° F. be plunged into 2.14 lbs. of water at the temperature of 64°, the resulting temperature be 147.4°; what is the capacity of the cobalt for heat?   *Ans.* 107.

6. If 15 lbs. of iron at the temperature of 1167° F. be plunged into 19 lbs. of water at the temperature of 65°, the resulting temperature is 156°; what is the specific heat of the iron?   *Ans.* 114.

74. The specific heat of gases is determined by transmitting a known weight of the gas under experiment, heated to $212°$ F., through a spiral tube contained in a vessel of water, the temperature of which is carefully noted at the beginning and end of the process.

75. In determining the specific heats of bodies, if we take equal weights we obtain a series of numbers all different, and exhibiting no simple relations among themselves; but if, instead of *equal* weights, we take quantities in proportion to the chemical equivalents or combining numbers of the various bodies, we obtain a series of numbers having a remarkably close relation to one another.

Thus, if we use weights in proportion to their chemical equivalents, the table on page 29 will become—

TABLE OF SPECIFIC HEAT OF ELEMENTARY ATOMS.

Iron	3.093	Tin	3.312
Lead	3.258	Platinum	3.205
Nickel	3.218	Mercury	3.719
Zinc	3.087	Silver	6.174
Copper	3.017	Gold	6.462
Sulphur	3.266	Antimony	6.561

NOTE.—From this table, it appears that the elementary atoms of the first nine bodies given have equal capacities for heat, and those of the last three double as much capacity. We may safely conclude that there exists some intimate, though as yet imperfectly understood relation between the thermal and the chemical nature of bodies. The same connection has been found to exist in certain chemical compounds, and, both for elementary and compound bodies, may be stated as follows:—

In bodies of similar chemical constitution, the specific heats are in an inverse ratio to their chemical equivalents or to some simple multiple or submultiple of the latter.

76. The selection of mercury for thermometric purposes was chiefly determined by its low capacity for heat. It is on account of its low capacity that mercury is sensitive; i. e., it both warms and cools rapidly, and hence it promptly follows every change of temperature.

NOTE.—The thermometer measures only the *intensity* of heat, while the calorimeter measures the *quantity*,—or rather the quantity above $32°$ F., the melting-point of ice.

77. The capacity for heat of different bodies increases as they expand and decreases as they contract; and hence when a body is suddenly made to expand without the application of heat, its temperature falls because a part of its sensible heat becomes insensible. So also when a body is suddenly condensed its temperature rises,—a part of its insensible heat becoming sensible.

This is shown very clearly in the case of gases by placing a delicate thermometer in the air contained in the receiver of an air-pump. Upon rapidly exhausting the air, the part remaining in the receiver expands, and as it expands, its capacity for heat increases; the consequence is that a part of the sensible heat passes into insensible, and the thermometer sinks. The same principle explains the action of the nephelescope and the sudden formation of clouds.

NOTE.—When the volume of a gas is doubled, its capacity for heat is nearly doubled. One volume of air expanded into two volumes loses from 40° to 50° F.; when one volume is compressed into a ½ volume, its temperature is raised 40° or 50° F.; and when suddenly condensed into $\frac{1}{4}$ of a volume, its temperature is raised sufficiently to ignite tinder.

LECTURE VI.

CHANGE OF FORM, LATENT HEAT, CALORIC OF FLUIDITY, MELTING POINTS, THEORY OF FREEZING MIXTURES.

FIRST, CHANGE OF FORM.

78. All solid inorganic bodies that, when subjected to an increasing temperature, do not suffer decomposition by the heat, finally reach a point at which they melt and assume the liquid form. In this phenomenon two points are to be carefully noticed, viz. :

1st. Under the same amount of pressure the melting-point is invariably the same for the same body.

2d. When the solid once begins to melt, its temperature ceases to rise until the whole of the body has assumed the liquid form ; or, in other words, when a body passes from the solid to the liquid state, it does so by the absorption of a certain amount of heat.

79. The melting-points of a number of common substances are given in the following—

TABLE OF MELTING-POINTS.

Iron	melts at.	2800° F.	Tallow	melts at.	92° F.
Gold	"	2016°	Oil of Anise	"	50°
Silver	"	1873°	Olive Oil	"	33°
Zinc	"	773°	Ice	"	32°
Lead	"	594°	Milk	"	30°
Bismuth	"	476°	Wines	"	20°
Tin	"	442°	Oil of Turpentine	"	14°
Sulphur	"	392°	Mercury	"	—39°
Wax	"	142°	Liquid Ammonia	"	—46°
Phosphorus	"	108°	Ether	"	—47°

NOTE.—If the bodies are in the fluid form they freeze upon reaching the temperature set opposite them.

80. Water and certain other liquids may, with proper precaution, be cooled down considerably below their freezing-points without congealing. Thus if a small quantity of water be placed in a glass vessel having a perfectly smooth interior surface, and protected from the slightest agitation, it may be cooled down to 7° or even 5° F., that is, 25 or 27 degrees below its proper freezing-point, before it becomes solid. When thus cooled below 32° F., the least agitation or the introduction of a small angular fragment of any substance at once induces the congelation of a part of the water, and the temperature of the ice and remaining water instantly rises to 32°. It is, however, impossible to raise the temperature of a solid the least degree above its melting-point without producing liquefaction. Hence 32° F. represents, not the freezing-point of water, which is variable, but the melting-point of ice, which is constant.

NOTE.—In freezing, the particles arrange themselves at certain angles, and hence arises the sudden expansion which water undergoes in becoming solid,—an expansion equal to $\frac{1}{9}$ of its bulk, i. e., 9 cubic inches of water become 10 cubic inches of ice. That the particles of water become differently arranged in the act of freezing, is illustrated by the fact that water in the process of congelation rejects any foreign matter that it may contain. Thus, incorporate with the water any coloring matter, or dissolve in it any salt, or even the most acrid poison, or mix with it the strongest acid or any spirituous liquid, and freeze the compound, gently moving or agitating it during the process, and the ice formed will be absolutely pure frozen water, colorless, tasteless, and harmless. The foreign ingredient, poison, or acid, or salt, or coloring matter, or spirit, has been forced out of the water, and will be found concentrated in the centre of the mass of ice.

81. The freezing-point of water may be lowered by dissolving any salt in it. Common salt is the most effective agent to use for this purpose, and appears to lower the freezing-point in proportion to the amount of it dissolved. Thus, sea-water, which contains $\frac{1}{36}$ of its weight of salt, freezes at 28° F., while water containing $\frac{1}{4}$ its weight, congeals at 4° F.

82. If 1 lb. of water at 32° be mixed with 1 lb. of water at 174°, the result will be 2 lbs. of water at a temperature the mean between 32° and 174° i. e., at 103°. But if 1 lb. of ice

at 32° be mixed with 1 lb. of water at 174°, the result will be 2 lbs. of water at 32°; in other words, the 1 lb. of ice, in passing into the liquid form, *absorbs and conceals* 142° of heat.

83. The heat that is thus absorbed by a body in passing into the liquid state, is discoverable neither by the senses nor by the most delicate thermometer, and is hence called *Latent Heat*, from the Latin *lateo*, "to lie hid."

84. The absorption of heat by a body passing from the solid into the liquid, or from the liquid into the gaseous state, may be illustrated as follows: Let us suppose that a portion of ice at 0°, contained in a closed vessel, is placed in a furnace the heat of which is kept so regulated that the ice shall uniformly absorb 1° per minute. For 32 minutes the temperature of the ice will regularly rise, and at the end of that time will be at 32°. The ice then begins to melt, and, although it still continues to absorb 1° of heat per minute, its temperature remains stationary at 32°, until, at the end of 142 minutes, all the ice is converted into water, the temperature of which is 32° F. From this point the temperature again regularly rises at the rate of 1° per minute, and this uniform increase goes on for 180 minutes, when the thermometer indicates a temperature of 212°, and the water begins to boil, passing into the form of vapour. Now again the temperature ceases to rise, and for 972 minutes remains fixed at 212°. After the lapse of 972 minutes all the water is converted into steam at 212°, and the temperature of this steam rises uniformly 1° per minute.

85. The heat that disapears when a solid assumes the liquid form is called *Caloric of Fluidity;* that which disappears when a liquid assumes the gaseous state is termed *Caloric of Elasticity.*

86. The following table shows the amount of heat absorbed by different bodies in passing from the solid to the liquid state:

TABLE OF CALORIC OF FLUIDITY.

Water	142°	Zinc	493°
Sulphur	145°	Tin	500°
Lead	162°	Bismuth	550°
Bees Wax	175°		

FREEZING MIXTURES.

87. All freezing mixtures depend essentially upon the fact that solid bodies can assume the liquid form only by the absorption of heat, and hence when this heat is not directly applied, it is abstracted from the surrounding bodies.

Thus, when a salt is dissolved in water it lowers the temperature of the water. Nitre, for instance, thus reduces the temperature of the water in which it is dissolved 15° or 18°, while a mixture of 5 parts sal ammoniac and 5 parts of nitre finely powdered and dissolved in 19 parts of water, may reduce the temperature from 50° F. to 10° F., or considerably below the freezing point.

88. The following table contains a list of the ingredients used in common freezing mixtures, and also indicates the degree of cold produced.

TABLE OF FREEZING MIXTURES WITHOUT ICE.

No.	Mixture.	Parts.	Thermometer sinks.	Degree of cold produced.
1	Nitrate of Ammonia Water	1 1	from +50° to +4°	46°
2	Muriate of Ammonia Nitrate of Potash Water	5 5 19	from +50° to +10°	40°
3	Sulphate of Soda Diluted Nitric Acid	3 2	from +50° to −3°	53°
4	Sulphate of Soda Muriate of Ammonia Nitrate of Potash Diluted Nitric Acid	6 4 2 4	from +50° to −10°	60°
5	Sulphate of Soda Nitrate of Ammonia Diluted Nitric Acid	6 5 4	from +50° to −14°	64°
6	Sulphate of Soda Hydrochloric Acid	8 5	from +50° to 0°	50°
7	Phosphate of Soda Nitrate of Ammonia Diluted Nitric Acid	5 3 4	from 0° to −34°	34°

FREEZING MIXTURES.

TABLE OF FREEZING MIXTURES WITH ICE.

No.	Mixture.	Parts.	Thermometer sinks.	Degree of cold.
1	Snow or Pounded Ice....... Common Salt..............	2 1	to —5°	*
2	Snow or Pounded Ice....... Common Salt.............. Sal Ammoniac.............	5 2 1	to —12°	*
3	Snow or Pounded Ice....... Common Salt.............. Sal Ammoniac............. Nitrate of Potash..........	24 10 5 5	to —18°	*
4	Snow or Pounded Ice....... Common Salt.............. Nitrate of Ammonia........	12 5 5	to —25°	*
5	Snow...................... Diluted Nitric Acid.........	7 4	from +32° to —30°	62°
6	Snow...................... Crys. Muriate of Lime	2 3	from +32° to —50°	82°
7	Snow...................... Potash....................	3 4	from +32° to —51°	83°
8	Snow...................... Diluted Nitric Acid.........	3 2	from 0° to —46°	46°
9	Snow...................... Crys. Muriate of Lime......	1 2	from 0° to —66°	66°
10	Snow...................... Diluted Sulphuric Acid.....	8 10	from —66° to —91°	25°

89. When a body passes from a liquid to a solid state, it gives up its latent heat. Thus, when water assumes the solid form it sets free the 142° of heat it had absorbed in liquefying.

This fact can be very clearly shown by placing in a stoppled bottle a hot saturated solution of sulphate of soda, and passing a thermometer air-tight through a cork, as represented in the accompanying figure. Upon allowing the solution to cool to the ordinary temperature, no crystallization takes place as long as the bottle is closely stoppled; but upon removing the stopper, solidification at once takes place, and the temperature rises, as is indicated by the thermometer,—indeed, if the bottle be grasped by the hand, it is sensibly warmer than before the crystallization commenced.

Fig. 9.

So also if a portion of water containing a thermometer be carefully cooled below 32°, say to 10° or 15° below the ordinary freezing point, upon throwing a small fragment of ice or any other substance in the water, a portion is instantly changed into the solid form, and the temperature of the ice formed, and the unfrozen water rises at once to 32° by the absorption of the heat disengaged by the part congealed.

90. The fact that water absorbs so large an amount of heat in assuming the liquid form and gives it up again in freezing, has a remarkable influence on our climate and the duration of our seasons. If, by the disengagement of a single degree of heat, water could assume the solid form, the process of freezing would go on with fearful violence, and there would be no gradual change from summer to winter ; and if, on the other hand, ice could melt by absorbing a single degree of heat, the vast accumulations of winter would liquefy so rapidly as to inundate the entire country.

Both the melting of ice and the freezing of water require time. The 142° of heat have, in the former case, to be absorbed, and in the latter case disengaged, and this serves as an effectual check upon sudden transitions from summer to winter or from winter to summer.

LECTURE VII.

SECOND CHANGE OF FORM, VAPORIZATION—BOILING POINTS, CALORIC OF ELASTICITY—NATURE OF VAPOURS—ELASTIC FORCE OF VAPOURS—DENSITY OF WATER-VAPOUR—EFFECTS OF PRESSURE AND COLD ON VAPOURS AND GASES.

91. When any liquid is subjected to an increasing temperature, it finally reaches a point at which it begins to boil and pass off rapidly into the state of vapour. In this phenomenon two points require to be carefully noticed, viz.:

>1st. The same liquid, under the same circumstances as regards the pressure upon its surface, &c., invariably begins to boil at the same thermometric point.

BOILING POINTS. 41

2nd. When a liquid once begins to boil, its temperature ceases to rise until after it has wholly assumed the form of vapour; or, in other words, when a liquid passes into the state of vapour, it does so by the absorption of a certain amount of heat.

92. The boiling points of a number of bodies are given in the following:

TABLE OF BOILING POINTS.

Hydrochloric Ether.....	52° F.	Nitric Acid.............	248° F.
Ether	96°	Oil of Turpentine.......	314°
Sulphide of Carbon......	118°	Phosphorus.............	554°
Ammonia...............	140°	Sulphuric Acid.........	620°
Alcohol................	173°	Whale Oil.,............	630°
Water..................	212°	Mercury................	662°

93. We have seen (in Art. 84) that water absorbs 972° of heat in passing into the form of steam or vapour, and it is to the possession of this large amount of latent heat that we are to attribute the efficiency of steam as an agent for warming.

NOTE.—The caloric of elasticity of steam would be almost sufficient, if the steam were a solid body, to render it visibly red hot in day light.

94. The latent heat contained in the steam generated by 1 lb. of water is sufficient to raise nearly $5\frac{2}{5}$ lbs. of water from the melting point of ice to the boiling point of water.

Thus since 180° of heat are required to raise 1 lb. of water from 32° to 212°, the steam generated by 1 lb. of water will raise $972 \div 180 = 5\frac{2}{5}$ lbs. of water from 32° to 212°.

NOTE.—When buildings are heated by steam conveyed through them in cast-iron pipes, it is customary to allow one cubic foot of boiler capacity for every 2000 cubic feet of space to be heated; and it is found that of the conducting steam pipe one square foot of surface must be exposed for every 200 cubic feet of space to be heated to the temperature of 75° F.

95. From the circumstance that the temperature of bodies heated by steam can never be raised above 212° F., and that

consequently all danger of empyreuma is thus avoided, steam is very much employed for heating extracts, organic substances, &c., and is much preferable to a fire for that purpose.

96. The amount of heat absorbed by different liquids in assuming the form of vapour is exhibited in the following:

TABLE OF CALORIC OF ELASTICITY.

Water.............. 972° F.	Ether. .... 162° F.
Alcohol............ 385°	Oil of Turpentine...... 133°

97. The most important features with regard to the nature of vapours may be illustrated by the following simple experiment:

Fig. 10. A glass tube, *a*, (Fig. 10,) half an inch in diameter and 20 to 25 inches long, open at one end and closed at the other, is filled to within half an inch or so of the top, with mercury, and the remaining space filled with ether. The thumb is then firmly pressed upon the open end, the tube inverted and placed in the mercury contained in a jar, *b*, having the same length as the tube, and a diameter three or four times as great. The ether at once rises, owing to its superior levity, and occupies the upper or closed extremity of the tube, where, the mercury being at the same level in the tube and jar, it is subjected to a pressure equal to that of the atmosphere. Now if the tube be raised, &c., the following facts will be observed:

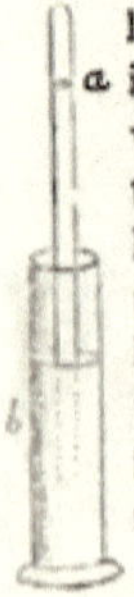

    1st. If the tube be raised in the jar as high as possible without admitting the atmospheric air, a portion of the ether or other liquid becomes converted into vapour and depresses the column of mercury in the tube; and if different liquids be tried in succession, it will be found that at the same temperature they depress the mercurial column to an unequal amount,—water, for example, less than alcohol, and alcohol less than ether. Hence,

I. *Decreasing the pressure upon the surface of a liquid facilitates its evaporation; and in a vacuum vapours form instantly, even at the lowest temperature.*

NOTE.—Hence, there are many liquids which would, if the pressure of the air were removed, become permanently gaseous.

II. *The elastic force of the vapour of different liquids may be measured by the amount to which they depress the mercurial column in a barometer tube. Thus at a temperature of* 80° *F. water depresses the mercurial column* 1 *inch, alcohol* 2 *inches, and ether* 20 *inches.*

    2nd. If the end of the tube be grasped in the hand or slightly warmed by exposure to the flame of a spirit lamp, the column of the mercury is still further depressed ; hence,

The elastic force of a vapour increases with its temperature.

    3rd. If the tube be warmed to the *boiling point* of the ether, or whatever other fluid is introduced into the upper part of the tube, the mercury is at once depressed to the same level as that in the jar ; hence,

The elastic force of the vapour of any liquid at its boiling point is equal to the pressure of the atmosphere, or, in other words, would sustain a column of mercury 30 *inches in height, or is equal to* 15 *lbs. to the square inch.*

    4th. If now the tube be allowed to cool, the vapour condenses and the mercury rises in the tube ; hence,

A vapour is condensed into a liquid by decreasing its temperature.

    5th. If, in place of cooling the tube, it be depressed in the jar so as to increase the pressure on the vapour contained within, a portion of this vapour at once condenses, and the mercury within the tube constantly maintains the same level as that in the jar ; hence,

I. *A vapour is condensed into a liquid by subjecting it to pressure; and*

II. *A vapour is at its point of maximum density when its temperature is the same as the boiling point of the liquid from which it is formed.*

    98. The elastic force of vapours increases very rapidly with their temperature,—each vapour appearing to follow a rate of

progression peculiar to itself. That of water-vapour is exhibited in the following:

TABLE OF ELASTIC FORCE OF WATER-VAPOUR IN VACUO.

Temperature.	Elastic force.
Water at −22° F. depresses the mercury in a barom. tube	0·0144 inch.
−4° " " "	0·0331 "
14° " " "	0·0818 "
32° " " "	0·1811 "
50° " " "	0·3608 "
68° " " "	1·6847 "
86° " " "	0·2421 "
140° " " "	5·8583 "
185° " " "	7·4808 "
212° " " "	29·9220 "

99. A vapour is said to be at its point of maximum density when we can neither increase the pressure upon it nor decrease its temperature without condensing a portion of it into liquid. We have seen that a vapour may be produced from a liquid under reduced pressure even at a very low temperature, but in that case the vapour is, comparatively speaking, very rare. The vapour is invariably most dense when at the boiling point of the liquid producing it. The comparative density and weight of water-vapour, at different temperatures, is shown in the following:

TABLE OF DENSITY OF WATER-VAPOUR.

Temperature.	Density.	Weight of 100 cub. in.
212° F.	1·000	14·962 grains.
150°	0·272	4·076 "
100°	0·074	1·113 "
60°	0·022	0·338 "
50°	0·016	0·247 "
32°	0·009	0·136 "

100. The distinction commonly made between a vapour and a gas is, that the former is more readily made to assume the liquid form. Gases are divided into those which are permanently elastic and those which are not permanently elastic; and the only respect in which the latter differ from vapours, is that

SIGNIFICATION OF VAPOURS.   45

they require a greater decrease of temperature or increase of pressure to condense them.

101. Among the gases which have not as yet been made to assume the liquid form by the conjoined effects of cold and pressure, may be mentioned *oxygen, hydrogen, nitrogen, nitric oxide, carbonic oxide, coal gas,* and *atmospheric air.* These refused to liquefy at the temperature of — 166° F. while subjected to pressures of from 27 to 58 atmospheres.

The subjoined table gives the results obtained by Faraday on the cold and pressure required to liquefy certain gases :

Gas.	Tension of vapour in atmospheres.	Temperature.	Remarks.
Sulphurous Acid	0·726 / 1·589 / 3·000	0° F. / 32° / 68°	Becomes a colorless transparent crystalline solid body at —105° F.
Sulphuretted Hydrogen	1·02 / 6·1 / 14·6	—100° / 0° / 52°	Becomes a white crystalline translucent body, resembling camphor, at —122°.
Carbonic Acid	1·14 / 6·97 / 22·84 / 29·09 / 38·50	—111° / —56° / 0° / 15° / 32°	Becomes a white non-crystalline solid, resembling snow, or, more nearly, anhydrous phosphoric acid, at a temperature of about —148°.
Chlorine	4	60°	Does not become solid at —220°
Nitrous Oxide	50	45°	Becomes a transparent crystalline colorless solid at — 150°
Cyanogen	1·25 / 2·37 / 6·90	0° / 32° / 63°	Becomes a transparent crystalline solid at —30°.
Ammonia	2·48 / 4·44 / 6·9	0° / 32° / 60°	Becomes a white translucent crystalline solid at —103°.
Hydrochloric Acid	1·8 / 15·04 / 26·20	—100° / 0° / 32°	Does not become solid at the lowest attainable temperature.
Olefiant Gas	4·6 / 26·9	—105° / 0°	
Hydriodic Acid	2·9	0°	Becomes a clear solid, like ice, at —60°.
Fluo-silicic Acid	9	—160°	Becomes solid at the lowest attainable temperature.
Arsenuretted Hydrogen	0·94 / 5·21 / 13·19	—75° / 0° / 60°	Does not become solid at —166°.

LECTURE VIII.

EBULLITION—THEORY OF BOILING—MEANS BY WHICH THE BOILING POINTS OF LIQUIDS MAY BE ELEVATED OR DEPRESSED.

---

102. When some water is placed in a vessel over a fire, small bubbles of vapour form at the bottom, rise a little way, collapse and disappear. As the process of heating goes on, these bubbles rise higher and higher, and at length reach the surface, where they escape with bubbling agitation, producing the phenomenon of *ebullition*.

103. Ebullition takes place in a liquid, or, in other words, the liquid *boils*, just as soon as the elasticity of the vapour-bubbles is equal to the pressure upon the surface of the liquid. Until the liquid reaches this point, the bubbles of vapour that form near the bottom of the vessel have their elasticity diminished by loss of heat as they rise through the cooler liquid above them, and are thus unable to maintain themselves, and are consequently crushed in and condensed. *Hence the boiling point of any liquid is that point or degree of temperature at which the elastic force of its vapour is equal to the pressure of the atmosphere.*

104. It follows directly from Art. 103 that we can artificially elevate the boiling point of water or any other liquid by increasing the pressure upon its surface. This is well illustrated by Papin's Digester, which is a vessel so contrived that the steam never escapes, but, accumulating in the upper part, exerts a constant and powerful pressure upon the surface of the water. The vessel is fitted with a safety valve, and in it water may be heated with facility to 350° or 400° F. In fact it is said that water may be made red hot in a Papin's Digester and still retain its fluidity. The chief use of the instrument is to intensely heat certain bodies which require a high temperature for their solution. Thus: bones which resist the action of water at 212° are reduced to a jelly in the Digester.

THEORY OF BOILING.

105. Generally speaking, the greater the specific gravity of a liquid the higher its boiling point, and hence the boiling point of water may be elevated by dissolving any salt in it. Some salts appear to raise the boiling point more than others, thus:

Water saturated with common salt (100 water to 30 salt) boils at 224°.
" " " potash (100 water to 74 potash) " 238°.
" " " chloride of calcium " 264°.

NOTE.—This property is of some practical importance, when it is required to subject a body to a steady temperature somewhat above 212°.

106. The only modes, then, by which the boiling point of water may be raised are:

1st. By increasing the pressure upon its surface; and
2nd. By dissolving a salt in it so as to increase its specific gravity.

It follows that once a liquid boils it can be made no hotter except by one of these two methods. A thermometer plunged in boiling water indicates no change of temperature, no matter how rapidly the process of ebullition may be made to proceed.

NOTE.—This fact is of considerable value in domestic economy. Meats, vegetables, soups, &c., cook just as rapidly when kept gently boiling as when placed on a great fire and made to boil with violence; the unnecessary expenditure of fuel in the latter case being altogether employed in converting a portion of the water into steam

107. It is also evident from Art. 103 that by decreasing the pressure on a surface of a liquid we lower its boiling point. This may be shown by placing a flask of water considerably below the boiling point or but little above blood heat, inside the receiver of an air-pump and rapidly exhausting the air. After a short time, as the exhaustion becomes tolerably complete, the water enters into a state of violent ebullition. In Leslie's process for freezing water (Art. 121), where a first-class air-pump is employed, the water may be seen boiling and freezing at one and the same time, or, in other words, it is made to boil at 32° F. The same fact, viz., that decrease of pressure lowers the boiling point, is very beautifully shown by boiling some water in a flask, and while it is in a state of ebullition firmly corking the flask. Now if the water be allowed to cool partially and the flask be then plunged in a vessel of cold water, the liquid in the flask again begins to boil with violence, and the colder the water in the outer vessel the more rapid the ebullition. To understand the reason of this, we have merely to remember that as the flask was corked while the water was boiling, the upper part, or the space between the water and the cork, is filled with vapour, and that upon plunging the flask into cold water, this vapour is condensed and thus a partial vacuum produced. The water then boils from the reduced pressure on its surface, and as fast as new vapour is generated it is condensed by the external cold water.

NOTE.—Mr. Howard's patent process for concentrating the syrup of sugar without scorching and browning it, depends upon the facility with which liquids are evaporated under reduced pressure. The boilers containing the syrup are fitted with air-tight lids, and the air, and the steam also as fast as it is generated, is pumped off by a powerful air-pump worked by a steam engine. By this process sugar syrup may be boiled at 150° F.

The same process is of great value in inspissating vegetable infusions, i. e. in reducing them to the state of extracts for medical purposes; as by this means they are obtained without exposure to a very high temperature and consequent loss of a large amount of the active principle.

108. Since the pressure of the air is greatest at the level of the sea, and regularly decreases as we ascend into the higher regions of the atmosphere, it is plain that water must boil at a lower temperature on elevations than at the sea-level. Thus travellers assert that at the summits of lofty mountains, water boils at so low a temperature that meat and vegetables cannot be cooked. It has been found by experiment that an elevation of 550 feet lowers the boiling point of water 1°, and Saussure ascertained the fact that at the top of Mont Blanc water boils at 184° F. It is also in close agreement with this fact that as we descend into deep mines, the boiling point of water rises above 212°.

109. The pressure of the air at the level of the sea is different at different times, causing the mercurial column in the barometer to vary from 27·74 to 30·6 inches in length, and this unequal pressure modifies to a considerable degree the boiling point of water, as seen in the following table :

Barometer in inches of mercury.   Water boils.
    27·74... 208° F.
    28·29... 209°
    28·84... 210°
    29·41... 211°
    29·92... 212°
    30·6.. 213°

Thus the unequal pressure of the atmosphere causes a difference in the boiling point of water equal to about 5°, and this fact must be attended to in fixing the boiling point of water on a thermometric scale. It is only when the barometer stands at 29·92 that the boiling point of water is 212°.

110. Besides the variation in the boiling point under increase of pressure or density, the nature of the containing vessel exerts a modifying influence. Thus in a rough metal vessel water boils at 212°, in a clean glass vessel at 214°. If the glass has been previously well cleaned with hot sulphuric acid, water may be heated to 221° before it boils. On the other hand, in a vessel coated on the inside with sulphur or shell-lac, water boils at 211°. The cause of this phenomenon appears to be but very imperfectly understood, as in the case when it is cooled considerably below its common freezing point, the water appears to be in a condition of unstable equilibrium, and the least agitation, or the introduction of an angular body, at once induces the suspended process.

LECTURE IX.

HIGH PRESSURE STEAM—ELASTIC FORCE OF CONFINED STEAM—VOLUME OF VAPOURS—RELATION BETWEEN THE SENSIBLE AND THE INSENSIBLE HEAT OF VAPOURS.

---

111. If the hand or any other part of the body be exposed for a moment or two to the steam generated by water boiling under ordinary circumstances, it is very severely scalded; but, when steam of high pressure, and which is consequently much hotter than ordinary steam, escapes through the safety valve of a boiler and issues into the air, the hand may be, with perfect safety, immersed in it. This singular property of high pressure steam is explained as follows—

Elastic bodies escaping from a state of compression expand beyond their original dimensions. They then contract, afterwards expand, again contract, and thus oscillate, as it were, within narrower and narrower limits until they finally regain their normal condition. Now when steam of high pressure escapes into the air it becomes very greatly expanded, and at the same time so mixed with air that it is prevented from subsequently collapsing. When however steam is mingled with two or three times its volume of air it becomes low pressure steam, is not easily condensed, and has its temperature reduced from $250°$ or $300°$ to $120°$ or $130°$, and at this temperature is not sufficiently hot to scald the hand.

112. If a portion of steam not accompanied by water be placed in a vessel and heated, it does not exert a greater elastic force than would an equal volume of atmospheric air inclosed and subjected to the same temperature. But when water is present, more steam continues constantly to rise and accumulate in the upper part of the containing vessel, and, adding its elastic force to that of the steam previously existing, the pressure becomes enormous.

113. The elastic force of steam at temperatures above 212° is determined by means of an arrangement illustrated by Fig. 11 : *a* is a stout globular copper vessel placed on a stand over the flame of a spirit lamp; it contains mercury to the depth of about 2 inches, and over that some water. *b* is a long tube, open at both ends, and having attached to it a scale carefully graduated in inches. The lower end of this tube reaches nearly to the bottom of the vessel *a*, and dips beneath the surface of the mercury. *c* Fig. 11. is a thermometer, the bulb of which is placed just inside the vessel *a*; and *f* is a stop-cock. The water is boiled for some time with the stop-cock *f* open so as to expel all the air; and during this time the thermometer steadily indicates a temperature of 212°, and the mercury in the tube is at the level of that in the vessel *a*, thus showing that steam at 212° has an elastic force equal to the pressure of the atmosphere. The stop-cock *f* is now closed, and the steam accumulating in the upper part of the globe acquires increased elastic force, and, pressing on the surface of the water and thus on the mercury, forces the latter to ascend in the gauge-tube *b*. For every 30 inches the mercury rises in the tube, the confined steam is said to have a pressure or elastic force of another atmosphere. Thus when the mercury in the tube is at the level of that in the vessel, the steam has an elastic force of one atmosphere. When the mercury in the tube is 30, 60, 90, 120, &c., inches above the level of that in the globe, the steam is said to have an elastic force of 2, 3, 4, 5, &c., atmospheres.

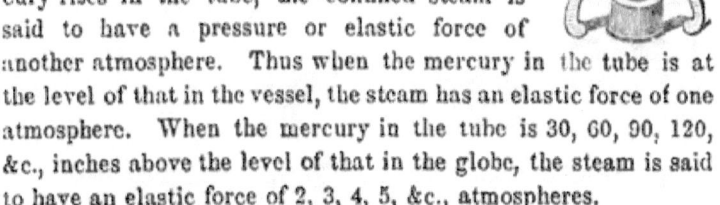

114. The elasticity of steam, at different temperatures, is expressed in atmospheres in the following:

TABLE OF ELASTIC FORCE OF STEAM.

Elasticity in Atmospheres.	Temperature.	Elasticity in Atmospheres.	Temperature.
1	212°F.	8	341·8°F.
1½	233·9°	9	350·8°
2	250·5°	10	358·3°
2½	263·8°	15	392·5°
3	275·2°	20	418·5°
3½	285·1°	25	439·3°
4	293·7°	30	457·2°
4½	300·3°	35	472·7°
5	307·5°	40	486·6°
6	320·4°	45	499·1°
7	331·2°	50	510·6°

115. Equal volumes of different liquids yield very different volumes of vapour.

Thus under ordinary circumstances:

1 cubic inch of water yields 1696 cubic inches of vapour.
1 " alcohol " 519 " "
1 " oil of turpentine " 192 " "

116. From Art. 96 (Chem. Art. 46) it appears that the denser the vapour the less its latent heat. Thus the caloric of elasticity of water-vapour is 972°, and that of alcohol-vapour 385°, i. e., water-vapour has 2½ times more latent heat than an equal weight of alcohol-vapour; but since the specific gravity of alcohol-vapour is 2½ times that of water-vapour, it is manifest that *equal volumes* of the two vapours contain equal amounts of latent heat.

117. Since the latent heat of different vapours is proportional to their volume, it follows that the same expenditure of heat will

generate the same bulk of vapour from all liquids, and hence no advantage would be gained by substituting any other liquid for water in the steam engine.

118. Vapours generated at a low temperature contain more latent heat than those generated at a high one. Thus water may be made to boil in a good vacuum at a temperature of 100° or 150°, but the steam produced is much more diffused and rare than that obtained at 212°, and hence (Art. 77) contains more insensible or latent heat. It has been determined by experiment that equal weights of steam of all temperatures, when condensed by water, raise the temperature of the water through the same number of degrees, or, in other words, the sensible and the insensible heat of steam, added together, amount to a constant quantity.

From this we may obtain a simple rule for determining the latent heat of water-vapour at any temperature. Neglecting the heat which it has at 0° F., the sensible heat of steam at 212° is 212°, and (Art. 96) the latent heat of steam at 212° is 972°. Hence the sum of the sensible and latent heat of steam at 212° is 212° + 972° = 1184°.

Then to find the latent heat of water-vapour at any other temperature, deduct this sensible heat from this constant number 1184°, and the remainder will be the latent heat:

Temperature.		Latent heat of equal weights of steam.
0°	1184° − 0° =	1184°
32°	1184° − 32° =	1152°
100°	1184° − 100° =	1084°
150°	1184° − 150° =	1034°
212°	1184° − 212° =	972°
250°	1184° − 250° =	934°
300°	1184° − 300° =	884°
400°	1184° − 400° =	784°

NOTE.—From this it is evident that no fuel is saved by distilling in vacuo; for to convert a cubic inch of water into steam requires the same amount of heat, no matter what the temperature at which the evaporation is effected.

LECTURE X.

SPONTANEOUS EVAPORATION.

119. It has been remarked (Art. 97) that when some water is admitted into a vacuum the latter becomes instantly filled with vapour. The tension of the vapour thus formed depends upon the temperature, and is measured by the amount of depression it causes in the barometric column when admitted into the Torricellian vacuum. Thus at —22° F. it lowers the mercurial column 0·0144 of an inch, at 32° F. 0·1811 of an inch, at 86° F. 1·2421 inch, at 140° F. 5·8583 inches, and at 212° F. 29·922 inches.

120. Evaporation always produces cold, since it requires a certain amount of heat to convert a liquid into a vapour. This circumstance may be illustrated by a number of facts.

1st. If some ether be dropped upon the hand and allowed to evaporate it produces a very decided sensation of cold.

2nd. The pulse glass (Fig. 12), which consists of a tube bent twice at right angles and terminated by a bulb at each end, is designed to show the same fact. The instrument is filled partially with alcohol and partially with alcohol-vapour. When one bulb is grasped by the hand, the warmth imparted is sufficient to boil the small portion of the liquid that wets the inside, and as this evaporates and distils over into the other bulb, a sensation of cold is produced.

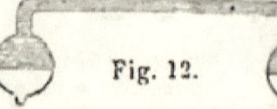

Fig. 12.

3rd. If a small vessel containing water be covered with a cloth kept moistened with ether, the evaporation of the latter produces sufficient cold to congeal the water.

121. Leslie's process for freezing water by its own evaporation depends on this principle. A little water in a cup is supported over a shallow vessel containing concentrated sulphuric acid, and the whole placed on the plate of an air pump and covered with as small a receiver as possible. All that is required is to produce a good vacuum at first. If this be attained and the sulphuric acid is concentrated, the water-vapour is absorbed by the acid as rapidly as it is formed, and the temperature of the water in the cup soon sinks to the freezing point.

NOTE.—Various other bodies, as, for example, chloride of lime, dry parched oatmeal, dry sole leather, &c., would answer for absorbents, though not as well as sulphuric acid. When the acid becomes too much diluted it may be concentrated again by boiling.

122. The Cryophorus, or *frost-bearer* of Wollaston, is also employed to show the congelation of water by its own evaporation. It consists of a tube terminated in bulbs as in Fig. 13, and containing nothing but water and water-vapour. When used, all the water is poured into the bulb a, and the instrument placed upright with the bulb b in a freezing mixture. The vapour in the lower bulb is condensed and thus a partial vacuum formed, which is immediately filled by a new portion of vapour from the water in the upper bulb. By this means a continuous and somewhat rapid process of evaporation takes place in the upper bulb, and finally the temperature of the water contained therein sinks to the freezing point.

Fig. 13.

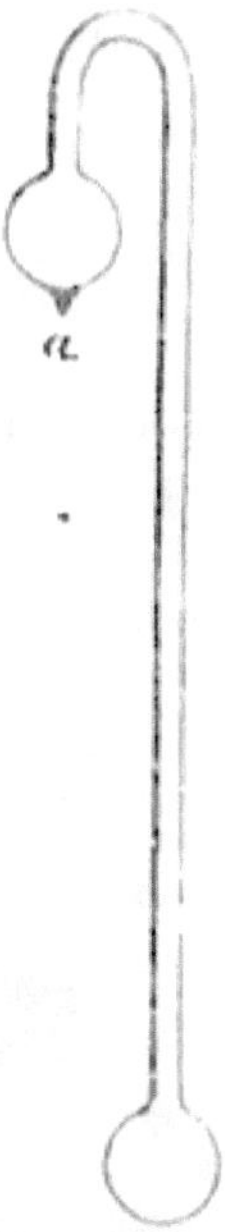

123. Evaporation into a space filled with air or any other gas follows the same law as evaporation into vacuo; the only difference being that in the one case the space becomes filled with vapour instantaneously, in the other it requires time. The quantity of vapour that rises into a portion of space occupied by air or a gas, is precisely the same as would have formed in a vacuum at the same temperature.

If some water be allowed to evaporate into a vacuum at 80° F. it will lower the mercurial column 1 inch, or, in other words, the tension of water vapour at 80°F. is $\frac{1}{30}$ of the usual tension of the air. So, if some dry air at 80°F. be placed over water, the vapour which rises will increase the tension of that air $\frac{1}{30}$ if the air be confined, or will increase its bulk $\frac{1}{30}$ if the air be allowed to expand.

124. Evaporation into air goes on at all temperatures; even in the depth of winter, a large portion of vapour is formed direct from the snow and ice that cover the face of the country. The rapidity and degree to which this spontaneous evaporation is carried on depends chiefly on three circumstances:

1st. The previous dryness of the air.
2nd. Its temperature.
3rd. The rapidity of its movements.

Thus, only as much vapour can rise into a portion of air as would rise into the same space if it were a vacuum, and hence it is evident that the amount of vapour that forms and passes into a given amount of air must depend upon the amount already present in it, or, in other words, upon its previous dryness. So also the higher the temperature, the greater the amount of vapour that rises; and finally evaporation is promoted by a wind which removes the air as fast as it becomes saturated.

125. Humid hot air contains much more vapour than humid cold air; hence when a portion of air saturated with moisture has its temperature lowered, a part of the vapour assumes the liquid form and is deposited in drops, forming *dew*.

Many familiar phenomena depend upon the partial condensation of the vapour present in the air. Thus when a decanter or other vessel of cold water is brought into a heated apartment it becomes rapidly covered with moisture. The cold decanter lowers the temperature of the stratum of air immediately surrounding it, and this, no longer able to retain all its moisture, deposits a portion on the cold glass. Hence also the deposition of moisture upon window panes in bed rooms and other apartments in winter. From the same cause when a warm thaw occurs after a severe frost, brick and stone walls are covered with a profusion of moisture.

126. Hygrometers and Hygroscopes are instruments designed for measuring the amount of vapour in the air at any particular time.

Fig. 14.

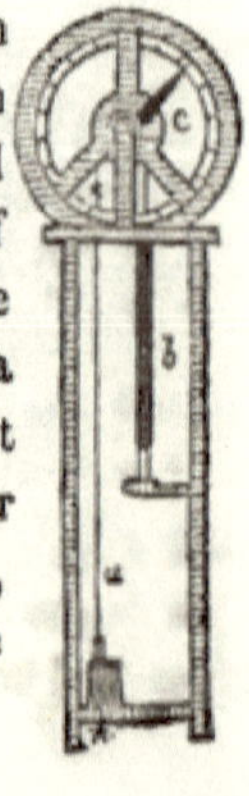

127. Saussure's Hair Hygrometer is represented in Fig. 14. It consists essentially of a human hair freed from grease by immersion in sulphuric ether. This prepared hair is fixed by one end to a hook in the lower part of the frame, is then passed over a pulley carrying the index *c*, and is attached by the other extremity to a delicate spring, *b*. As the hair becomes moist it lengthens, and the spring *b* contracting draws it over the pulley and thus moves the index to the right; again, as the hair dries, it contracts and thus moves the index in the opposite direction.

HYGROMETERS.

128. Another mode of determining the amount of vapour in the air is by means of the Psycrometer, or wet-bulb thermometer. This consists of two delicate thermometers attached to a frame (Fig. 15), one having its bulb covered with muslin kept constantly moistened by water which passes along the string in connection with the reservoir. Evaporation produces cold, hence the wet-bulb thermometer indicates a temperature lower than the dry-bulb thermometer, in proportion as the evaporation is more or less rapid. If the air be very dry this process is very rapid, and the wet-bulb thermometer indicates a temperature much lower than the other; if, on the other hand, the air be saturated with moisture, no evaporation takes place, and the thermometers both indicate the same temperature.

Fig. 15.

129. The dew-point is much more easily determined by means of Daniell's Hygrometer. This instrument consists of a tube terminated in bulbs, as represented in Fig. 16, and containing nothing but ether and ether-vapour. The bulb *a* is covered with muslin, and the bulb *b* contains a delicate thermometer. The instrument acts upon the principle of the Cryophorus. When an observation is to be made, the muslin about *a* is kept moistened with ether, which by its evaporation produces cold. The vapour contained in *a* is thus condensed, and evaporation of the ether in *b* promoted. By this means the temperature of *b* is gradually lowered, and finally reaches the point at which the surrounding air parts with a portion of its moisture and deposits it as dew upon the cooled glass.

Fig. 16.

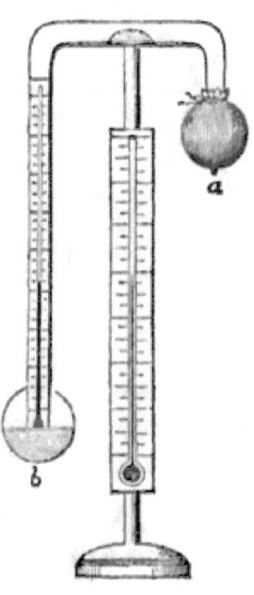

LECTURE XI.

SPHEROIDAL STATE OF MATTER.

130. If into a red-hot crucible we pour a small quantity of water, and continue to keep the crucible intensely heated, the water assumes the form of a sphere, and, gliding with a peculiar rotatory motion over the bottom of the capsule, evaporates very slowly and without ebullition; in other words, it does not reach its boiling point, and in fact does not become sufficiently hot to scald the hand if thrown upon it. The water when in this condition is said to be in the *spheroidal state*. Now, if the crucible be allowed to cool, as soon as it has reached a temperature not more than 75° or 80° above the boiling point of water, the spheroidal condition is lost and the liquid begins to boil with explosive violence, being rapidly dissipated in steam.

NOTE.—This is explained by supposing that at a very high temperature that species of attraction which water has for the surface of almost all solids gives place to a sort of repulsive action. Hence when water is dropped upon an intensely heated surface, it does not come in contact with it, but becomes surrounded by an envelope of steam or vapour of high tension, which, being a very imperfect conductor of heat, tends to retard the passage of heat to the liquid; but when the temperature of the surface declines, the tension of this vapour is lessened, and at the same time the repulsive action between the heated surface and the water is diminished, the heat is rapidly transmitted to the liquid, and it suddenly bursts into ebullition.

NOTE 2.—A rude method of testing the heat of smoothing-irons is based upon this principle. A drop of saliva is thrown upon its surface, and if the iron be sufficiently heated the drop glides over it without wetting it, but if not hot enough it adheres and rapidly boils off.

131. Other liquids besides water may be thrown into the spheroidal state, and the temperatures at which they pass into this condition are proportional to their boiling points. In the following table the first column gives the name of the substance, the second its ordinary boiling point, the third the temperature at or above which the heated surface must be in order to throw the liquid into the spheroidal state, and the fourth column the temperature, as indicated by a thermometer, of the liquid while in the spheroidal state.

Water,	212° F.	288° F.	206° F.
Alcohol,	173°	273°	168°
Ether,	96°	142°	93.5°
Hydrochloric Ether,	52°		51°
Sulphurous Acid,	14°		13°

The numbers in the fourth column are in all probability somewhat too high on account of the difficulty of preventing the thermometer from being influenced to some extent by the heat **radiated** by the heated surface. We **may** safely infer that—

The temperature of a liquid in a spheroidal state is invariably some degrees below its boiling point.

132. The spheroidal state of matter was first examined by **Leidenfrost** in the year 1756, and has since been extensively investigated by M. Boutigny. According to the definition of the latter,

A body is said to be in the spheroidal state, when its temperature remains unchanged while resting on a surface with which it has no actual contact, **and the temperature of which surface may be raised indefinitely.**

NOTE.—When a drop of liquid is in the spheroidal state on a flat surface, that there is no contact is proved by the fact that the light of a lamp is visible between the spheroid and the metal plate. Concentrated nitric acid does not, while in the spheroidal state, act upon the hot silver or other metallic surface upon which it **rests**, although it instantly attacks and corrodes the metal if sufficiently **cold**. Acids and alkalies may be thrown together into an intensely heated platinum crucible and **no** chemical action ensues; the two bodies, forming themselves into separate globules, roll around, singularly repelling each other.

133. All **bodies are** capable of assuming the spheroidal state, and **when in** that condition possess the remarkable property of reflecting nearly all the heat that is radiated to them.

134. Taking advantage of the fact that the temperature of liquids in the spheroidal state is always some degrees below the boiling point, Faraday has succeeded in freezing water, and even **mercury, in a red-hot** capsule.

Thus if into a capsule heated to redness, or better still to whiteness, some *liquid* sulphurous acid be thrown, it passes into the spheroidal condition, and reaching only the temperature of 13° F. slowly evaporates. Now when some water is permitted to drop gradually into the spheroidal acid, the latter rapidly abstracts from the water-drops the heat they contain, and, thus reducing their temperature, freezes them.

In order to congeal mercury, a small capsule filled with it is plunged into a mixture of solid carbonic acid and ether in the spheroidal state contained in a red-hot crucible. The mixture of carbonic acid and ether abstracts heat from the mercury, and the latter is, in a few moments, thrown out from the glowing crucible a solid frozen mass.

135. It has been proved by numerous and repeated experiments that perfect immunity from the caloric of intensely heated bodies may be secured by previously wetting the part to which the application is made with water or some more volatile fluid. Thus if the hand be moistened with ether or alcohol, it may be safely plunged into boiling water, or if it be moistened with either of these or with water it may be dipped into molten lead or iron without being burned. It is even said that when the hand has been previously moistened with liquid sulphurous acid, a sensation of cold is experienced while it is immersed in the glowing metal.

NOTE.—This is explained by the fact that when the moistened hand is plunged into the melted metal the moisture slowly passes into the state of vapour and forms a species of non-conducting glove around the hand. The dry parts not immersed suffer much more from the radiated caloric than do the parts actually dipped beneath the surface of the metal.

136. The trial by ordeal of walking on hot plough-shares, frequently employed in the Middle Ages as a test of guilt, was always successful if the plough-shares were sufficiently hot, i. e., if they were heated above the temperature of 490° or 500°, or if they were red-hot, because then a cushion of vapour was formed between the foot and the iron, and effectually protected the former from injury. But if the iron were only heated to 200° or 250°, the foot came in direct contact with it and was severely burned. The same explanation holds with regard to passing a bar of red hot iron across the tongue,—a feat often exhibited by blacksmiths.

APPENDIX TO HEAT.

SOURCES OF HEAT.

137. The Sun.—The amount of heat annually received by the earth from the sun, has been estimated to be sufficient to melt a stratum of ice 101 feet thick.

The atmosphere is supposed to absorb 40 per cent. of the heat of the sun's rays.

The total heat emitted by the sun is 2381 million times as great as that received by the earth.

The heat at the surface of the sun is seven times as great as that of a blast furnace, the temperature of which is certainly not less than 3500° F.

138. The Stars.—It is estimated that the fixed stars (all of which are suns) furnish to the earth an amount of heat equal to four-fifths of that supplied by the sun, and that without this auxiliary source of heat neither animal nor vegetable life could exist upon the earth.

139. The Earth.—The temperature of the earth's surface is not uniform but decreases from the equator to the poles.

The temperature falls as we ascend, and also as we descend to a certain point which is variable, but which is nowhere more than 100 feet below the surface. At a distance of from 40 to 100 feet below the surface, the temperature remains unchanged, i.e., is always the same as the *mean* temperature of the surface. Even at the moderate depth of 4 or 5 feet (covered) the thermometer ceases to mark the *daily* range of temperature. At a distance of from 40 to 100 feet below the surface, the internal and external heat may be said to be balanced.

Below this stratum of constant temperature the thermometer rises 1° F. for every 60 feet descent. This is proved by various circumstances, as descent into deep mines, Artesian wells, the occurrence of thermal springs, &c.

It follows that at a very moderate depth water would boil, metals would melt, rocks would fuse, and the hardest substances in nature would become converted into a red hot liquid mass.

The distance in which this latter occurs is variously estimated at from 21 to 100 miles. We may safely conclude that the crust of the earth is not more than 50 miles in thickness or $\frac{1}{80}$ of the earth's radius; but it is not everywhere of the same thickness, as is proved by the fact that the temperature rises much more rapidly as we descend in some places than in others.

The temperature at the earth's centre must be inconceivably great. It has been estimated at 450000° F. (A temperature of 12000° F. melts the hardest known substances.)

Hence we must regard the earth as a mass of molten fire with a comparatively thin enveloping crust (comparable to the skin of onion) on which we all act our varied parts unconscious of the fire which rages beneath us.

The internal heat radiates so slowly to the surface, that its effect is scarcely perceptible, not raising the thermometer more than $\frac{1}{17}$ of a degree Fahr.

The internal heat received by the surface in the course of a year would melt a crust of ice $\frac{1}{4}$ of an inch in thickness, (M. de Beaumont,) while the absolute quantity of heat received by the earth's surface annually from the sun, would melt a crust of ice 101 feet in thickness. (Puillet.)

The cooling of the earth's crust was much more rapid formerly than now, and consequently, the increase of temperature in proportion to descent was much greater. It has been estimated that more than 30,000 years would be required to lessen by one-half the present rate of increase, i. e., to reduce the increase for every 60 feet descent from 1° to $\frac{1}{2}$° F.

140. Extremes of Terrestrial Temperature.—Captain Parry records a temperature of —59° F. at Melville Island in 1819; Captain Black at Fort Reliance, Lat. 60° 46′ N. a temperature of —70° F.; Dr. Smith records a temperature of 114° F. in the shade, and 144° F. in the sun, at Mosul, near Bagdad. Thus the range in the shade is about 200° in different latitudes. In this latitude there is often a difference of more than 100° F. between the maximum of summer and the minimum of winter.

141. Chemical Action.—Equivalents of the different acids combining with the same base produce the same quantity of heat.

Equivalents of different bases combining with the same acid, produce different quantities of heat, the most powerful base evolving the most heat.

When a neutral salt is converted into an acid salt there is no disengagement of heat.

When a neutral salt is converted into a basic salt there is a disengagement of heat (Graham, Hess, and Andrews)

142. Animal and Vegetable Heat.—The temperature of organized beings is generally higher than that of the medium in which they live. This vital heat is developed by the so called *vital* action, which is merely another name for chemical action occurring within the body of the plant or animal.

In birds and mammals, the heat evolved is sufficient to maintain the temperature of the body at from 90° F. to 100° F.; in the *cold blooded* animals less heat is generated, but the blood is always a few degrees warmer than the surrounding medium.

The temperature of plants is usually about 1° higher than the surrounding air, but in some exceptional cases, as for example when just expanding their flower buds, the temperature may be 50° or 60° above that of the air.

143. Heat and mechanical force, like force and velocity, are mutually exchangeable terms. Thus a given amount of heat will perform a certain amount of work, and a certain amount of force as friction, or percussion will supply a definite amount of heat.

For instance, the mechanical effect produced by the combustion of one bushel of coals weighing 84 lbs., is sufficient to raise 120,000,000 lbs. one foot. (See Part 1, Arts, 163, 168.)

LIGHT.

LECTURE XII.

THEORIES, DEFINITIONS, PHOTOMETERS AND PHOTOMETRY.

144. Two theories have been advanced by philosophers, with respect to the nature of Light:

1st. The Corpuscular Theory of Sir Isaac Newton.
2nd. The Wave Theory of Huygens.

145. The Corpuscular Theory, theory of emission, or Newtonian Theory, assumes that all luminous bodies are constantly emitting or throwing out infinitely small particles of their substance, and that these, moving with exceeding great velocity, penetrate the transparent coats of the eye, and, falling upon the nervous tissue, produce the sensation of light.

146. The assumptions in the Wave Theory are chiefly two, viz.—

1st. That all space is filled by an extremely rare elastic fluid or medium called the *luminiferous ether*.—This ether is supposed not only to fill the space above and beyond the atmosphere and extending out to the sun, and planets, and fixed stars, but also to penetrate the atmosphere, and even the densest liquids and solids occupying their intermolecular spaces.

2nd. That the particles of a luminous body are in a state of perpetual and very rapid vibration, and that these vibrating particles impinge upon the luminiferous ether and produce in it a series of undulations or waves, which, moving with greater or less rapidity, strike upon the retina and thereby give rise to the sensation of light.

147. It will thus be observed that the corpuscular theory regards light as acting upon the optic nerve in a manner analogous to that in which odorous bodies act upon the olfactory nerve; while the wave theory explains the action of light upon the optic nerve as being similar to that of sound upon the auditory nerve.

148. It is not absolutely necessary to pin our faith to either of these theories in order to acquire a tolerably clear idea of the principal facts in the science of light. The wave theory is the more generally adopted at the present day, because it affords a clearer and more simple explanation of many phenomena, as is proved by the researches of Fresnel, Young, Fraunhöfer, Herschel, and others; yet a large number of very remarkable facts are not clearly elucidated by the undulatory hypothesis; and the corpuscular theory of Newton, developed by Laplace and Biot, and supported by Brewster and Brougham, is capable of affording an explanation of some luminous effects which do not appear to be the result of undulations.

DEFINITIONS, &C.

149. Light is that which enables us to see bodies.

150. All visible bodies are divided into:

    I. Self-luminous bodies.
    II. Non-luminous bodies or Illuminated bodies.

151. All self-luminous bodies discharge, and all illuminated bodies reflect, light of the same color as themselves.

152. Light is emitted from **every** visible point of a luminous body or of an illuminated body in **every direction** in which the point is visible.

153. Light moves in straight lines, and consists of separate and distinct parts called **rays** of light.

154. A ray of light is the smallest portion that we **can either stop or allow to pass.**

FORMATION OF SHADOWS.

155. A pencil of light consists of a greater or smaller number of rays.

156. Transparent bodies are those which allow so large a quantity of light to pass, that objects are distinctly visible through their substance.

157. Opaque bodies are those which do not permit light to pass through their substance.

158. Translucent bodies are those which are semi-transparent, or which allow a measure of light to pass, but not sufficient to enable one to discern objects through them.

159. When an opaque body is placed before a luminous one, the rays of light proceeding from the latter being unable to pass through it or to bend round it are more or less completely intercepted, and the result is the production of a shadow on that side of the opaque body remote from the source of light.

160. If the luminous body be one of any considerable magnitude, the shadow projected by the opaque one consists of a central part, totally devoid of light, called the *umbra*, and an external shell of partial obscuration called the *penumbra*.

161. If the luminous body be a mere point, there is no shading off from the dark umbra to the illuminated portion; in other words there is no penumbra.

162. A body always casts a shadow having the same geometrical outline as itself.

163. If the opaque body be a sphere and be placed before a luminous body having some considerable magnitude:—then

1st. If the opaque body be of the same size as the luminous body, the shadow will be cylindrical and extended to infinity.

2nd. If the opaque body be smaller than the luminous, the shadow will be convergent, and the rapidity with which it converges will depend upon the distance between the opaque and luminous bodies; and

3rd. If the opaque body be larger than the luminous body, the shadow will diverge, and the rapidity of its divergence will depend upon the distance between the luminous and opaque bodies.

PHOTOMETERS, &C.

164. The illuminating power of a light depends upon several circumstances.
1st. The absolute intensity of the light.
2nd. The color of the light.
3rd. The magnitude of the luminous surface.
4th. The distance of the luminous body from the object illuminated.
5th. The angle at which the rays of light fall upon the object.
6th. The degree to which the rays are absorbed in passing through the air, &c., &c.

165. Photometers are instruments designed to measure the relative intensities of different lights, and depend essentially upon the principle that the illuminating powers of lights of the same absolute intensity and having equal magnitudes vary inversely as the square of the distance between the light and the object illuminated.

166. The methods of photometry commonly employed are:
1st. Rumford's method, by comparison of shadows.
2nd. Ritchie's method, by comparison of illuminated surfaces.
3rd. The method by extinction of shadows.

167. The apparatus necessary in Rumford's method consists of a white screen and a small opaque rod. It proceeds upon the principle that when two lights both cast a shadow of the same opaque body, the more intense light casts the deeper shadow.— The lights are placed in such a manner that the two shadows of the rod, which are cast so as to be in juxtaposition, are of the same depth or intensity, when the illuminating powers of the lights are compared by comparing their distances from the rod. Thus, the magnitude of the lights being the same—if they are equally distant from the rod, their intensities are equal—if the one be twice as remote as the other, its intensity will be *four* times as great, &c.

168. Ritchie's Photometer, Fig. 17, consists of a box $a\,b$ about 8 or 10 inches in length and 1 inch in diameter, and having in the middle a small triangular wedge, with its sides, $m\,s, m\,g$, inclined at an angle of about 45 degrees to the bottom. This wedge is neatly covered with white paper. At the summit of the box there is a conical tube having an aperture d to which the eye is applied. The lights to be examined are placed at l and l', and are altered in position until both surfaces of the wedge $s\,m\,g$ are equally illuminated, when, as before, the illuminating powers of the lights are as the squares of their distances from the central point m.

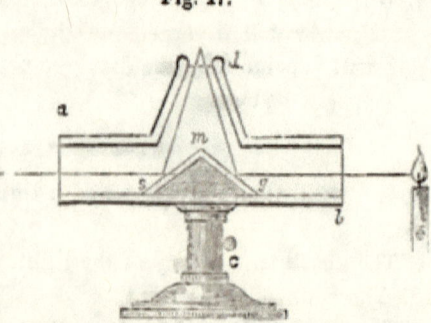

Fig. 17.

169. The method by extinction of shadows depends upon the following principle: If an opaque object is placed between a luminous body and a screen it casts a shadow. Now if a second light be introduced, it may be so placed with reference to the screen as to just obliterate all trace of the shadow. The *intensities* of the lights are then as the squares of their distances from the *screen*.

LECTURE XIII.

DECOMPOSITION OF LIGHT, NEWTON'S SPECTRUM, BREWSTER'S SPECTRUM, CALORIFIC RAYS, ACTINISM, FRAUNHOFER'S SPECTRAL LINES.

170. White light, as emitted from the sun or any luminous body, is a compound of differently colored lights and may be decomposed, analyzed, or separated into its elementary parts by two methods, viz:—

    1st. By Refraction.
    2nd. By Absorption.

NEWTON'S SPECTRUM.

171. Light is decomposed by refraction by placing a triangular glass prism opposite a small hole perforated in the shutter of a darkened room, and causing the admitted ray to fall, after passing through the prism, upon the wall or a screen.

Fig. 18.

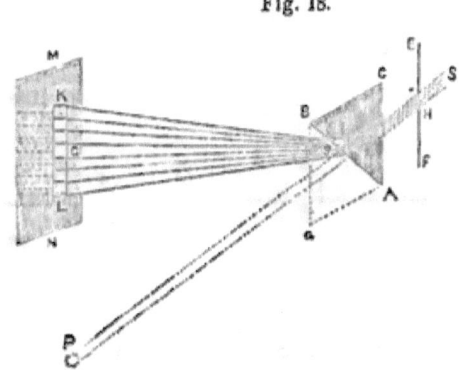

172. When a ray of light is thus decomposed, its elementary constituents arrange themselves on the screen so as to form an elongated colored figure, called the *Prismatic Spectrum*.

Thus, *S H* is a ray of white light passing through a small hole in the shutter *E F*, and then through the triangular glass prism *A B C*. The beam of light, instead of passing on in a straight line to *P*, is bent out of its course and dispersed into a spectrum, *K L*, exhibiting the seven prismatic colors.

173. The order of the colors in the prismatic spectrum is, commencing with the least refrangible ray, as follows:

> Red.
> Orange
> Yellow
> Green.
> Blue.
> Indigo.
> Violet.

174. The cause of the dispersion of light in the prismatic spectrum is found in the unequal refrangibility of the different colors. Thus red, being nearest the line of direction of the original ray of white light, is said to be the least refrangible, while violet, the most remote, is called the most refrangible color.

NOTE.—The whole length of the spectrum, and also the relative lengths of the colored spaces, differ with the substance of which the prism is made—depending upon what is called the *dispersive power* of the body.

175. The colored spaces in the spectrum are not all equally long,—and indeed it is a very difficult matter to detect the boundary line between any two adjacent colors. After many trials, however, Newton and Fraunhöfer have determined the lengths of the colored spaces to be as follows:—

MAGNITUDE OF COLORED SPACES.

	R	O	Y	G	B	I	V
Newton...	45	27	40	60	60	48	80
Fraunhöfer	56	27	27	46	48	47	109

NOTE.—The spectrum was in each case supposed to be divided into 360 equal parts, and Newton's numbers are for a crown glass prism, while Fraunhöfer's are for a prism of flint glass.

176. If a second prism, a *B A*, of precisely the same kind, be applied to the first, *B A C*, as indicated in Fig. 18, the seven prismatic colors are *recompounded* into ordinary white light; and the beam of light thus produced passes on to P, the point on which it would have fallen had no prism whatever been interposed. So if a circular disc of card-board be divided into colored spaces, as in Fig. 19, and be made to rapidly rotate upon its axis, the colors, if pure, blend into one another and produce white light. Similarly, impalpable powders of the different colors may be mixed together so as to appear white or grayish white.

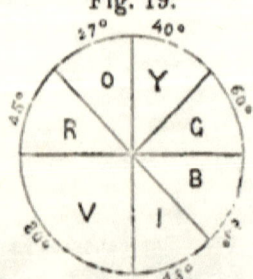

Fig. 19.

177. The illuminating power of the spectrum is greatest in the yellow space, and decreases towards either end. Thus, representing the maximum illuminating effect, as in the yellow, by 1000, we have the following:

TABLE OF ILLUMINATING POWERS.

R	O	Y	G	B	I	V
94	640	1000	480	170	31	6

178. By placing delicate thermometers in the differently colored portions of the spectrum and allowing them to remain until each color had exerted its maximum effect, Herschel discovered that the calorific rays of greatest intensity are accumulated outside the spectrum, a little beyond the red space. Sir Henry Englefield subsequently determined the heating powers of the different colors to be as follows:

Blue,   56°
Green,   58°
Yellow,   62°
Red,   72°
Beyond Red 79°

NOTE.—The thermometer fell again to 72° when returned into the red part of the spectrum.

179. The place of maximum chemical effect in the spectrum may be determined by casting it on a sheet of paper imbued with chloride of silver, when it will be found that the discoloration is most rapid and complete in, or rather beyond, the violet band, and thence decreases to the red extremity. The difference of chemical or actinic power is also observed when small bottles filled with a mixture of chlorine and hydrogen are simultaneously immersed in the colored spaces. The chemical rays possess the power of causing these gases to combine with explosive violence; and it is found that this effect is produced most rapidly beyond the violet extremity of the spectrum, in what Herschel terms the *lavender* band, and that actinism is scarcely at all manifested beyond the yellow portion of the spectrum.

180. When light is admitted into a darkened room through a slit or fissure in the shutter not more than one thirtieth of an inch

in width, the spectrum formed by the interposed prism is found to be crossed by numerous black lines which invariably maintain the same position with respect to the colored bands. These lines were first discovered by Wollaston, but were more carefully examined by Fraunhöfer of Munich, who enumerated 354. Subsequently Sir David Brewster determined the existence of 2000, and he has inserted that number in his map of the solar spectrum. None of the lines exactly correspond with the boundaries of the colored spaces.

Fig. 20.
Violet.

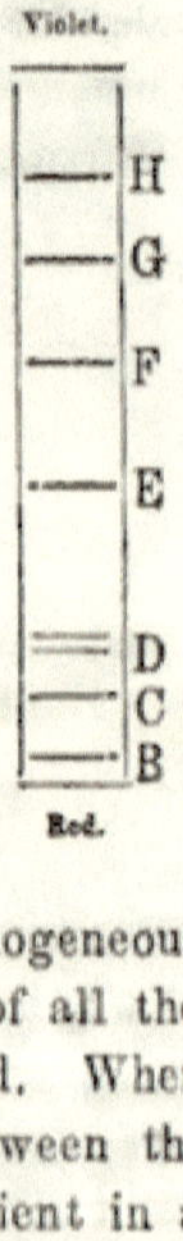

181. From their distinctness, seven of the lines alluded to are much used as land-marks or points of reference, and are distinguished as the *spectral lines B, C, D, E, F, G, H,* of Fraunhöfer.

Of these, *B* lies in the red near its outer margin; *C* is a broad black line beyond the middle of the red; *D* is a strong double line in the orange; *E* is in the green; *F* is a very strong line in the blue; *G* is in the indigo, and *H* in the violet.

NOTE.—These lines are of great use in enabling us to measure accurately the refractive and dispersive powers of different bodies.

H
G
F
E
D
C
B
Red.

BREWSTER'S SPECTRUM.

182. When a beam of white light is transmitted through a piece of blue glass, the transmitted light is of a blue color. This blue, however, is not a simple homogeneous color, like the blue of the spectrum, but is composed of all the colors of white light which the glass has not absorbed. When we interpose a piece of glass of this description between the prism and the spectrum, the latter is found to be deficient in a certain portion of its colored rays. Thus the glass is found to have absorbed a great part of the red, the whole of the orange, most of the green, a considerable part of the blue, less of the indigo, and very little of the violet. In the spectrum, the yellow, which is scarcely at all absorbed, is found to extend over the space formerly occupied by the orange on the one side and the green on the other. Hence, by absorption, orange light has been decomposed into red and yellow, and green light into yellow and blue.

183. From repeated observations on the absorption of light by different colored media, Brewster has come to the conclusion that the solar spectrum consists of three superimposed spectra of equal lengths, viz.:

>1st. A Red Spectrum.
>2nd. A Yellow Spectrum.
>3rd. A Blue Spectrum.

The maximum of the *primary red* spectrum is about the middle of the red space of the solar spectrum; the maximum of the *primary yellow* spectrum is in the middle of the yellow space; and the maximum of the *primary blue* spectrum is in the boundary between the blue and indigo spaces. The two minima of each of the three primary spectra coincide at the two extremities of the solar spectrum.

184. The coloration of the different parts of the solar spectrum is accounted for by Brewster's theory as follows:

I. Red, yellow, and blue light exist in every part of the spectrum.

II. A certain portion of these three primary colors combine so as to form white light in every part of the spectrum.

III. In the red space there is more than a sufficiency of red light to produce white light by combination with all the yellow and all the blue, i. e., surplus or uncombined red rays produce the characteristic color of that portion of the spectrum.

IV. At the space next above the red, all the blue light is combined with a part of the yellow and a part of the red to form white light, and the surplus red and yellow unite to produce orange.

V. In the yellow band, all the red and all the blue combine with a part only of the yellow to form white light, and the remaining yellow colors the space.

VI. In the space next above the yellow, all the red neutralizes a portion only of the yellow and of the blue, and the surplus of these two colors combine to form green.

VII. In the blue portion, all the red, nearly all the yellow, and a small part of the blue, or more properly of the indigo, combine to form white, and the remaining indigo unites with the remaining yellow to produce blue light.
VIII. The indigo band is produced by all the red and all the yellow, requiring a small portion only of the indigo for the production of white light.
IX. In the violet space there is rather more red than yellow, and the surplus red combining with the indigo, or the so called blue, produces violet light.
X. By absorbing at any point of the spectrum the excess of any color above what is necessary to produce white light, we may cause white light to appear, and this white light cannot be decomposed by refraction.
XI. Representing primary red light by the letter R, primary yellow by Y, and primary blue by B, the proportions of these primary colors that enter into the composition of different parts of the spectrum are as follows :—

COLOR.	PROPORTION OF PRIMARY RAYS.	
White	20 R +	30 Y + 50 B
Red	8 R	
Orange	7 R +	7 Y
Yellow		7 Y
Green		10 Y + 10 B
Blue		6 Y + 12 B
Indigo		13 B
Violet	5 R	+ 15 B

LECTURE XIV.

ABSORPTION OF LIGHT, NATURAL COLORATION OF BODIES, COMPLEMENTARY COLORS.

ABSORPTION OF LIGHT.

185. When a ray of light falls on a surface, it may be either
Absorbed,
Transmitted, or
Reflected.

ABSORPTION OF LIGHT.

Commonly, however, it happens that the light thrown on a surface is partly absorbed, partly transmitted, and partly reflected, or partly absorbed and partly reflected.

186. Bodies differ very greatly in their capacity for absorbing common light; but even the most transparent, as **air and water, absorb some, and the** amount absorbed increases with **the thickness of the stratum of the** transmitting **medium through which the light passes.**

Thus, on the summits of lofty mountains many stars are visible which are never seen on the plains below; and objects are not visible through depths of water exceeding thirty or forty feet, even when remarkably clear.

187. In the following list **the bodies decrease in** absorptive power from the first **to the last:**

Charcoal	—	Rock Crystal	—
Coal		Selenite	
Hot Nitrous Acid Gas		Glass	
Metals		Mica	—
Black Hornblende	—	Water and transparent fluids	
Black Pleonaste		Air and colorless gases.	
Obsidian			

NOTE.—Charcoal in the form of gas or flame, and in a particular form of aggregation, as in the diamond, is transparent. Also some of the metals, as gold and silver, are translucent in thin films—gold transmitting green, and silver blue light.

188. Several hypotheses have been advanced to account for the phenomenon of absorption, but none have, as yet, been deemed very satisfactory. The principal are the following:—

I. That the particles or rays of light are actually stopped by the particles of the body, and remain within it, in the form of imponderable matter (Brewster).

II. That the light is lost within the body by the interference of the different parts of the ray, which after taking two routes of different lengths, meet again in a condition to *interfere* (Herschel).

III. The absorption of light arises from the multitude of reflections in the interior of the body (Newton).

NATURAL COLORATION OF BODIES.

189. Ink, black pleonaste, obsidian, and some other bodies absorb all the colors of the spectrum equally; but, as a general thing, the different colored rays are not absorbed in equal proportions. Hence arises the natural color of bodies.

190. The principal points to remember in regard to the causes of the reflected colors of bodies are the following:—

I. A body which absorbs all the white light that falls upon it, appears *black*.

II. A body that reflects all the light that falls upon it, or that reflects all the prismatic colors in proper proportions to compose white light, appears *white*.

III. A body which appears *red*, when placed in ordinary white light, exhibits that color because it absorbs all the blue and yellow rays, and reflects only the *red*.

IV. A body that appears *blue* in ordinary white light, exhibits that tint because it absorbs all the yellow and red rays, and reflects only the blue.

V. A body that appears *orange* in ordinary white light, exhibits that color because it absorbs all the blue rays, and reflects the red and yellow rays in proper proportion to form orange, &c.

VI. All bodies, of whatever color, exhibit that color only when placed in white light, or in compound light of which that color is a constituent, or in homogeneous light of that color.

VII. Thus, a body which reflects homogeneous red when placed in white light, and which does not reflect white light from its outer surface, will appear *black* if placed in homogeneous blue, or indigo, or green, or yellow light, because it absorbs all these colors. If placed in homogeneous *red* light, it reflects all the light thrown upon it, and appears red; if in homogeneous orange, or violet light, it absorbs the yellow or blue, and reflects the red, and hence appears red.

VIII. Similarly, a body which is green in white light, is blue in homogeneous blue light, since there is no yellow to reflect; is yellow in homogeneous yellow light, since there is no blue to reflect; is yellow in orange light, because it absorbs the red and reflects the yellow; and is black in homogeneous red light.

COMPLEMENTARY COLORS.

191. The transmitted tints of bodies arise from the unequal absorption or reflection of the colored rays of light. All the rays stopped either by reflection or absorption, or both, will form by their union a compound color, which will be complementary to the transmitted color

192. Complementary colors are those which by their union produce white light. To find the complementary color of any of the prismatic colors, take, in a pair of compasses, half the length of the spectrum; then setting one leg on the given color, the other will fall on the complementary color.

TABLE OF COMPLEMENTARY COLORS.

Red	Bluish Green.
Orange	Blue.
Yellow	Indigo.
Green	Reddish Violet.
Blue	Orange Red.
Indigo	Orange Yellow.
Violet	Yellow Green.
Black	White.
White	Black.

LECTURE XV.

THEORY OF TRANSVERSE VIBRATIONS, CAUSE OF COLOR AND BRILLIANCY OF LIGHT, INTERFERENCE OF LIGHT.

THEORY OF TRANSVERSE VIBRATIONS.

193. According to the Wave theory, light is caused by undulations in the ether, and, since it is proved by astronomical observation that light travels at the rate of 192,000 miles per second, the undulations that produce light must advance with that velocity.

194. In producing these undulations, the particles of ether do not move forward at all, but simply vibrate or oscillate up and down, and thus, without advancing themselves, propagate an onward motion. (See Part I. Art. 349, NOTE.)

NOTE.—This can be satisfactorily illustrated by tying one end of a tolerably long rope to a wall, and holding the other end in the hand so as not to have it drawn tight, agitating the free extremity up and down. A series of waves or undulations is propagated along the rope, but the particles of which the rope is composed do not themselves advance in the least.

195. It is customary to make a distinction between the terms undulation and vibration, the latter being regarded as the cause and the former as the effect. Thus, in the experiment with the rope, the movement of the hand up and down is the vibration or cause, and the wave-like movement that runs along the rope is the undulation or effect.

196. The vibrations that produce luminous undulations in the ether are always transverse to the direction of the ray. Thus, if the ray is running north and south, the vibration producing it was made east and west, or in any other direction at *right angles* to a line running north and south. The undulations of the air, on the contrary, which give rise to the phenomena of sound, are produced by vibrations which are normal to the ray, i. e. made in the same direction in which the ray is moving.

NOTE.—Although we can only perceive by the eye movements produced by the transverse vibrations of the ether, and by the ear movements produced by normal vibrations in the air, it has been suggested that other creatures may be able to distinguish, by their senses of sight, or hearing, or feeling, movements in the ether produced by normal, and in the atmosphere produced by transverse vibrations.

197. The amplitude of a wave or undulation in a fluid is determined by the distance to which it rises or falls above or below its original position in the fluid in a state of rest; or, the amplitude of the wave may be said to be measured by "the magnitude of the excursions of the vibrating particles."

198. The length of a wave is measured by the distances between the crests of two adjacent waves or undulations.

199. The brilliancy of all light depends upon the amplitude of the waves producing it,—the greater the amplitude, the more brilliant the light. The color of the light depends upon the length of the wave,—the longest waves producing red, the shortest waves violet light, and waves of intermediate length the other colors in the order of their refrangibility.

PHENOMENON OF INTERFERENCE.

200. If two ethereal undulations in opposite phases meet, they destroy each other's effect, and, producing quiescence among the particles of the ether, give rise to blackness or the absence of light. In this case the waves are said to *interfere*.

NOTE 1.—Waves are said to be in opposite phases when the convexity of the one corresponds to the concavity of the other.

NOTE 2.—A corresponding phenomenon occurs in the science of sound, when two sounds or atmospheric waves meet and destroy one another, producing silence. (See Part I., Art 381.)

201. Two waves do not interfere if they meet after they have travelled through parts of equal lengths, or through paths that differ in length by 1, 2, 3, 4, 5, &c., entire waves.

202. Two waves interfere when they have travelled through unequal paths, the inequality in length not being 1, 2, 3, 4, 5, &c., entire waves; and the interference is complete when the

inequality in the lengths of the paths of the two waves is ½, 1½, 2½, 3½, 4½, &c., waves.

203. Some idea of the mode in which the wave lengths of light have been determined may be gathered from the following experiment. Through a pin-hole, *s*, Fig. 21, in the shutter of a darkened room, allow a sunbeam to enter, and at a short distance from the aperture place a thin wire, *a b*, (seen endwise in the figure,) horizontally across the centre of the admitted beam of light; finally, a little beyond the wire, set a white paper screen, *c d*. It will now be found that between the boundaries *x* and *y*, there is formed, not a continuous shadow, but a succession of bands, alternately black and white, as exhibited in Fig. 22. At the centre, *e*,(Figs. 21 and 22,) there is a white stripe, followed on each side by a dark one; these in turn succeeded by white bars, and so on. The explanation is simple. The waves of light bend round the wire, just as water waves, and also sound-waves bend round angular or rounded bodies. Wherever two waves fall upon the screen, having travelled through paths that are equal or which differ by 1, 2, 3, &c., entire waves, they exalt each other's effects and thus produce a white stripe; when, however, the two waves proceeding from *e* and *b* have come through paths which differ from one another by ½, 1½, 2½ waves, they completely interfere, and the result is a black bar. At *e*, the two waves *ae* and *be* meet after coming through equal paths, hence the white stripe; at *f* the two waves *a f* and *b f* meet after coming through paths differing in length by half a wave, hence the formation of a dark band; at *g* the two waves *a g* and *b g* meet after travelling through paths differing in length by *one entire* wave, hence they exalt each other's effects, and produce a white bar and so on. Between these points the waves meet so as to interfere more or less perfectly, and hence arises the *shading off* of one stripe into another.

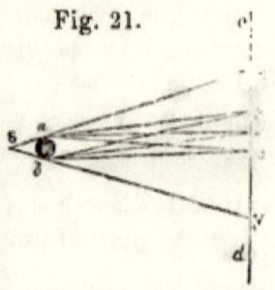

Fig. 21.

Fig. 22.

Now if we can ascertain the difference in the lengths of the two lines $a\,f$ and $b\,f$, we get the length of the wave by simply doubling it, &c., and, since we may make the experiment with any colored light, we may determine the wave-lengths of the various colors.

204. Very carefully conducted investigations by Newton, Brewster, Herschel, and others, with respect to the wave-lengths, &c., of light, have given results represented in the following:

TABLE OF WAVE-LENGTHS OF LIGHT.

Color of Rays.	Lengths of waves in parts of an inch.	No. of waves in one inch.	No. of waves that impinge during one second.
Red............	0·0000256	39180	477 Trillions.
Orange..........	0·0000240	41610	506 "
Yellow..........	0·0000227	44000	535 "
Green...........	0·0000211	47460	577 "
Blue............	0·0000196	51110	622 "
Indigo..........	0·0000185	54070	658 "
Violet...........	0·0000174	57490	699 "
Extreme Violet..	0·0000167	59750	727 "
White..........	0·0000225	44444	541 "

NOTE 1.—More recent experiments have determined the very remarkable fact that the length of the wave producing extreme violet light being taken as *one*, that producing the brightest yellow will be one-and-a-half, and that producing extreme red will be two, or, in other words, the wave of red light is twice, and the wave of yellow light one-and-a-half times as long as the violet wave.

NOTE 2.—The third line of the above table is found by dividing 192000 miles, the velocity of light per second, by the numbers in the first line, or by multiplying the inches in 192000 miles by the numbers of the second line.

LECTURE XVI.
COLORS OF THIN FILMS, COLORS OF GROOVED SURFACES.

205. The brilliant colors displayed by soap bubbles, thin plates of glass, mica, or other transparent bodies, are due to the interference of the rays reflected from the two surfaces. This interference, if complete, stops the luminous undulation altogether and produces blackness; if only partial, the amount of retardation determines the peculiar tint reflected. In all cases the

color transmitted by the film or thin plate is complementary to that reflected.

206. In order to observe the colors of thin films of air, Sir I. Newton placed a double convex lens, whose radius of curvature was 50 feet, upon a ground plate of glass. Upon then powerfully pressing their edges towards one another by several clamps, he made the lenses touch each other at their middle points and very gradually recede from each other towards their edges. The result was the production of a series of colored rings concentrically arranged around the point of apparent contact. As before remarked, the transmitted ring is always complementary to the reflected ring. The following is the result of Newton's experiments—the colors being arranged in the order of their occurrence from the point of apparent contact of the lenses:

Reflected Rings	Transmitted Rings
Black	White.
Blue	Yellowish Red.
White	Black.
Yellow	Violet.
Red	Blue.
Violet	White.
Blue	Yellow.
Green	Red.
Yellow	Violet.
Red	Blue.
Purple	Green.
Blue	Yellow.
Green	Red.
Yellow	
Red	Greenish Blue.
Green	Red.
Red	Bluish Green.
Greenish Blue	Red.
Red	

207. The following are the thicknesses, expressed in millionth parts of an inch, of plates of air, water, and glass, required to produce the different colored rings:

COLORS OF THIN FILMS.

Series or Orders of Colors.	Colors seen by Reflection.	Thickness of Films producing them.		
		Air.	Water.	Glass.
First	Very black	0·50	0·38	0·33
	Black	1·00	0·75	0·66
	Blackish	2·00	1·50	1·30
	Pale sky-blue	2·40	1·80	1·55
	White (like polished silver)	5·25	3·88	3·40
	Straw color	7·11	5·03	4·60
	Orange-red (dried or'ge-peel)	8·00	6·00	5·17
	Red (geranium sanguineum)	9·00	6·75	5·80
Second	Violet (vapour of iodine)	11·17	8·38	7·20
	Indigo	12·83	9·62	8·18
	Blue	14·00	10·50	9·00
	Green (that of the sea)	15·12	11·33	9·70
	Lemon-yellow	16·29	12·20	10·40
	Orange (fresh orange rind)	17·22	13·00	11·11
	Bright red	18·33	13·75	11·84
	Dusky red	19·67	14·75	12·66
Third	Purple (flower of flax)	21·00	15·75	13·05
	Indigo	22·10	16·57	14·25
	Prussian blue	23·40	17·55	15·10
	Grass-green	25·20	18·90	16·25
	Pale yellow	27·14	20·33	17·50
	Rose-red	29·00	21·75	18·70
	Bluish-red	32·00	24·00	20·66
Fourth	Bluish-green	34·00	25·50	22·00
	Emerald-green	35·29	26·50	22·80
	Yellowish-green	36·00	27·00	23·22
	Pale rose-red	40·33	30·25	26·00
Fifth	Sea-green	46·00	34·10	29·66
	Pale rose-red	52·50	39·38	34·00
Sixth	Greenish-blue	58·75	44·00	38·00
	Pale rose-red	65·00	48·75	42·00
Seventh	Greenish-blue	71·00	57·57	45·80
	Pale reddish-white	77·00	53·25	49·66

By aid of this table, the thickness of thin films of air, water, or glass, may be readily determined by observing the colors they reflect. The comparative thickness of plates of two substances, reflecting the same color, are in the inverse ratio of their indices of refraction.

NOTE 1.—It thus appears that a film of air less than one half of the millionth part of an inch in thickness, and films of water and glass less than one-third of the millionth part of an inch in thickness, cease to reflect light, and appear, consequently, black.

NOTE 2.—These rings may be observed by placing two pieces of clear window glass together and pressing them in the centre by means of a pointed body. The plates need not be very thin.

NOTE 3.—When observed in homogeneous light, the rings simply exhibit the same color as the light itself, and alternating with dark or non-luminous rings.

208. Other examples of the production of colors by thin films are met with when a small quantity of any volatile oil is spread over the surface of a liquid or of a solid, the films of certain chemical compounds deposited by galvanic electricity upon the surface of metals, the film of oxide formed on plates of lead, the films gradually deposited on the window-panes of stables, &c., &c. The beautiful iridescent and opalescent paper of De la Rue, owes its peculiar loveliness to the action of a thin film. A very minute quantity of spirit varnish is thrown on the surface of water, and spreads itself out on all sides until it forms a film of exquisite thinness. A sheet of paper or any other substance is then introduced beneath the film, and carefully and gently raised so as to bring with it the film of varnish, which, upon the evaporation of the water, remains permanently attached to the surface of the paper and exhibits the prismatic colors with marvellous clearness.

209. The colored rings observed by looking at the flame of a candle or at the sun, or at any other luminous body, through a glass plate having minute particles of dust, lycopodium seed, &c., or of water as by breathing on it, or small fibres, as those of silk or cotton, scattered over it, are due to the interference of the luminous waves inflected round the atoms or fibres. The finer the particles of dust or moisture, &c., the more distinct are the colors produced.

COLORS OF GROOVED SURFACES.

210. The beautiful tints presented by the surface of *mother-of-pearl* and other natural or artificial bodies having surfaces minutely grooved or striated, are likewise produced by interference, the depressions being of such a depth as to cause a minute inequality in the lengths of the paths of the incident rays of light. That this is the case is proved by the fact that if white wax or sealing-wax is softened and *pressed* on the surface of mother-of-pearl, becoming similarly grooved, it exhibits the same play of colors.

NOTE.—The grooves on the mother-of-pearl, are often as many as 3000 to the inch. Fine steel has been cut in fine lines so as to display the same kind of iridescence as mother-of-pearl.

LECTURE XVII.

SOURCES OF LIGHT, HEAT AS A SOURCE OF LIGHT, CHEMICAL ACTION AS A SOURCE OF LIGHT, PHOSPHORESCENCE AS A SOURCE OF LIGHT, FLUORESCENCE AS A SOURCE OF LIGHT.

211. The principal sources of light are the following :
    1st. The sun and the stars.
    2nd. Heat.
    3rd. Electricity.
    4th. Chemical action.
    5th. Phosphorescence.
    6th. Fluorescence.

212. We are unacquainted with the cause of the light emitted by the sun, but we know that it infinitely exceeds that from all *our* other sources whatever. The light is supposed to be emitted, not by the body of the sun itself, but by one of its outer gaseous envelopes. The stars, which are all in reality suns, emit light of an analogous kind and probably in a similar manner to that of our sun.

HEAT AS SOURCE OF LIGHT.

213. Heat is one of the most important artificial sources of light. All solid and liquid bodies which are not decomposed, shine

when their temperature is raised to about 1000° F. The color first presented by the shining hot body is red, and, as the temperature rises above 1000° F., orange, yellow, green, and the other prismatic colors, present themselves in regular succession, until at last the body reaches the temperature of 2130°, when all these tints are simultaneously emitted and the body is said to be white hot.

NOTE.—This sequence of color is very beautifully manifested in the process of *tempering* steel. The metal is first made exceedingly hard by heating to bright redness or even whiteness, and then plunging it into cold brine, or oil. When thus treated, it becomes so hard as to resist the action of a file and even to scratch glass. To temper this it is placed on a hot iron plate and gradually heated. As the heat permeates the steel, its surface passes through the various shades of color enumerated above. When we perceive the straw color, the steel is a little softened, and, being fit for the manufacture of various tools, is called *drill*-tempered steel; when the blue tint appears, it has been still more softened, and is what is termed *spring*-tempered steel, &c.

214. The light emitted by the ignited solid increases very rapidly as the temperature rises above 1000° F. The following table is given by Draper, and shows the intensity of the light evolved by platinum at different temperatures:

TABLE OF LIGHT EVOLVED BY HEATED PLATINUM.

Temperature of the Platinum.	Intensity of its Light.
980°	0·00
1900	0·34
2015	0·62
2130	1·73
2245	2·92
2360	4·40
2475	7·24
2590	12·34

215. When two charcoal points, connected with the two poles of a powerful galvanic battery in action, are brought within a short distance of one another, a luminous arch is produced

SOURCES OF LIGHT.

between them, and the light is so intense that its brightness is said to reach to one-fifth or even one-fourth that of an equal surface of the sun. (See Arts. 481–484.)

CHEMICAL ACTION AS A SOURCE OF LIGHT.

216. Chemical action is so constant a source of light, that we define combustion, which is merely one form of chemical action, to be " chemical combination attended by the evolution of *light* and heat." All flames are regarded as incandescent shells formed of a series of concentric and differently colored layers, the innermost one being red, and having a temperature of about 1000° F. Upon this the other colors, orange, yellow, green, blue, &c., are placed in succession, the exterior stratum being violet. When we look at such a flame, these differently colored shells, being all commingled, appear to yield white light; but a prism separates them one from another, and thus proves their individual existence. If we could obtain a horizontal section of such a flame, it would exhibit all the prismatic colors.

287. Many bodies in burning emit lights of peculiar tints. The flames thus obtained are mostly compound in their color, and may be decomposed by the spectrum, so as to present all the prismatic colors. Thus, the red of cyanogen and the blue of sulphur or carbonic oxide, are compound colors. Certain flames, as that of hydrogen, are deficient in some of the rays only, while others, as that of a solution of soda in alcohol, are homogeneous or monochromatic.

NOTE.—The principal artificially colored lights of pyrotechnists and others, are obtained as follows:

Blue or Bengal Light ..
$\begin{cases} \text{Dry nitrate of potassa} \ldots 6 \text{ parts} \\ \text{Sulphur} \ldots \ldots \ldots \ldots \ldots 2 \text{ "} \\ \text{Tersulphide of antimony} \ .1 \text{ "} \end{cases}$ All in fine powder and well mixed.

Green Light ....
$\begin{cases} \text{Dry nitrate of baryta} \ldots 4\frac{1}{2} \text{ parts} \\ \text{Sulphur} \ldots \ldots \ldots \ldots \ldots 1\frac{1}{2} \text{ "} \\ \text{Chlorate of potassa} \ldots \ldots 1 \text{ "} \\ \text{Lampblack} \ldots \ldots \ldots \ldots \frac{1}{4} \text{ "} \end{cases}$

Mix the lampblack, sulphur, and nitrate of baryta together in fine powder, and *afterwards* add the chlorate of potassa in rather coarse powder without rubbing it with the other substances.

Red Light ....
$\begin{cases} \text{Dry nitrate of strontia} \ldots 8 \text{ parts} \\ \text{Sulphur} \ldots \ldots \ldots \ldots \ldots 2\frac{1}{4} \text{ "} \\ \text{Chlorate of potassa} \ldots \ldots 2 \text{ "} \\ \text{Lampblack} \ldots \ldots \ldots \ldots \frac{1}{2} \text{ "} \end{cases}$

Observe same caution in mixing as in case of green-light compound.

213. A very intimate relation exists between the intensity of the chemical action occurring in any given case of combustion, and the color of the resulting flame. Chemical changes are regarded as being accompanied by a vibratory movement among the particles of the uniting bodies; and the more energetic the chemical action, the more rapid are these vibratory movements. The vibrating particles impinging upon the ether impart their movements to it, and the numerous undulations thus arising in the latter, are more or less rapid in proportion as the vehemence of the chemical action is greater or less. But the more rapid the pulsation, the shorter the wave, and the more refrangible the ray. Very intense chemical combination, therefore, tends to produce blue or violet light, while red, orange, and yellow flames are caused by a more incomplete combustion. Thus, sulphur and carbonic oxide give a blue flame on account of their strong affinity for oxygen and the facility with which they obtain the maximum quantity with which they are capable of combining by combustion.

Cyanogen, on the other hand, burns with a red flame, because, in the decomposition of the gas during combustion, nitrogen, an incombustible element, is set free, and this, surrounding the flame, prevents the free access of the air, and thus causes the combustion to proceed somewhat imperfectly. Similarly, an oil-lamp insufficiently supplied with air affords but a dull red light, but upon conveying air into the interior of the flame, as is done in the Argand burner, the light becomes brilliantly white.

NOTE.—The chief varieties of strong artificial lights occasionally employed for illuminating purposes, are:

I. THE DRUMMOND LIGHT, or OXY-HYDROGEN LIGHT. This is produced by projecting, with due caution, on a piece of prepared lime or chalk, a jet of a mixture of two volumes hydrogen and one volume oxygen.

II. THE BUDE LIGHT is obtained by passing a steady current of oxygen through an Argand lamp, having a very thick wick, supplied with a highly carbonized oil, as whale oil. The oxygen is forced through the centre pipe of the burner by means of a constant but very low pressure.

III. THE OXY-CALCIUM LIGHT is obtained by urging the flame of a spirit lamp or of a common coal-gas burner against a ball of lime by means of a jet of oxygen escaping from a moderate but steady pressure.

IV. THE ELECTRIC LIGHT, for a description of which see Art. 485.

PHOSPHORESCENCE AS A SOURCE OF LIGHT.

219. All solid non-metallic bodies exhibit more or less perfectly the phenomenon of phosphorescence, i. e., of shining after exposure to the sun's light.

220. In the greater number of bodies this emission of light lasts but a moment; in some, however, it continues for a considerable length of time and is marked by great brilliancy. Among the best *phosphori*, as such bodies are called, we may mention certain varieties of the diamond, and of fluor-spar, sulphide of barium, sulphide of calcium, dried paper, silk, sugar, borax, &c., among inorganic bodies; and rotten wood, decaying fish and other animal matter, certain marine animalcules, the glow-worm, the fire-fly, &c., in the organic kingdom.

221. The phosphorescence of inorganic bodies may be explained upon the undulatory theory as follows:—

The luminous waves of the ether striking upon the surface of a phosphorus gradually throw the molecules of the latter into more or less intense vibration. Upon the withdrawal of the source of light, the undulations caused by it in the ether instantly cease, but, owing to the greater density of the phosphorus, its particles for a time retain their vibratory movements, and these impinging upon the ether continue to impress undulations upon it. The vibrations of the particles of the phosphorus gradually decline, and thus the phosphorescence becomes extinct.

222. The Newtonian theory supposes that certain bodies possess the power of *absorbing* light while exposed to the sun's rays, and afterwards *emitting* it in the dark.

223. Phosphorescence is not attended with heat to any appreciable degree, and the intensity of the light emitted is very low—an apparently very luminous diamond yielding a light several thousand times less intense than the flame of a very small oil lamp. The lower the temperature of the phosphorus when exposed to the source of light, the more decided and long continued its subsequent phosphorescence, and, indeed, a phosphorus which has just ceased to emit light becomes again luminous if exposed to a higher temperature.

224. The phosphorescence of animal and vegetable substances is due, probably, to chemical action alone, since in all cases the luminosity ceases upon the withdrawal of oxygen or of the air.

225. The more refrangible rays of the spectrum are most potent in producing phosphorescence in a body, and in some cases the invisible rays beyond the violet extremity are particularly powerful in this respect. The red and the other rays of low refrangibility, not only produce no phosphorescence, but tend to counteract the influence of the rays at the other extremity of the spectrum.

The wave-lengths of the light emitted by the phosphorus are usually greater than those of the exciting rays, i. e. the phosphorescent light is of a color belonging to a part of the spectrum nearer to the red than the light which excited the phosphorus.

FLUORESCENCE OR EPIPOLIC DISPERSION.

226. When a ray of ordinary white light is allowed to fall upon fluor-spar or upon solution of sulphate of quinine or of certain other bodies, a lively diffused blue light is thrown back. It is believed that this blue light is produced by an exceedingly thin stratum of the liquid adjacent to the surface by which the ray entered, and to this remarkable surface action the name of epipolic dispersion has been given. (Greek *epipolés*, " on the top of," i. e. " at the surface.")

227. The phenomenon of epipolic dispersion has been thoroughly investigated by Professor Stokes of Cambridge, and his explanation is now very generally received, although many persons yet prefer Sir David Brewster's explanation by *internal dispersion*. Stokes appears to prove satisfactorily that this diffused blue light consists of the chemical rays rendered visible by a change in their refrangibility.

228. It is not merely the most refrangible rays that are capable of becoming epipolized, i. e. rendered less refrangible—the yellow, the red, and all the other rays are alike influenced. It follows of course that it is not blue light that is always produced by epipolic action. The depression of the light in the scale of colors is invariable, i. e. the length of the wave is always increased and its velocity of undulation diminished.

229. The term *Fluorescence* is now commonly applied to the

phenomenon just described, because it does not, like the terms epipolic action, internal dispersion, true diffusion, &c., involve any theory.

230. The number of fluorescent bodies is somewhat limited. Fluor-spar, a solution of sulphate of quinine, and an aqueous solution of horse-chestnut, diffuse a blue light; many compounds of sesqui-oxide of uranium give a greenish-blue light, especially the nitrate of the glass called *canary-glass* (glass colored yellow by oxide of uranium); a decoction of madder and alum gives a yellow or orange-yellow fluorescence; tincture of turmeric, a greenish light; and an alcoholic solution of chlorophyll diffuses a red light.

NOTE.—Fluorescence is entirely dependent upon the incidence of certain rays, and is therefore quite distinct from phosphorescence; and, although the former may give a blue light very much resembling the latter, they are by no means to be confounded. As a general rule, phosphorescent bodies are not fluorescent.

LECTURE XVIII.

CATOPTRICS.

REFLECTION FROM PLANE MIRRORS, REFLECTION FROM CONCAVE MIRRORS, REFLECTION FROM CONVEX MIRRORS, RULES FOR FINDING THE FOCAL DISTANCE OF MIRRORS.

231. Catoptrics is that branch of optical science which investigates the laws that govern the *reflection* of light by mirrors, &c.

232. Mirrors are highly polished solid bodies capable of reflecting a large proportion of the rays of light incident upon them.

The term mirror is commonly restricted to reflectors made of glass coated on one side with an amalgam of tin.

Specula are highly polished *metallic* reflectors. They are made of steel, of silver, or of the so called speculum metal, the best variety of which consists of 32 parts copper and 15 parts tin.

NOTE.—Specula are better reflectors than glass mirrors, as in the latter a portion of the incident rays are reflected from the first surface and render the image less perfect than that obtained by the use of a speculum.

233. Mirrors and specula are plane, concave, or convex. A plane mirror is a flat surface like a common looking-glass; a concave mirror is a reflecting surface curved like the inside of a watch-glass; a convex mirror is a reflecting surface curved like the outside of a watch-glass.

234. Parallel rays of light are such as lie in the same plane and being produced ever so far both ways do not meet. Converging rays are such as continually approach each other in one direction, so that if sufficiently produced they will meet in a point. Diverging rays are such as continually recede from each other.

235. When a ray of light falls upon a surface and is reflected, the angle contained by the line of incidence and the perpendicular to the point at which the ray strikes the surface is called the *angle of incidence;* the angle contained between the perpendicular and the line of reflection is called the *angle of reflection.* The two following facts are to be carefully noted:

1st. The incident ray, the perpendicular to the point of incidence, and the reflected ray, are all in the same plane.

2nd. The angle of reflection and the angle of incidence are equal.

NOTE.—In order to trace the course of a ray of light incident on a plane mirror we draw a line at right angles to the mirror at the point of incidence and make the angle of reflection equal to the angle of incidence. For a concave mirror, we join the point of incidence with the geometrical centre of curvature, and, considering this as the perpendicular, make the angle of reflection equal to the angle of coincidence. For a convex mirror, we join the point of incidence with the geometrical centre of curvature, and continuing this line through the mirror, we regard it as the perpendicular.

REFLECTION FROM PLANE MIRRORS.

236. Rays of light incident upon a plane mirror retain their relative directions after reflection, i. e. parallel incident rays continue to be parallel after reflection; diverging incident rays continue to diverge after reflection, and converging incident rays continue to converge after reflection.

Fig. 23.

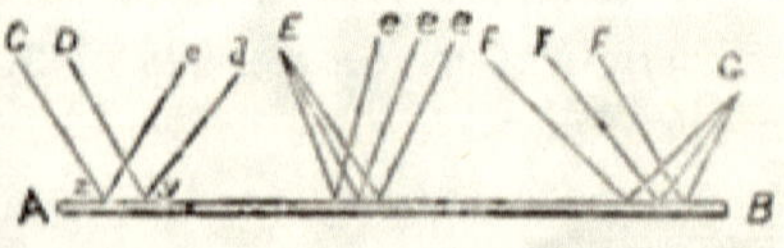

REFLECTION FROM CONCAVE MIRRORS.

237. *Parallel rays* incident upon a concave mirror are reflected to a point whose distance from the face of the mirror depends upon the curvature of the mirror.

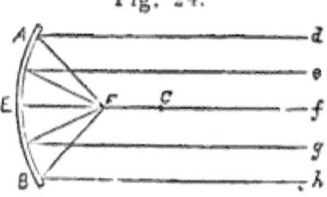

Fig. 24.

238. The point to which a concave mirror reflects the rays incident upon it, is called the *focus* or "fire place" of the mirror; and the focus for *parallel rays*, as *F* in Fig. 24, is called its *principal focus*.

239. *Diverging rays* incident upon a concave mirror are reflected to a focus, *f*, Fig. 25, which is always more remote from the mirror than its *principal* focus, *F*. If the radiant point, *P* (Fig. 25), be made gradually to approach towards the mirror, the following facts are observed:—

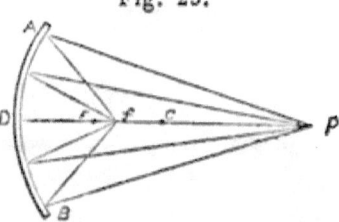

Fig. 25.

I. As *P* approaches the mirror *f* recedes from it.
II. When *P* coincides with *C*, the geometrical centre of curvature, *f* is also coincident with *c*.
III. When *P* approaches the mirror so as to take the position *f*, the focus *f* has receded so as to assume the position *P*.
IV. When *P* reaches the point *F*, the incident rays are reflected so as to be parallel to one another, i. e. the point *f*, or the focus, has become *infinitely remote*.
V. When *P* passes beyond *F*, the rays falling from it upon the mirror are reflected so as to diverge.

240. From the foregoing illustration it appears that when the radiant point is at *P* the rays are reflected to a focus in *f*, but when the radiant point is at *f* the rays are reflected to a focus in *P*. On account of this relation between *P* and *f*, the radiant point and the focus, they are called *conjugate foci*. The distance *f D* is called the *conjugate focal distance* of the mirror to distinguish it from *F D*, which is the *principal* focal distance.

NOTE.—When the radiant point is between the mirror and its principal focus, the reflected rays diverge from the face of the mirror. Now if these diverging rays be considered as passing back through the mirror, they will appear to *converge* towards a point behind it; this point is called their *virtual focus*.

241. *Converging rays* incident upon a concave mirror are reflected to a focus which is always nearer to the mirror than the principal focus. The conjugate focus is virtual, i. e. is behind the mirror. Here we note the following facts :—

    I. As the convergence of the rays is decreased, the focus approaches the principal focus, and the virtual conjugate focus recedes indefinitely.

    II. As the convergence is increased, both foci approach the mirror.

REFLECTION FROM CONVEX MIRRORS.

242. *Parallel rays* incident upon a convex mirror are reflected so as to diverge from one another. Their focus is virtual, and, for rays falling on the mirror near its middle point, the distance is about half the radius of curvature.

243. *Diverging rays* incident on a convex mirror are reflected so as to diverge more rapidly. Their focus is virtual, and their focal distance is always less than half the radius of curvature, but continually approaches that magnitude as the radiant point recedes from the mirror.

244. *Converging rays* incident on a convex mirror are reflected *parallel* if the incident rays converge towards the principal virtual focus; *convergent*, if the incident rays converge towards a point nearer to the mirror than the principal virtual focus; and *divergent*, if the incident rays converge towards a point beyond the principal virtual focus of the mirror.

RULES FOR FINDING THE FOCAL DISTANCE OF MIRRORS.

245. Let f = focus, f' = virtual focus, F = principal focus, r = radius of curvature of the mirror, d = distance of radiant point, d' = virtual point of convergence.

CONCAVE MIRRORS.

PARALLEL RAYS. $F = \frac{1}{2} r.$

Or: Principal focus is equal to half the radius of curvature.

EXAMPLE 1.—What is the principal focal distance of a concave mirror having a radius of curvature of 40 feet?

SOLUTION.

$F = \frac{1}{2} r = \frac{1}{2}$ of $40 = 20$ ft. *Ans.*

EXAMPLE 2.—What is the principal focal distance of a concave mirror having a radius of curvature of 17 ft. 11 inches?

SOLUTION.

$F = \frac{1}{2} r = \frac{1}{2}$ of 17 ft. 11 inches $= 8$ ft. $11\frac{1}{2}$ inches. *Ans.*

DIVERGING RAYS. $f = \dfrac{dr}{2d-r}.$

Or: The conjugate focus is found by multiplying the distance of the radiant point by the radius of curvature of the mirror, and dividing the product by the difference between twice the distance of the radiant point and the radius of curvature.

EXAMPLE 3.—What is the conjugate focal distance, for divergent rays, of a concave mirror whose radius of curvature is 25 ft.—the radiant point being 40 feet from the mirror?

SOLUTION.

Here $d = 40$ feet and $r = 25$ ft.

Then $f = \dfrac{dr}{2d-r} = \dfrac{40 \times 25}{2 \times 40 - 25} = \dfrac{1000}{55} = 18$ ft. $2\frac{2}{11}$ inches. *Ans.*

EXAMPLE 4.—What is the conjugate focal distance for divergent rays on a concave mirror whose radius of curvature is 64 ft., the radiant point being 64 ft. from the mirror?

SOLUTION.

Here $d = 64$ feet and $r = 64$ feet.

Then $f = \dfrac{dr}{2d-r} = \dfrac{64 \times 64}{2 \times 64 - 64} = \dfrac{64 \times 64}{64} = 64$ ft. *Ans.*

EXAMPLE 5.—What is the conjugate focal distance for diverging rays incident on a concave mirror whose radius of curvature is 19 feet, the radiant point being 9 ft. 6 in. in front of the mirror?

SOLUTION.

Here $d = 9\frac{1}{2}$ ft. and $r = 19$ ft.

Then $f = \dfrac{dr}{2d-r} = \dfrac{9\frac{1}{2} \times 19}{2 \times 9\frac{1}{2} - 19} = \dfrac{9\frac{1}{2} \times 19}{19 - 19} = \dfrac{9\frac{1}{2} \times 19}{0} = \infty$ *i. e.* the rays are reflected parallel.

CONVEX MIRRORS.

CONVERGING RAYS. $f = \dfrac{d'r}{2d'+r}$

Or: The focal distance is found by multiplying the radius of curvature of the mirror by the distance of the point to which the rays converge behind the mirror, and dividing the product by the sum of twice the distance of the virtual point of convergence and the radius of curvature.

EXAMPLE 6.—What is the focal distance for converging rays which fall on a concave mirror whose radius of curvature is 22 feet, the incident rays converging towards a point 18 feet behind the mirror?

SOLUTION.

Here $d' = 18$ feet and $r = 22$ feet.

Then $f = \dfrac{d'r}{2d'+r} = \dfrac{18 \times 22}{2 \times 18 + 22} = \dfrac{396}{58} = 6$ ft. $9\frac{27}{29}$ inches. *Ans.*

EXAMPLE 7.—What is the focal distance of the converging rays incident on a concave mirror whose radius of curvature is 40 feet, the incident rays converging towards a point 20 feet behind the mirror?

SOLUTION.

Here $d' = 20$ feet and $r = 40$ feet.

Then $f = \dfrac{d'r}{2d'+r} = \dfrac{20 \times 20}{2 \times 20 + 40} = \dfrac{800}{80} = 10$ feet. *Ans.*

CONVEX MIRRORS.

PARALLEL RAYS. $F' = \frac{1}{2}r.$

Or: The principal virtual focus is equal to half the radius of curvature.

EXAMPLE 8.—What is the principal focus for parallel rays incident on a convex mirror whose radius of curvature is 36 feet?

SOLUTION.

$F' = \frac{1}{2}r = \frac{1}{2}$ of $36 = 18$ feet.

EXAMPLE 9.—What is the principal focus for parallel rays incident on a convex mirror whose radius of curvature is 8 ft. 10 inches?

SOLUTION.

$F' = \frac{1}{2}r = \frac{1}{2}$ of 8 ft. 10 in. $= 4$ ft. 5 in. *Ans.*

DIVERGING RAYS. $f' = \dfrac{dr}{2d+r}$

Or: The virtual conjugate focus is found by multiplying the radius of curvature by the distance of the radiant point from the mirror, and dividing the product by the sum of the radius and twice the distance of the radiant point.

CONVEX MIRRORS.

EXAMPLE 10.—What is the conjugate focal distance for diverging rays falling on a convex mirror whose radius of curvature is 28 feet, the radiant point being 28 feet before the mirror?

SOLUTION.

Here $d = 28$ feet and $r = 28$ feet.

Then $f' = \dfrac{dr}{2d + r} = \dfrac{28 \times 28}{2 \times 28 + 28} = 9$ ft. 4 inches. *Ans.*

EXAMPLE 11.—What is the conjugate focal distance of a convex mirror whose radius of curvature is 6 feet, for diverging rays proceeding from a point 104 ft. distant?

SOLUTION.

Here $d = 104$ and $r = 6$.

Then $f' = \dfrac{dr}{2d + r} = \dfrac{104 \times 6}{2 \times 104 + 6} = \dfrac{624}{214} = 2$ ft. $10\tfrac{100}{107}$ inches. *Ans.*

CONVERGING RAYS. $f' = \dfrac{d'r}{2d'-r}$

Or: The virtual conjugate focus is found by multiplying the radius of curvature by the distance, behind the mirror, of the point to which the rays appear to converge, and dividing the product by the difference between the radius of curvature and twice the distance of the virtual point of convergence.

EXAMPLE 12.—What is the focal distance for converging rays incident upon a convex mirror whose radius of curvature is 40 feet, the incident rays converging towards a point 14 feet behind the mirror?

SOLUTION,

Here $d' = 14$ feet and $r = 40$ feet.

Then $f = \dfrac{d'r}{2d'-r} = \dfrac{14 \times 40}{2 \times 14 - 40} = \dfrac{560}{12} = 46$ ft. 8 in. *Ans.*

EXAMPLE 13.—What is the focal distance of a convex mirror whose radius of curvature is 7 feet, for incident rays which converge towards a point $3\tfrac{1}{2}$ feet behind the mirror?

SOLUTION.

Here $d' = 3\tfrac{1}{2}$ feet and $r = 7$ feet.

Then $f' = \dfrac{dr}{2d'-r} = \dfrac{3\tfrac{1}{2} \times 7}{2 \times 3\tfrac{1}{2} - 7} = \dfrac{24\tfrac{1}{2}}{7-7} = \dfrac{24\tfrac{1}{2}}{0} = \infty$ i. e. the rays are reflected so as to be parallel.

EXAMPLE 14.—What is the focal distance of a convex mirror whose radius of curvature is 30 feet, for incident rays which appear to converge towards a point 50 feet behind the mirror?

SOLUTION.

Here $d' = 50$ feet and $r = 30$ feet.

Then $f' = \dfrac{d'\,r}{2d' - r} = \dfrac{50 \times 3}{2 \times 50 - 30} = \dfrac{1500}{70} = 21$ ft. $5\frac{1}{7}$ ins. *Ans.*

EXERCISE.

15. What is the principal focus of a concave mirror having a radius of curvature of 7 feet 11 inches? *Ans.* 3 feet $11\frac{3}{4}$ inches.

16. What is the principal focus of a convex mirror whose radius of curvature is 11 feet 9 inches? Is the focus real or virtual?
Ans. 5 feet $10\frac{1}{2}$ inches; virtual.

17. What is the conjugate focal distance of a concave mirror whose radius of curvature is 19 feet, for rays emanating from a luminous point 107 feet distant. *Ans.* 10 feet $5\frac{21}{145}$ inches.

18. What is the conjugate focal distance of a convex mirror whose radius of curvature is 15 feet (1) for parallel rays incident upon it? (2) for rays appearing to converge to a point 6 feet behind the mirror? (3) for rays emanating from a luminous point 20 ft. in front of the mirror? (4) for luminous rays appearing to converge to a point 40 feet behind the mirror? (5) for rays appearing to converge to the principal virtual focus of the mirror?

Ans. (1) 7 ft. 6 in.; (2) 30 ft.; (3) 5 ft 5 $\frac{5}{11}$ in.; (4) 9 ft. $2\frac{10}{13}$ in.; (5) ∞

19. What is the conjugate focal distance of a concave mirror whose radius of curvature is 11 feet, (1) for parallel incident rays? (2) for rays converging towards a point 6 feet behind the mirror? (3) for rays emanating from a luminous point 40 feet before the mirror? (4) For incident rays converging towards a point 35 feet behind the mirror?

Ans. (1) 5 ft. 6 in.; (2) 2 ft. $2\frac{6}{17}$ in.; (3) 6 ft. $4\frac{3}{13}$ in.; (4) 4 ft. $9\frac{1}{27}$ in.

20. What is the principal focus of a convex mirror whose radius of curvature is 19 feet. *Ans.* 9 ft. 6 in.

21. What are the principal foci of mirrors whose radii of curvature are respectively 4 feet, 11 feet, 8 feet, and 6 feet 4 inches?

Ans. 2 ft., $5\frac{1}{2}$ ft., 4 ft., 3 ft. 2 in.

LECTURE XIX.

FORMATION OF IMAGES BY MIRRORS, RULES FOR THE FORMATION OF IMAGES BY MIRRORS.

246. The image of an object is a picture of it formed on the retina of the eye, or in the air, or on a screen, as, for example, a white wall or a sheet of paper.

247. Images are formed by mirrors or by lenses, or by allowing

FORMATION OF IMAGES BY PLANE MIRRORS.

he rays of light that emanate from the object to enter through a small aperture into a dark chamber and there fall on a white screen.

248. The mode in which an image is formed by the method last mentioned may be understood from the following illustration:

Let A be a small aperture in $C D$, the shutter of a darkened room. Before the orifice let there be placed an object, $B\ G\ R$; an inverted image of this will be produced on the wall or screen in the darkened room.

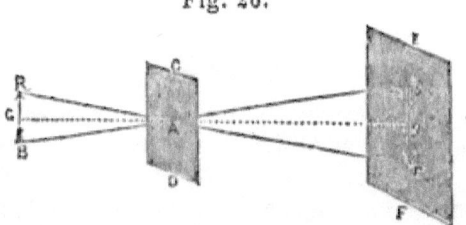

Fig. 26.

Light moves only in straight lines. All the rays that proceed from B are intercepted by the shutter except those that pass in the direction $B\ A$, and these continuing their rectilineal course finally fall upon the screen at b; similarly, those that proceed from R fall upon the screen at r, and those from G pass direct to g. Of course rays from points between B and G fall on the screen at points between $b\ g$, and so on. Thus there is formed on the screen, $F\ E$, an *inverted* image of the object, $B\ R$.

NOTE.—Since only a small proportion of the rays that emanate from the object can enter the aperture, the image formed is necessarily somewhat indistinct. If the aperture be enlarged, more light enters but the image is still more indistinct, as the rays that proceed from adjacent points of the object are cast on the same point of the screen and thus create confusion.

FORMATION OF IMAGES BY PLANE MIRRORS.

249. When an object is placed before a plane mirror, as a looking-glass, an image of the same size and form is produced and lies apparently as much behind the mirror as the object is before it.

Thus, in Fig. 27 let $M N$ be an object placed before the mirror, $A B$, and let the eye be placed at E. Then, of the rays diverging from the point M, those that fall upon the mirror at the points $D\ F$, are reflected to the eye as though they proceeded from the virtual focus m. Similarly, those from N are reflected as though they radiated from n. The line joining M and m and also that joining N and n are perpendicular to the mirror; and the points m and n are as much behind the mirror as the points M, N are respectively before it.

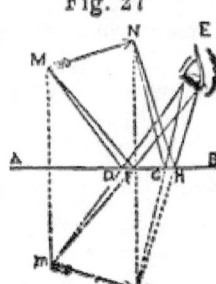

Fig. 27

FORMATION OF IMAGES BY CONCAVE MIRRORS.

NOTE 1.—When a mirror is placed at an angle of 45° to the horizon, an erect object placed before it will appear horizontal and vice versâ, because the image has the same inclination to the mirror as the object, and twice 45° make 90°.

NOTE 2.—Since the angle of incidence is equal to the angle of reflection, they are together double of the angle of incidence, and hence the surface of the mirror which reflects the rays from the object is only half as long or as broad as the object itself. It follows from this that a person may see his whole length in a mirror but half his height.

250. An object placed between two parallel plane mirrors gives an indefinite number of images. These appear to be in a straight line and are produced by repeated reflections, and, in consequence of the loss of light by each additional reflection, the images become less and less brilliant as they recede from the object.

251. The kaleidoscope (*kalos*, "beautiful," *eidos*, "form," and *scopeo*, "I see,") is constructed on the principle that when two mirrors are inclined to one another at certain angles they give a multiplied image of an object.

Two mirrors inclined at an angle of 30°, 45°, or 60°, are placed in a paper tube, one end of which is closed by ground and the other by plane glass. Between the extremity of the mirror and the ground glass end a number of small fragments of colored glass, tinsel, and glass filaments twisted more or less, are placed in a cell with room to tumble around as the tube is turned; upon looking through the instrument towards the light and slowly turning it on its axis, an endless variety of symmetrical combinations present themselves and are indescribably beautiful and brilliant.

NOTE.—The number of times each image is repeated depends upon the angle made by the faces of the two mirrors, being equal to 360° divided by that angle. Thus if the mirrors make with one another an angle of 60°, the image will be multiplied $\frac{86°}{360°}=6$ times; if they make angle of 45° there will be $\frac{360°}{45°}=8$ repetitions, &c.

FORMATION OF IMAGES BY CONCAVE MIRRORS.

252. When an object is placed before a concave mirror, a real image is produced in all cases, except when the object is placed between the mirror and its principal focus; under which circumstances the image is virtual.

FORMATION OF IMAGES BY CONCAVE MIRRORS.

The following explains the formation of an image by a concave mirror. Let AB be a mirror whose centre of curvature is C, and let MN be an object placed beyond C. The rays MA, MD, MB, &c., proceeding from M to the mirror, are all reflected in the manner described in Art. 235 so as to paint the extremity M at m. Similarly the rays NB, ND, NA, &c., proceeding from N, are reflected to a focus at n. The result is the formation of an inverted image of the object MN, and this image is very bright, because a great number of rays concur to produce each of its parts.

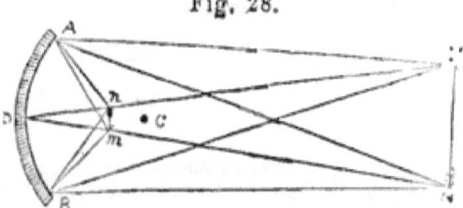

Fig. 28.

253. In the formation of an image by a concave mirror the following points are worthy of notice:

- I. As the object approaches the centre of curvature, the image also approaches it. When the object is in the centre of curvature, the image coincides with it both in position and in size.
- II. When the object is beyond the centre of curvature, the image will be between the centre of curvature and the principal focus, and will be smaller than the object.
- III. When the object is between the centre of curvature and the principal focus, the image will be beyond the centre of curvature and will be magnified.
- IV. When the object is in the principal focus, the image is infinitely remote; in other words, no visible image is produced.
- V. When the object is between the mirror and its principal focus, a magnified *virtual* image is formed.
- VI. When the object is on one side of the principal axis of the mirror, the image is on the other side.
- VII. When the distance of the object from the mirror is known, the distance of the image may be determined, and *vice versâ*, by the rules in Art. 245.
- VIII. The size of the image is to the size of the object as the distance of the image from the mirror is to the distance of the object from the mirror.
- IX. The image is always inverted.

102 FORMATION OF IMAGES BY CONVEX MIRRORS.

254. Concave mirrors have been used as light-house reflectors and as burning mirrors. When used as reflectors they are commonly made of copper, coated with silver and polished, and are parabolic in form. A light, as that of a lamp, placed in the focus of such a mirror, has its divergent rays reflected parallel.

255. Parallel rays of light that fall upon a concave mirror near its axis are not reflected to the same point as those that fall further from it, so that, unless the aperture of the mirror is limited to 8° or 10°, the image produced by either the concave or convex mirror, is more or less indistinct. This imperfection in concave and convex mirrors is termed *spherical aberration by reflection*, and is remedied by making the mirror parabolic in form.

NOTE.—By the crossing of the reflected rays there is produced a curve more brilliant than the other parts of the image; this is called the *caustic curve*.

FORMATION OF IMAGES BY CONVEX MIRRORS.

256. A convex mirror always gives an image which is virtual erect, and less in size than the object.

Let $A B$, Fig. 29, be a convex mirror, $M N$ an object placed before it, and E the position of the eye of the observer. The rays $M D$, $M F$, are reflected from the mirror as though they radiated from the point m behind the mirror; similarly the rays $N G$, $N H$, proceeding from N, are reflected to the eye as though they radiated from the point n; hence the formation of the image $m\, n$.

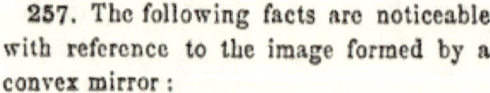

Fig. 29.

257. The following facts are noticeable with reference to the image formed by a convex mirror:

I. The image occupies the same place, however much the position of the eye may be varied.

II. The image will approach the mirror as the object approaches it, and will recede towards the principal virtual focus as the object recedes from the mirror.

III. The size of the image is to the size of the object as the distance of the image from the centre of curvature is to the distance of the object from the centre of curvature.

CONSTRUCTION OF IMAGES. 103

IV. When the object is in the principal axis of the mirror, the image is also in the principal axis; but when the object is on one side of the principal axis, the image is on the same side.

258. To construct an image of a body by means of a convex or concave mirror use the following—

RULE.

I. Take any point in the object and from it draw a secondary axis.

II. Take any ray whatever incident from the assumed point and join the point of incidence with the centre of curvature of the mirror. This line will be perpendicular to the mirror at that point, and will shew the angle of incidence.

III. Draw from the point of incidence, on the other side of the perpendicular, a straight line, making with it an angle equal to the angle of incidence.

IV. The line thus determined is the path of the reflected ray, and, being produced until it meets the secondary axis, determines the spot in which the image of the assumed point is formed.

V. Determine the position of several other points of the object in the same manner.

259. The position, size, and distance of the image may be determined by Art. 245, VI and VIII of Art. 253, and III and IV of Art. 257.

EXAMPLE 1.—An object 17 inches long is placed 11 feet before a concave mirror whose radius of curvature is 18 feet; if the head of the figure coincides with the principal axis of the mirror, determine the position and magnitude of the image.

SOLUTION.

I. Here $d = 11$ feet, and $r = 18$ feet.

Then $f = \dfrac{dr}{2d-r} = \dfrac{11 \times 18}{2 \times 11 - 18} = \dfrac{198}{4} = 49$ ft. 6 inches $=$ distance of image from mirror.

II. Dis. of object : dis. of image : : size of object : size of image.

Or; 11 ft. ; 49 ft. 6 in. : : 17 inches : $\dfrac{594 \times 17}{132} = 76\frac{1}{2}$ in. $=$ length of image.

III. The image is inverted, having its head still coincident with the principal axis of the mirror.

EXAMPLE 2.—An object 22 inches in length is placed 6 feet from a convex mirror whose radius of curvature is 14 feet; the foot of the object being below the principal axis, determine the distance, size, and position of the image.

SOLUTION.

Here $d = 6$ and $r = 14$.

I. $f = \dfrac{dr}{2d+r} = \dfrac{6 \times 14}{2 \times 6 + 14} = \dfrac{84}{26} = 3$ feet $2\frac{10}{13}$ inches = distance of virtual image from the mirror.

II. 72 inches: $38\frac{10}{13}$ inches : : 22 inches : $\dfrac{38\frac{10}{13} \times 22}{72} = 11\frac{11}{13}$ inches = size of image.

III. Image is erect, with its foot on the same side of the principal axis as the foot of the object.

EXERCISE.

3. An object 2 feet in length is placed 5 feet before a concave mirror whose radius of curvature is 8 feet; the centre of the object being in the principal axis of the mirror, determine the distance, position, and size of the image.

Ans. Distance from mirror = 20 feet; length of image = 8 feet; image inverted, and still has its centre in the principal axis.

4. An object 14 inches long is placed 43 inches before a plane mirror; determine the position and size of the image.

Ans. Distance from mirror = 43 inches; length of image = 14 inches: image erect.

5. An object 16 inches in length is placed 27 inches before a convex mirror whose radius of curvature is 40 inches; determine the distance, position, and size of the image, the object being completely above the principal axis of the mirror.

Ans. Distance from mirror = $11\frac{37}{47}$ inches; length of image = $6\frac{38}{47}$ in.; image erect, and completely above the principal axis.

6. An object 12 inches in length is placed 4 feet 7 inches before a concave mirror whose radius of curvature is 30 inches; the head of the object being above the principal axis, determine the distance, position, and size of the image.

Ans. Distance from mirror = $11\frac{11}{4}$ inches; length of image = $2\frac{2}{4}$ in.; image inverted, and has its head below principal axis.

7. An object 20 inches in length is placed 100 feet before a convex mirror whose radius of curvature is 15 feet; the head of the object being in the principal axis of the mirror, determine the position, distance, and size of the image.

Ans. Distance from mirror = 6 feet $11\frac{3}{13}$ inches; length of image = $1\frac{17}{13}$ inches; image inverted, with its head still in principal axis.

8. An object 4 inches in diameter is placed 22 inches before a convex mirror whose radius of curvature is 1 foot 10 inches; the lower edge of the object being below the principal axis of the mirror, determine the position, distance, and size of the image.

Ans. Distance from mirror = $7\frac{1}{3}$ inches; diameter of image = $1\frac{1}{3}$ inches; image erect, with lower edge still below the principal axis.

LECTURE XX.

DIOPTRICS.

DEFINITIONS, LAWS OF REFRACTION, INDICES OF REFRACTION, PHENOMENON OF TOTAL REFLECTION, DIFFERENT KINDS OF LENSES, PROPERTIES OF DIFFERENT KINDS OF LENSES, RULES FOR FINDING THE FOCAL LENGTHS OF LENSES.

DEFINITIONS.

260. DIOPTRICS is that branch of optical science which investigates the *progress of those rays* of light which enter transparent bodies and are *transmitted* through them.

261. When a ray of light is passing through the same medium it invariably preserves its rectilineal course; but when it passes from one medium into another of different density, it becomes bent or *refracted* out of its original path.

Thus, if a straight rod is placed obliquely, partly immersed in water, it appears bent just at the surface of the water. If a shilling be placed in the bottom of a basin on a table, and the observer move back until he has completely lost sight of the coin, it again becomes visible to him upon a second person carefully pouring water into the bowl.

262. Let $B\ C$, Fig. 30, be the surface of some water in a vessel, and $S\ A$ a ray of light incident on it at A, $N\ A\ N'$ the perpendicular to the surface, $A\ R$ the direction of the reflected ray, and $A\ T$ the direction of the refracted ray; then:

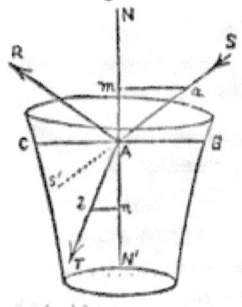

Fig. 30.

The angle $S\ A\ N$ is the *angle of incidence*.

The angle $N\ A\ R$ is the *angle of reflection*.

The line $N\ A\ N'$ is called the *normal*.

The angle $T\ A\ N'$ is called the *angle of refraction*.

Let $A\ a$ be taken equal to $A\ b$, and from a and b let fall the perpendiculars $a\ m$ and $b\ n$ to the normal $N\ A\ N'$; then:

The line $a\ m$ is called the *sine of the angle of incidence*.

The line *b n* is called the *sine of the angle of refraction.*

The line *a m* divided by the line *b n* is called the index of refraction, and is commonly represented by the letter *n*.

263. The general laws of the refraction of light may be thus stated:

I. *The incident ray, the refracted ray, and the normal, are all in the same plane, and the sine of the angle of incidence bears a constant ratio, in the same medium, to the sine of the angle of refraction,* or $\frac{a\,m}{b\,n} = n =$ a constant quantity.

II. *When a ray of light passes from a rarer into a denser medium, as from air into water, it is bent towards the normal or perpendicular.*

III. *When a ray of light passes from a denser into a rarer medium, it is refracted from the normal or perpendicular.*

IV. *When a ray of light is incident perpendicularly on a refracting surface, it suffers no refraction or change in its direction.*

V. *The index of refraction is always the same for the same medium, whether the angle of incidence be great or small.*

264. The index of refraction differs from different bodies, being, as a general rule, greatest in combustible bodies, and increasing also with the density of the body. The indices of refraction of a few of the most remarkable bodies are exhibited in the following—

TABLE OF INDICES OF REFRACTION.

SUBSTANCE.	INDEX OF REFRAC.	SUBSTANCE.	INDEX OF REFRAC.
Vacuum	1·000000	Crown Glass	1·500
Hydrogen	1·000138	Flint Glass	1·639
Oxygen	1·000272	Sulphur	2·040
Nitrogen	1·000300	Phosphorus	2·224
Air	1·000294	Diamond	2·487
Water	1·366	Chromate of Lead	2·936

265. The preceding table gives the index of refraction of a ray of light passing from a vacuum into various media. In order to

determine the index of refraction for light passing from one medium into another, we must divide the index of refraction of the second medium by that of the first.

Thus, the index of refraction of a ray of light passing from water into crown glass is $\frac{1\cdot500}{1\cdot366} = 1\cdot098$; of a ray of light passing from water into air the index of refraction is $\frac{1\cdot000294}{1\cdot366} = 0\cdot732$, &c.

266. When light falls upon a polished metallic reflector, it is partly reflected by the surface, and partly absorbed or otherwise lost; when it falls upon a glass reflector or other transparent medium, a second portion is reflected from the second surface. In all cases the amount of light reflected by the first surface is greatest when the incident rays are perpendicular to the surface. The number of rays reflected out of 100 rays incident at different angles by different reflectors is shown by the following—

TABLE SHEWING RAYS REFLECTED OUT OF 100 INCIDENT RAYS.

Angle of Incidence.	Crown Glass.	Plate Glass.	Flint Glass.	Speculum Metal.	Polished Steel.
10°	3·608	3·546	3·819	70·85	60·52
20°	3·837	3·790	4·117	69·43	.....
30°	4·189	4·164	4·574	68·11	58·69
40°	4·767	4·778	5·320	66·91	.....
50°	5·810	5·882	6·656	65·87	54·96
60°	7·964	8·155	9·369	65·03	.....
70°	13·448	13·891	16·015	64·41	.....
80°	32·396	33·155	36·422	64·04	.....
90°	75·776	74·261	72·074	63·91	53·60

TOTAL REFLECTION.

267. Under ordinary circumstances, when light falls upon a transparent body, it is partially reflected by the first and second surfaces, and partially transmitted; when, however, the rays fall very obliquely upon the *second* surface of the transparent medium, they are wholly reflected, i. e. they do not pass through the surface into the rarer medium beyond. This phenomenon is known

as the *Total Reflection* of light, and can, of course, (Art. 563,) only take place when the exterior medium is less dense than that in which the rays are passing.

268. When light passes from a denser to a rarer medium, the angle of refraction is greater than the angle of incidence. In the case of water and air, the angle of refraction is 90° when the angle of incidence is 48° 35'; so that if a ray of light passes through water making an angle greater than 48° 35' with the perpendicular, the refracted ray makes an angle greater than 90° with the perpendicular, and consequently does not pass from the water at all. Light passing through common glass at an angle greater than 41° 49', suffers total reflection.

NOTE 1.—To an eye placed beneath the surface of water all the objects above the horizon would be seen within an angle of 97° 10', or double the angle of total reflection for water.

NOTE 2.—The brilliancy of the light which has suffered total reflection far exceeds that reflected from the best metallic reflectors. This may be shown by nearly filling a wine-glass with water and holding it up so that the surface of the water may be seen from beneath. When thus placed it presents an appearance equally brilliant with that of burnished silver, on account of the perfect reflection of the incident light. No object above the surface of the water in the glass will be visible.

LENSES.

269. A LENS is a transparent body, as glass or crystal, having one or both of its sides segments of spheres.

270. The principal lenses and other optical glasses are shown in sections in Fig. 31

Fig. 31.

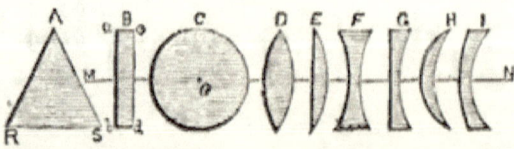

I. An *optical prism A*, is a triangular prism having two plane surfaces, *A R*, *A S*, called *refracting surfaces*, and a face, *R S*, called the *base* of the prism. The angle *R A S* is called the *refracting angle* of the prism.

II. A *Plane Glass*, *B*, is a plate of glass having two parallel plane surfaces, *a b*, *c d*.

III. A *Spherical Lens*, *C*, is a geometrical sphere.

IV. A *Double Convex Lens*, *D*, has both its surfaces convex, either equally or unequally.

V. A *Plano-Convex Lens*, *E*, has one surface plane and the other convex.

VI. A *Double-Concave Lens*, *F*, has both its surfaces concave, either equally or unequally.

VII. A *Plano-Concave Lens*, *G*, has one surface plane and the other concave.

VIII. A *Meniscus*, *H*, has one surface concave and the other convex, and their relative curvatures are such that they meet if produced. Since the centre of the meniscus is thicker than its edge, it may be regarded as a convex lens.

IX. A *Concavo-Convex Lens*, *I*, has one surface concave and the other convex, but their curvatures are such that they would never meet if continued. The concavo-convex lens has its centre thinner than its edge, and may hence be regarded as a concave lens.

NOTE.—In Fig. 31 these lenses, &c., are seen only in sections, so that if they were revolved around their central axis, M N, they would severally, except the prism, describe the solid lenses they are designed to represent.

271. When a ray of light passes through a prism near the refracting angle, it is turned towards the back of the prism, and hence the image is removed towards the refracting angle.

Thus, let a ray of light, *a b*, be incident upon the surface, *A C*, of the prism *A C B*; it is first refracted in the direction *b f*, and upon emerging it is still further refracted to *d*. An eye placed at *d* would therefore see an object at *a* as though it occupied the position *a'*. If the refracting angle be turned down, all objects appear to be elevated when seen through the prism.

Fig. 32.

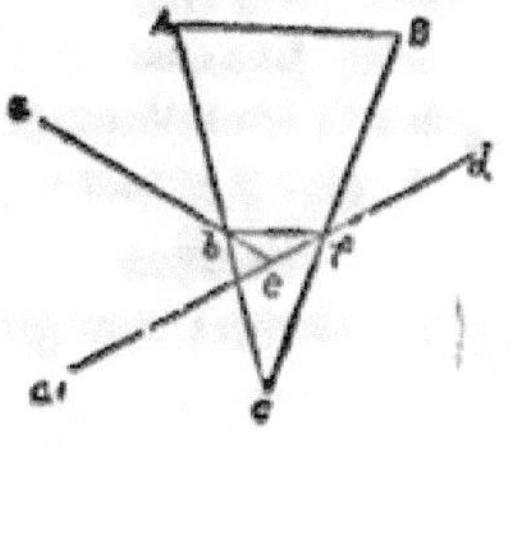

NOTE.—The angle *a c a'* is called the *angle of deviation*.

272. The following particulars in connection with a prism are to be carefully noted:

Fig. 33.

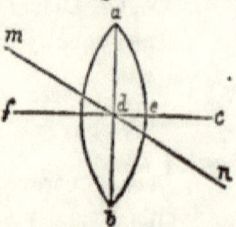

I. The points f and c are called the *geometrical centres*, or *centres of curvature*.

II. The point d is the *optical centre*, $a b$ is the *aperture*, cf is the *principal axis*, and any other line, $m n$, passing through d is a *secondary axis*.

III. All the rays, such as $m n, f c$, &c., that pass through the optical centre, d, are called *principal rays*.

273. A double convex lens may be regarded, in its action upon light, as being formed of two prisms, of small refracting angles, placed back to back.

Fig. 34.

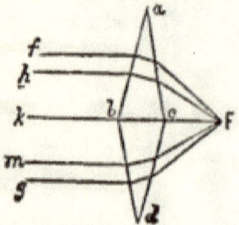

Thus, let $a b c$ and $d b c$ be two prisms of small refracting angles placed back to back. We have seen that light, in its passage through a prism, is bent towards the back of the prism; hence parallel rays, f, h, k, m, g, falling upon the surface $a b d$ are refracted to a focus in F; or if diverging rays from F fall upon the surface $a c d$, they are refracted as parallel rays f, h, k, m, g.

274. A double concave lens may be regarded, in its action upon light, as being formed of two prisms of small refracting angles, united by those refracting angles.

Thus, let $r o s$ and $s t v$ be two such prisms united by their refracting angles at s. Then, as before, since a ray of light in passing through a prism is bent towards the back, the parallel rays e, h, f, falling on the surface $o s t$, become divergent in passing through the lens; and converging rays, g, n, k, falling on the surface $r s v$, emerge on the other side as parallel rays, e, h, f.

Fig. 35.

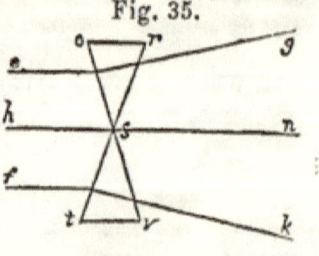

275. Convex lenses are proved by the laws of refraction to possess the following properties:

I. Every *principal ray* that falls upon a convex lens of limited thickness is transmitted unchanged in direction.

II. Incident rays parallel to the axis of the lens are refracted to a focus; and the focus for these parallel rays is called the *principal focus* of the lens.

FOCAL LENGTHS OF LENSES. 111

III. Rays diverging from the principal focus of a convex lens are refracted parallel.

IV. Diverging rays, emanating from a point in the axis more distant than the principal focus, converge after refraction, and the point of convergence approaches the principal conjugate focus as the point, from which the rays radiate, recedes.

V. Rays radiating from a point in the axis nearer than the principal focus diverge after refraction, but the divergence of the refracted rays is less than that of the incident rays.

276. The principal properties of concave lenses are the following:

1. Rays parallel to the axis are rendered divergent by a concave lens.

II. Diverging rays are made still more divergent by a concave lens.

III. Incident rays converging towards the principal focus are made parallel by a concave lens.

IV. Incident rays that converge towards a point more remote than the principal focus are rendered divergent by passage through the lens.

V. Incident rays that converge to a point between the lens and its principal focus, are refracted to a point beyond this principal focus.

277. The focal lengths of glasses of all kinds may be found by the following formulas:

Let r = radius of curvature of one surface.
r' =   "   "   " other "
d = distance of source of light.
d' =   "   " virtual point of convergence of the rays incident upon the lens.
t = thickness of lens.

FOCAL LENGTHS OF LENSES.

CONVEX LENSES.
Parallel Rays.

I. Double equi-convex lens, $\quad F = r.$

II. Double unequi-convex lens, $\quad F = \dfrac{2\,r\,r'}{r+r'}$

III. Plano-convex lens with plane surface exposed to rays, $\quad F = 2\,r.$

IV. Plano-convex lens with convex surface exposed to rays, $\quad F = 2\,r - \tfrac{2}{3}\,t.$

V. Meniscus, $\quad F = \dfrac{2\,r\,r'}{r-r'}$

Diverging Rays.

VI. Double equi-convex lens, $\quad F = \dfrac{d\,r}{d-r}.$

VII. Double unequi-convex lens, $\quad F = \dfrac{2\,d\,r\,r'}{d\,(r+r')-2\,r\,r'}.$

VIII. Plano-convex lens, $\quad F = \dfrac{2\,d\,r}{d-2\,r}.$

IX. Meniscus, $\quad F = \dfrac{2\,d\,r\,r'}{d'(r-r')+2\,r\,r'}.$

Converging Rays.

X. Double equi-convex lens, $\quad F = \dfrac{d'\,r}{d'+r}.$

XI. Double unequi-convex lens, $\quad F = \dfrac{2\,r\,r'\,d'}{d'\,(r+r')+2\,r\,r'}.$

XII. Plano-convex lens, $\quad F = \dfrac{2\,d'\,r}{d'+2r}.$

XIII. Meniscus, $\quad F = \dfrac{2\,d'\,r\,r'}{d'\,(r-r')+2\,r\,r'}.$

CONCAVE LENSES.

PARALLEL RAYS. The *virtual* focus is found by formulas, I, II, III, and IV, and for the concavo-convex lens by formula V.

DIVERGING RAYS. The *virtual* focus is found by formulas X, XI, XII, XIII.

CONVERGING RAYS.—The focal lengths are found by formulas VI, VII, VIII and IX.

EXAMPLES.

EXAMPLE 1.—What is the focal length, for parallel rays, of a convex lens whose radii of curvature are each 7 inches?

SOLUTION.

Formula 1. $F = r = 7$ inches. *Ans.*

EXAMPLE 2.—What is the focal length, for parallel rays, of a glass sphere whose diameter is $2\frac{1}{2}$ inches?

SOLUTION.

Formula 1. $F = r = \frac{1}{2}$ of $2\frac{1}{2} = 1\frac{1}{4}$ inches. *Ans.*

EXAMPLE 3.—What is the focal length, for parallel rays, of a meniscus whose radii of curvature are respectively 6 and 5 inches?

SOLUTION.

Formula V. $F = \dfrac{2\,r\,r'}{r - r'} = \dfrac{2 \times 6 \times 5}{6 - 5} = \dfrac{60}{1} = 60$ inches. *Ans.*

EXAMPLE 4.—What is the focal length of a double convex lens whose radii are respectively 4 and 5 inches, for rays emanating from a point 20 feet distant?

SOLUTION.

Formula VII. $F = \dfrac{2\,d\,r\,r'}{d(r + r') - 2\,r\,r'} = \dfrac{2 \times 240 \times 4 \times 5}{240(4 + 5) - 2 \times 4 \times 5} = \dfrac{9600}{2120} = 4.528$ inches. *Ans.*

EXAMPLE 5.—What is the focal length, for parallel rays, of a plano-convex lens whose radius of curvature is 10 inches, and thickness $\frac{1}{2}$ an inch, the rays falling on the convex side?

SOLUTION.

Formula IV. $F = 2r - \frac{2}{3}t = 2 \times 10 - \frac{2}{3}$ of $\frac{1}{2} = 20 - \frac{1}{3} = 19\frac{2}{3}$ inches.

EXAMPLE 6.—What is the virtual focal length of a double concave lens whose radii of curvature are 11 inches and 9 inches, the incident rays converging towards a point 20 inches from the lens?

SOLUTION.

Formula VII. $F = \dfrac{2\,d\,r\,r'}{d(r + r') - 2\,r\,r'} = \dfrac{2 \times 20 \times 11 \times 9}{20(11 + 9) - 2 \times 11 \times 9} = \dfrac{3960}{202} = 19.6$ inches. *Ans.*

EXAMPLE 7.—What is the virtual focal length of a concavo-convex lens whose radii of curvature are 11 and 7 inches, the rays emanating from a point 5 feet before the lens?

SOLUTION.

Formula XIII. $F = \dfrac{2\,d\,r\,r'}{d(r - r') \times 2\,r\,r'} = \dfrac{2 \times 60 \times 11 \times 7}{60(11 - 7) + 2 \times 11 \times 7} = \dfrac{9240}{394} = 23.45$ inches. *Ans.*

PROBLEMS.

EXERCISE.

8. What is the focal length, for parallel rays, of a glass lens in the form of a sphere having a diameter of one-sixteenth of an inch?

Ans. $\frac{1}{32}$ of an inch.

9. What is the focal length of a double convex lens whose radii of curvature are 10 and 3 inches, for incident rays appearing to converge to a point 40 inches from the mirror?   Ans. 4·1379 inches.

10. What is the focal length, for parallel incident rays, of a meniscus whose radii are 15 and 17 inches?   Ans. 255 inches.

11. What is the virtual focal length of a double concave lens whose radii of curvature are 16 and 20 inches, for incident rays diverging from a point 20 feet from the lens?   Ans. 16·55 inches.

12. What is the focal length, for parallel rays, of a double convex lens whose radii are each one-third of an inch?   Ans. $\frac{1}{6}$ of an inch.

13. What is the focal length of a plano-convex lens whose radius of curvature is 8 inches, for rays converging towards a point 4 inches from the lens?   Ans. $\frac{1}{6}$ of an inch.

14. What is the focal length of a meniscus whose radii of curvature are $8\frac{1}{4}$ and $8\frac{2}{3}$ inches, for rays diverging from a point 40 inches before the lens?

Ans. $3\frac{61}{127}$ inches.

15. What is the focal length of a double convex lens whose radii of curvature are 14 inches and 13 inches, for divergent rays proceeding from a point 100 inches distant from the lens?   Ans. $15\frac{85}{146}$ inches.

16. What is the focal length of a meniscus whose radii of curvature are 21 and 29 inches for incident rays convergent towards a point 10 feet from the lens?   Ans. 67·107 inches.

17. What is the focal length, for parallel rays, of a plano-convex lens whose radius of curvature is 20 inches, and thickness $1\frac{1}{2}$ inches, the rays being incident upon its convex surface?   Ans. 39 inches.

18. What is the focal length of a concavo-convex lens whose radii of curvature are 15 and 16 inches, for incident rays converging towards a point 100 inches from the lens?   Ans. $82\frac{2}{9}$ inches.

19. What is the focal length of a plano-convex lens, for parallel rays, the radius of curvature of the lens being 30 inches and the plane face being exposed to the rays?   Ans. 60 inches.

LECTURE XXI.

FORMATION OF IMAGES BY LENSES, MAGNIFYING POWER OF LENSES, SPHERICAL ABERRATION, CHROMATIC ABERRATION.

278. Images are formed by lenses in precisely the same manner as by mirrors, and are, like those produced by the latter, either real or virtual.

279. The formation of an image by a convex lens may be understood by a reference to the accompanying figure.

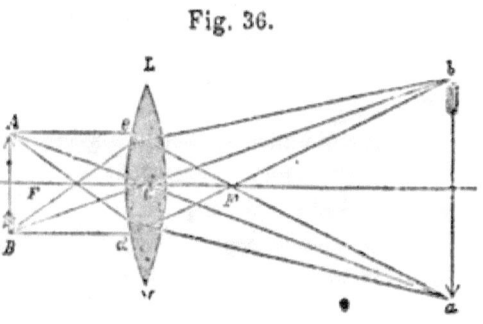

Fig. 36.

$A B$ is an object on one side of the lens, $L M$, and further removed from it than its principal focus, F. All the rays that emanate from A, as $A e a, A c a, A d a$, are made to converge to a focus, a, where they paint an image of the point A. Similarly all the rays that proceed from B are united in the point b, and thus an inverted image is formed on the remote side of the lens.

280. If the object be placed between the lens and its principal focus, as in Fig. 37, the rays *diverge* on leaving the lens, and form a virtual, magnified, and erect image on the same side as the object and more remote from the lens.

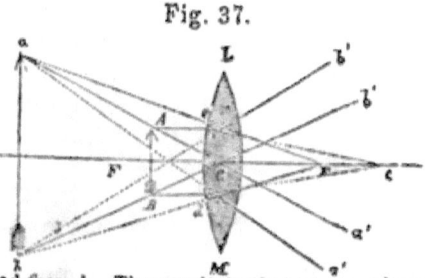

Fig. 37.

Let $A B$ be an object placed before the lens, $L M$, and within its focus. Then all the rays that emanate from A, as $A e F, A c a', A d a'$, are refracted by their passage through the lens and appear to proceed from a. Similarly, the rays from B, as $B d F$, $B c b', B e b'$, appear to proceed from b. The result is that an eye placed at F receives the rays of light issuing from the object $A B$ as though they proceeded from $a b$.

Note.—As the image ab and the object AB both subtend the same angle, acb, to the eye and the former is more remote, it is of course magnified. The enlarged image obtained by a single lens used as a microscope is of the kind here described.

281. A concave lens gives a reduced virtual image on the same side of the lens as the object.

282. The following points are to be remembered in connection with the formation of images by lenses:

I. All real images are inverted, and all virtual images are erect.
II. The size of the image is to the size of the object as the distance of the image from the lens is to the distance of the object from the lens.
III. If an object be placed before a double equi-convex lens at the distance of twice its focal length, the image is on the other side of the lens, at an equal distance from it, and of equal size.
IV. As the object approaches nearer to the convex lens, the image recedes, and *vice versa*.
V. When the object is in the focus of the convex lens, the rays are refracted parallel, and the image is infinitely distant.
VI. When the object is more remote from the convex lens than its focus, the image is real and inverted. It is magnified if the object is distant less than twice the focal length of the lens, but is diminished if the object is distant more than twice the focal length of the lens.
VII. When the object is between the convex lens and its focus, the image is virtual, erect, and magnified.
VIII. The larger the lens, the greater the number of rays of light it receives from the object, and consequently the brighter the image.

MAGNIFYING POWER OF LENSES.

283. The apparent size of an object depends upon the angle at which it is seen, because the eye judges of the magnitude of an object by the direction or divergence of its limiting rays.

Thus, if the lines drawn from the extremities of an object placed at a certain distance before the eye, meet on the retina making an angle of say 30°, the object will appear twice as large as when removed to such a distance as to subtend an angle of only 15°, &c. The nearer, then, an object can be brought to the retina, the greater will be the **angle** under which it is viewed, and consequently the greater its apparent magnitude.

284. If a man be placed at the distance of say 200 feet from the eye, the image formed on the retina subtends so small a visual angle, and is hence so indistinct, that we are unable to discern his features with any degree of clearness. Now suppose we place midway between the man and the eye a convex lens of 50 feet focal length, we shall obtain (Art. 282, III.) an inverted image of the man 100 feet behind the lens, and this image will be of the size of life. The eye now, being only 6 inches from the image, can examine minutely the details of his personal appearance. The *effect* of the lens has therefore been to bring the man from the distance of 200 feet to the distance of 6 inches, or, in other words, to bring him 400 times nearer to the eye, and it has hence *apparently magnified* him 400 times.

285. By using a lens of less focal length, we might have *actually* as well as apparently magnified the image of the man. Thus, suppose the man to be, as before, 200 feet from the eye, and that between the eye and the man, 25 feet before the latter, we place a lens whose conjugate focal lengths are 25 and 175 feet. Then the man being 25 feet before the lens, his image will be 175 feet behind it, and will be magnified in the proportion of 175 to 25, i. e. 7 times. At the same time, the lens has had the effect of bringing the image 400 times nearer the eye, and hence its apparent **magnitude has been increased** $7 \times 400 = 2800$ **times.**

286. If, in the last case, we change the relative positions of the object and the eye, the image would be actually diminished 7 times in magnitude; but as it is still brought 400 times nearer the eye, its apparent magnitude will be increased $\frac{19^2}{2} = 57\frac{1}{2}$ times.

287. The distance of distinct vision is, for most persons, about 10 inches, i. e. unaided by glasses they perceive a small object when placed at that distance from the eye more clearly than when at a greater or less distance. This arises from the fact that in order to produce a clear well-defined image on the retina, the rays must enter the eye very nearly parallel to one another. When we bring an object very near to the eye, we give it great apparent magnitude, but it becomes very indistinct. But if we bring an object nearer to the eye than the limit of distinct vision, and then by any contrivance cause the rays that proceed from it to enter the eye in a state of parallelism, we magnify the image without militating against its clearness. Now we have seen that when the rays emanate from the focus of any lens, they emerge parallel, so that when an object, or the image of one. is placed in the focus of a lens held close to the eye, and having a short focal length the rays will enter the eye under the conditions requisite to give clearness of vision, and the image will be magnified in proportion to the proximity of the object to the eye. Thus, suppose the focal length of the lens is $\frac{1}{4}$ of an inch, then its magnifying power will be 10 inches, the limits of distinct vision, divided by $\frac{1}{4}$ of an inch, the focal length of the lens, i. e. 40 times; and since the apparent superficial magnitude is always as the square of the apparent linear magnitude, the magnifying effect of such a lens is described by saying it is equal to 40 linear or 1600 superficial powers.

SPHERICAL ABERRATION.

288. The rays refracted from a convex or concave surface do not all meet in the same point, but those which enter the lens at its principal axis are refracted to a focus more remote or nearer the lens that those which enter at its edge. This imperfection is called the *spherical aberration of lenses.*

289. Let $L\,M$, Fig. 38, be a plano-convex lens with its plane surface exposed to the parallel rays $B\,L$, $C\,K$, $D\,P$, $E\,M$. Let

SPHERICAL ABERRATION. 119

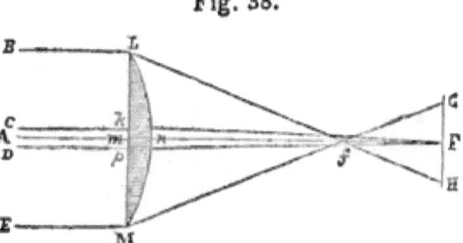

Fig. 38.

$C\,k$ and $D\,p$ be incident upon the lens very near its principal axis, $A\,m\,n\,F$, and let F be their focus after refraction; also let $B\,L$ and $E\,L$ be incident near the edge of the lens; it will be found upon tracing their course by the rules before laid down, that they meet in a focus, f, much nearer the lens than F. Let the rays Mf and Lf be continued till they meet $G\,H$, a plane perpendicular to the line $A\,F$, then

> The distance Ff is called the *longitudinal spherical aberration of the lens.*
>
> The distance $G\,H$ is called its *lateral spherical aberration.*

290. The following will give some idea of the amount of longitudinal spherical aberration of different lenses:

I. In a plano-convex lens, placed as in Fig 38, the aberration is to equal 4·5 times $m\,n$, the thickness of the lens.

II. In a plano-convex lens with its convex side exposed to the parallel rays, the aberration is only 1·17 times its thickness.

III. In a double equi-convex lens the aberration is 1·67 of its thickness.

IV. In a double convex lens having its radii of curvature as 2 to 5, the aberration is about 4·5 times the thickness of the lens if the side whose radius is 5 is turned towards the parallel rays, but is only about 1·17 times the thickness of the lens if the other side is exposed to the parallel rays.

V. The lens with least spherical aberration is a double convex lens whose radii are to each other as 1 to 6. When the more convex side of such a lens is exposed to the parallel rays, the aberration is only 1·07 of the thickness; but when the flatter side is thus exposed, the aberration is as much as 3·45 of the thickness of the lens.

291. The effect of spherical aberration is, obviously, to produce indistinctness in the image. This arises from the fact that all the rays that emanate from any point of the object are not refracted to the same focus, and the result is the production of several images—the rays from which cross one another and interfere, so as to produce caustics and render the principal image obscure.

292. Lenses whose sections are ellipses or hyperbolas are perfectly free from spherical aberration; but owing to the great difficulty of accurately grinding them to these forms, the lenses employed in optical instruments are always simply convex or concave, and other means are made use of to obviate the difficulty arising from aberration.

293. These means are chiefly two in number. The first and simplest consists in placing, between the lens and the object, a perforated metallic or other disc, which is technically called a *diaphragm*. The perforation is of such a size as to allow only those rays to enter the lens that would fall upon its middle part; in other words all the rays that would pass through the lens near its margin are stopped, and the image is thus rendered much more distinct. The second method consists in uniting a meniscus with a double convex lens. The radii of curvature of these lenses have to bear certain proportions to one another, and these proportions have been computed by Sir J. Herschel. When used as a magnifying glass, as in the microscope, the meniscus is directed to the object, but when used for forming an image, or as a burning glass, the convex lens is directed to the object.

CHROMATIC ABERRATION.

294. When a ray of ordinary white light is refracted by a lens of any form, consisting of a single refracting medium as glass or a gem, it is decomposed as by a prism, and dispersed into a more or less perfect spectrum. It follows that when a single lens is placed before an object, the rays of white light proceeding from the latter are decomposed. The violet rays, being most refrangible, are refracted to a focus nearer to the lens than the focus of the yellow rays, and these latter nearer than that of the red rays. The image formed by such a lens is coloured violet if it is formed in the focus of the violet rays, and is bordered or fringed with red and yellow; it is yellow if formed in the focus of the yellow rays, and is fringed with blue or red, &c. This imperfection in lenses is known as *chromatic aberration.*

295. It was believed by Newton that it was impossible to refract light without decomposing it, and he was led to this belief by supposing that the dispersing power of a body was always in proportion to its refracting power. It is now known, however, that the dispersive power of a body is not always proportional to its index of refraction. Crown-glass and flint-glass have very nearly the same index of refraction, yet the dispersive power of the latter is nearly twice that of the former. This circumstance enables us to correct chromatic aberration.

296. A convex lens causes the violet rays of light to converge more powerfully than the red rays, while a concave lens causes the violet rays to diverge more powerfully than the red rays. It is plain that, by combining together a convex and a concave lens, we may overcome the difficulty of chromatic aberration; but if we make both lenses of the same kind of glass, the concavity of the one will be exactly equal to the convexity of the other, and the magnifying power of the convex lens is destroyed. Now flint-glass disperses twice as powerfully as crown-glass, so that a concave lens of flint-glass, which is just sufficient in power to correct the chromatic aberration of a convex lens of crown-glass, is not capable of completely neutralizing its magnifying power. A compound lens of the kind here described is called an *achromatic lens.*

NOTE.—The combination employed to produce achromatism overcomes also to a certain extent the spherical aberration of the lens.

LECTURE XXII.

OPTICAL INSTRUMENTS.

THE SIMPLE MICROSCOPE, THE COMPOUND MICROSCOPE, THE TELESCOPE, THE MAGIC LANTERN, THE CAMERA OBSCURA.

297. A MICROSCOPE (*micros*, "small," and *skopeo*, "I see") is an optical instrument used for magnifying very small objects in order to enable us to examine them more minutely.

298. Microscopes are simple or compound, achromatic or non-achromatic.

299. A SIMPLE MICROSCOPE consists essentially of a single lens, which magnifies the object by enabling us to bring it in close proximity to the eye without rendering it indistinct. (See Arts. 280, 287.)

NOTE.—*Two* or *three* or more lenses may be combined so as to act as a single lens, and constitute a simple microscope. Two lenses thus acting constitute what is called a *doublet*, three lenses a *triplet*, &c.

300. The following are the principal simple microscopes occasionally employed:

I. A minute hole perforated in a piece of black card-board by a fine needle.

II. A drop or globule of Canada balsam suspended in a hole made in card-board or a sheet of metal.

III. A glass sphere or globule made by holding a glass thread in the flame of a spirit lamp until it melts and runs into a sphere.

IV. A drop of water, oil, varnish, or Canada balsam, suspended from the lower surface of a clear glass plate.

V. A glass magnifying lens properly ground and polished.

VI. A lens of garnet, diamond, or other precious stone similarly ground and polished.

VII. The Wollaston lens, which is formed by two plano-convex or double-convex lenses placed in a brass cup or tube and separated by a diaphragm of blackened wood.

VIII. The Coddington lens, the most perfect of all simple microscopes, consists of a spherical lens with its equatorial portions ground away so as to limit the central aperture.

301. A COMPOUND MICROSCOPE consists of two or more lenses so arranged that one forms an enlarged image of the object, and the others magnify this image.

The mode in which this is accomplished may be understood by a reference to Fig. 39. The minute object, $M M$, to be examined, being placed a short distance beyond the principal focus of the object-glass $A B$, a magnified inverted image is formed at $m n$. A second lens, the eye-glass, being so placed that this image shall fall in its principal focus, acts as a simple microscope in enlarging the image. Commonly, however, a third lens $E F$, called the field-glass, is placed between the object-glass $A B$, and the eye-glass $C D$. It has the effect of intercepting the extreme pencils of light $m n$, which would otherwise not have fallen on the eye-glass.

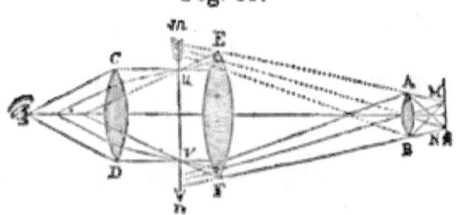

Fig. 39.

NOTE.—The lens $A B$ is called the *object-glass* or *objective*, the lens $E F$ the *field-glass*, and the lens $C D$ the *eye-glass* or *ocular*; and the first and last may, like the simple microscope, be doublets, triplets, &c.

302. COMPOUND ACHROMATIC MICROSCOPES are of various forms, and are supplied with a variety of delicate mechanical contrivances to enable the operator properly to adjust the instrument. In all, however, the essential parts are the three lenses above described. Commonly the object-glass consists of a triple achromatic objective, and the field-glass and eye-glass are combined into one eye-piece, and are so arranged as to correct both the spherical and the remaining chromatic aberration.

303. The *angular aperture* of a microscope is the angular breadth of the cone of light the object-glass receives from the object and transmits through the instrument. Of course it depends upon the diameter of the lens and the distance of the object.

Note.—The principal English manufacturers of microscopes are Ross, Powell, Smith, and Beck. A first-rate achromatic compound microscope made by one of these is worth from $100 to $500, and in some cases a single lens of high power costs from $20 to $50. The prize microscope of Mr. Ross had the following lenses:

1 inch focal length	....	27° angular aperture.	
$\frac{1}{2}$ "	"	.... 60°	"
$\frac{1}{5}$ "	"	.... 113°	"
$\frac{1}{8}$ "	"	.... 107°	"
$\frac{1}{12}$ "	"	.... 135°	"

304. The following are the principal rules with regard to the power of a microscope:

I. The illuminating power varies nearly as the square of the angular aperture.

II. The penetrating power varies directly as the angular aperture.

III. The visual power varies as the square root of the angular aperture.

IV. The disturbance arising from spherical aberration varies as the square of the angular aperture.

V. The defining power, or sharpness of minute detail, varies as the degree of perfection with which the spherical and chromatic aberration is corrected.

VI. The magnifying power of the compound microscope is found by multiplying together the magnifying power of the objective and of the eye piece.

305. The Solar Microscope is simply a variety of magic lantern (Art. 314) in which the light of the sun is thrown by an inclined reflector through the back of the instrument upon the object to be magnified so as to strongly illuminate it, and thus allow higher magnifying powers to be used. The image is cast on a screen, and may thus be exhibited to many persons at the same time.

306. The Oxy-hydrogen Microscope differs from a solar microscope merely in employing the light obtained by casting a burning jet of a mixture of hydrogen and oxygen gases upon a piece of chalk or lime. As in the case of the solar microscope,

the image is cast upon a screen, and so as to be viewed by many persons at once.

307. The magnifying power of a microscope may be computed as follows: Let $d =$ distance of distinct vision $= 10$ inches, $p =$ magnifying power of lens, and $f =$ focal length of lens. Then for a simple microscope or a magnifying lens $p = \dfrac{d}{f}$.

EXAMPLE 1.—What is the magnifying power of a lens whose focal length is $\frac{1}{5}$ of an inch?

SOLUTION.

$$p = \frac{d}{f} = \frac{10}{\frac{1}{5}} = 50 \text{ linear, or } 50^2 = 2500 \text{ superficial dimensions.}$$

EXAMPLE 2.—What is the magnifying power of a simple microscope whose focal length is $\frac{1}{30}$ of an inch?

SOLUTION.

$$p = \frac{d}{f} = \frac{10}{\frac{1}{30}} = 300 \text{ linear, or } 300^2 = 90000 \text{ superficial dimensions.}$$

For a compound microscope, find the magnifying power of the objective by dividing the distance of the image formed by it by the distance of the object, and multiply the result by the magnifying power of the eye-viece as obtained above.

EXAMPLE 3.—In a compound microscope the object is placed $\frac{1}{8}$ of an inch from the objective, and the eye-glass has a focal length of $\frac{3}{4}$ of an inch, the distance between the objective and the focus of the eye-glass being 8 inches, what are the linear and superficial magnifying powers of the microscope?

SOLUTION.

8 inches $\div \frac{1}{8} = 64 =$ linear magnifying power of objective,

$$p = \frac{d}{f} = \frac{10}{\frac{3}{4}} = \frac{40}{3} = 13\tfrac{1}{3} = \text{ linear magnifying power of eye-glass.}$$

Then $64 \times 13\tfrac{1}{3} = 853\tfrac{1}{3} =$ linear, and $(853\tfrac{1}{3})^2 = 728177\tfrac{7}{9} =$ superficial magnifying power of the combination.

EXERCISE.

4. What is the magnifying power of a lens whose focal length is $\frac{3}{8}$ of an inch?   *Ans.* $26\tfrac{2}{3}$ linear dimensions.

5. What is the magnifying power of a simple microscope whose focal length is $\frac{1}{4}$ inch to a person whose limit of distinct vision is 7 inches?
                    Ans. 28 linear dimensions.

6. What is the magnifying power to a good eye of a compound microscope, having an eye-piece ½ inch focal length, the object being placed ¼ of an inch from the objective, and the distance between the objective and the focûs of the eye-piece 6 inches? What would be the magnifying power to a person whose limit of vision is only 6 inches?

Ans. (1) 480 linear dimensions.
(2) 288 linear dimensions.

7. The eye-piece of a microscope has a focal length of ⅓ of an inch, the object is placed ⅔ of an inch from the objective, and the distance between this latter and the focus of the eye-piece is 11 inches. What is the magnifying power of the instrument? *Ans.* 1026⅔ linear dimensions.

8. A near-sighted person whose limit of distinct vision is only 4½ inches, uses a compound microscope with an eye-piece ½ inch focal length, the object being ⅔ inch from the objective, and the focus of the eye-glass 8 inches from the objective. What, to him, is the magnifying power of the instrument? *Ans* 192 linear dimensions.

THE TELESCOPE.

308. TELESCOPES (from *tele*, "far off," and *skopeo*, "I see") are instruments constructed for viewing distant objects. They are either refracting or reflecting, the latter differing from the former merely in having one or more reflecting mirrors or specula.

NOTE.—The telescope was invented in the thirteenth century, and was introduced into England by Roger Bacon. James Gregory was the first to describe, and Sir Isaac Newton the first to construct, a reflecting telescope.

309. THE ASTRONOMICAL TELESCOPE consists of two convex lenses, viz. an object-glass and an eye-glass. The object-glass is placed at one end of a tube longer than its focal length, and the eye-glass in a smaller tube which slides in and out of the larger, so as to allow of the focus being properly adjusted. An inverted image of any distant object is formed by the object-glass in the focus of the eye-glass, and this latter magnifies it, and transmits the rays in a state of parallelism to the eye. The astronomical telescope always gives an inverted image, and its power is found by dividing the focal length of the object-glass by the focal length of the eye-glass. (See Fig. 40.)

310. THE TELESCOPE OF GALILEO (used in 1609, and the oldest in form) consists of a double convex lens of long focus, used as an object-glass, and a concave lens of short focus as eye-piece. The lenses are placed at a distance apart equal to the difference of their principal foci. The light from a distant object collected by the large surface of the convex lens is converged towards a focus beyond the concave eye-glass, and is by it refracted to the eye in a state of parallelism. The magnifying power is found, as in the astronomical telescope, by dividing the focal length of the objective by the focal length of the eye-piece.

NOTE 1.—The telescope of Galileo gives an erect and very clear image of the object, but owing to the divergence of the rays through the eye-glass, the field of view is small.

NOTE 2.—The opera-glass consists of two small Galilean telescopes placed side by side, so as to be used by both eyes at once.

NOTE 3.—The *Night-glass* used by seamen is formed like a large opera-glass. It has low magnifying power, but concentrates a large number of the rays emitted by a distant object, and transmits them to the eye in the condition required for distinct vision.

311. The TERRESTRIAL TELESCOPE differs from the Astronomical merely in having two additional lenses for the purpose of refracting the image to the eye in an erect position.

The terrestrial telescope is shown in Fig. 40. If the lenses $E\ F$ and $G\ H$ be removed, and the eye placed at L, we have the astronomical telescope and see the image inverted. The lense $E\ F$ serves to erect the

Fig. 40.

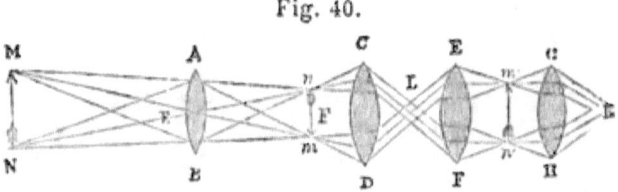

image, but it, at the same time, renders the rays convergent; the second lens, $G\ H$, throws these rays into a state of parallelism, and they reach the eye in the condition requisite for distinct vision.

312. REFLECTING TELESCOPES are of various forms, and are named after their inventors. They are used almost exclusively for astronomical purposes, and many of them are of very great power. The instrument described by Gregory, and hence called the GREGORIAN TELESCOPE consists of a concave mirror having the centre cut away. The rays of light emanating from a distant object are collected by this, and reflected so as to form an

inverted image. They are then received on a small concave mirror placed fronting the great one, and are thus reflected through the orifice of the latter, giving an erect image which is properly magnified by an eye-glass.

The NEWTONIAN TELESCOPE consists of a concave speculum placed in the bottom of a tube with the axis parallel to that of the tube. The rays reflected from it are received by an inclined plane mirror, by which they are reflected so as to form an image on the side of the tube. This image is, as before, properly magnified by an eye-piece.

HERSCHEL'S TELESCOPE consists of a metallic speculum set in a tube with its axis inclined towards the side of the latter, so as to cast the image (of course inverted) outside of the tube. The image is then examined by the aid of a magnifier.

In the Gregorian telescope the observer faces the object, in the Newtonian he faces the tube, and in Herschel's he has his back towards the object.

NOTE 1.—Newton was the first to construct a reflecting telescope, and the one made with his own hands is yet in the possession of the Royal Society. Sir William Herschel constructed 200 seven-feet Newtonian reflecting telescopes, 150 ten-feet, and 80 twenty-feet focal length. He finished his great telescope, 40 feet in length, on the 27th August, 1789, and on the same day discovered with it the sixth satellite of Saturn. Its speculum was $49\frac{1}{2}$ inches in diameter and weighed 2118 lbs.

NOTE 2.—The celebrated telescope of Lord Rosse is the largest reflecting telescope ever constructed. It was several years in being made, and was completed in 1845. The tube is of wood hooped with iron, and is 7 feet in diameter and 54 feet in length. The speculum is 6 feet in diameter, and weighs about 9000 lbs.

Since the speculum of this telescope is 72 inches in diameter, if we assume the pupil of the human eye to be $\frac{1}{10}$ of an inch in diameter, the speculum is 720 times as great in diameter as the human eye, and 518400 times as great in surface. Now if one-half of the light be lost by reflection from the mirror, we shall have concerned in forming the image 259200 times as much light as ordinarily enters the eye. This will, in a measure, account for the remarkable power of the instrument.

313. The lenses employed in good astronomical telescopes require to be achromatic, and it is difficult to obtain them of large size. This arises from the fact, that, as before explained, the achromatic lens consists of a convex lens of crown-glass combined with a concave lens of flint-glass, and in practice, it

is found almost impossible to obtain flint-glass in large pieces of uniform density, free from flaws, veins, and other imperfections.

NOTE 1.—Some idea of the difficulty of obtaining large achromatic lenses may be gleaned from the fact, that the object-glass of the great achromatic reflecting telescope of Cambridge, Mass., is but sixteen inches in diameter, and yet it cost, unmounted, the enormous sum of $15000. And it is recorded as a perfect marvel that a Mr. Bontemps, in the employment of Chance Brothers & Co. of Birmingham, has succeeded in producing a disc of flint-glass 29 inches in diameter, $2\frac{1}{2}$ inches thick, weighing 200 lbs., and so free from imperfections as to be very nearly faultless. When combined with a crown-glass lens into an achromatic objective, it will be worth many thousands of pounds sterling.

NOTE 2.—THE MAGNIFYING POWER of a telescope is measured by the apparent enlargement of the image.

THE ILLUMINATING POWER of a telescope is the amount of light which it collects from the object and transmits to the eye, as compared with the amount of light the unaided eye would collect from the same object.

THE PENETRATING POWER of a telescope is the ratio of the distance from which the eye and the telescope would collect, for the purposes of vision, an equal amount of light. The penetrating power is equal to the square root of the illuminating power.

THE VISUAL POWER of a telescope is found by multiplying the penetrating power by the magnifying power, and extracting the square root of the product.

If $D =$ diameter of the objective, $d =$ diameter of the pupil of the eye, $n =$ number of lens through which the light has to pass before reaching the eye, $x =$ the amount of light transmitted by each lens, commonly about $\frac{9}{10}$, $V =$ visual power, $P =$ penetrating power, $I =$ illuminating power, and $M =$ magnifying power.

$$\text{Then } M = \frac{\text{focal length of object-glass}}{\text{focal length of eye-glass}}; \ I = \frac{D^2 x^n}{d^2};$$

$$P = \sqrt{\frac{D^2 x^n}{d^2}} = \frac{D}{d}\sqrt{x^n}; \ V = \sqrt{MP} = \left\{ \frac{MD x^{\frac{n}{2}}}{d} \right\}^{\frac{1}{2}}$$

314. THE MAGIC LANTERN is an instrument used for projecting on a screen a magnified image of an object painted in transparent colors on glass.

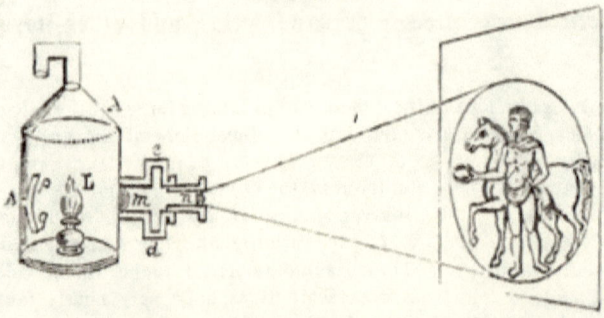

It consists essentially of a dark chamber, or tin box, *A A'*, which contains the source of illumination, the lenses, &c. The parabolic reflector *p q*, receives the diverging rays of light from the lamp, *L*, and reflects them parallel upon the convex illuminating lens, *m*. The lens *m* concentrates the light upon the object which is painted on a slide that fits into *e d*. The rays proceeding from the strongly illuminated object pass through a second convex lens, *n*, by which they are converged upon a screen, so as to give a magnified image. (See Art. 279.)

315. The magnifying power of the Magic Lantern is equal to the distance of the screen from the lens *n*, divided by the distance of the object from the same lens. It follows that we may increase the size of the image at pleasure by either increasing the distance between the lantern and the screen, or by decreasing the distance between the object and the lens, proper adjustments being attached to the instrument to enable us to do the latter. Since, however, the amount of light transmitted through the lens *n* remains unchanged, the brilliancy of the picture decreases as its size is enlarged.

Note.—In order to enable us to cast a large picture, we may make use of a more powerful light than that obtained by a common lamp, as for example the Bude light or the oxy-calcium light.(See Art. 218). If we employ the concentrated light of the sun, or the oxy-hydrogen light, we have the so-called solar microscope or the oxy-hydrogen microscope.'

Note 2.—It will be remembered that a single convex lens like that employed in the lantern gives an inverted image; hence in order to have the picture erect on the screen, the object must be inverted in the lantern.

Note 3.—It is advisable, when possible, to cast the picture on a white wall, as then all the rays are reflected to the eye, and a brighter picture obtained than when a screen is employed. This is evident when we consider that the screen partly reflects the light and partly transmits it, the picture being equally well seen either before or behind it. If a screen is used, it should be waxed or kept wetted, in order to prevent rays being thrown from the lens to the eye through the pores of the muslin.

316. THE CAMERA OBSCURA ("dark chamber"), in its common form, consists of a box, Fig. 42, with a convex lens *C*, which receives the light proceeding from an external object, and refracts it divergently upon a plane reflector, *A*, placed at an angle of 45° to the top of the box. This reflects or casts an image upon a ground glass screen, *B*.

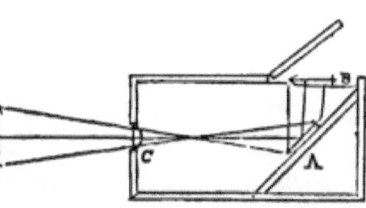

Fig. 42.

NOTE.—The picture thus obtained is inverted only as regards right and left portions, and is very distinct and vivid with all its natural colors, the external light of course being excluded as much as possible from the screen *B*. Other forms of the instrument are employed, but they are the same in principle as the one here described. In the camera employed by photographers, the lens *C* is movable by a rack and pinion adjustment, so as to bring it to a focus, and the image is received upon a prepared plate placed vertically in the chamber.

LECTURE XXIII.

THE EYE AND VISION.

317. THE HUMAN EYE is a most perfect and wonderful optical instrument. It is globular in form, is placed in a deep bony socket called the *orbit*, and is further protected by *eyelids*, *eyelashes*, and an *eyebrow*. The ball of the eye consists essentially of three distinct coats or membranes, enclosing three distinct fluids or humors.

318. The parts of the eye which require description in this connection are the following:

I. The Sclerotic Coat and the Cornea
II. The Choroid coat.
III. The Retina and Optic Nerve.
} The three coats of the eye.

IV. The Crystalline Lens.
V. The Aqueous Humor.   The three fluids of the eye.
VI. The Vitreous Humor.
VII. The Iris and the Pupil.
VIII. The external appendages of the eye.
IX. The means adopted for keeping the surface of the eye moist.
X. The means by which the movements of the eye are effected.

319. THE SCLEROTIC COAT (*skleros*, "hard") is the outer membrane of the eye. It is dense, hard, and pearly-white in color, being transparent only in front, where it becomes more convex, and is called the CORNEA (*cornu*, "a horn.") The cornea may, in fact, be regarded as a distinct membrane set into a groove in the sclerotic, as a watch-glass is set into the rim of a watch; it is, however, so firmly united to the sclerotic that they are commonly taken as one.

320. THE CHOROID COAT (*chora*, "a region") is a strong membrane consisting chiefly of blood-vessels and nerves. It lines the sclerotic coat, and is covered anteriorly by the *pigmentum nigrum*, or black pigment, a layer of cells which have the power of secreting a black granular matter in their interior. The choroid coat becomes modified in the front part of the eye, and is then called the iris.

321. The RETINA (*rete*, "a net work") is an exceedingly delicate film or net-work of nervous fibres spreading out from the optic nerve. The retina covers the choroid coat, or rather the *pigmentum nigrum*, which overlies the latter. It does not extend over the whole interior surface of the eye, but proceeds forward nearly as far as the iris. The optic nerve penetrates the choroid and sclerotic coats, and passes through the back of the orbit to the brain.

322. The IRIS (*iris*, "a rainbow") is a membrane of various colors forming a curtain or diaphragm. It is the colored portion of the eye, and is adherent by its outer margin to the choroid coat. The central aperture of the iris is called the *pupil*, and is capable of enlargement and contraction by means of certain fibres of the iris.

APPENDAGES OF THE EYE. 133

323. THE CRYSTALLINE LENS is placed behind the iris and very near to it. It resembles thick jelly or soft gristle in consistence, but being placed in a membrane or capsule so as to have the form of a lens, it receives its common name. It is, however, sometimes spoken of as the *crystalline humor*. The crystalline lens is more convex in front than behind, and consists of several layers which increase in density from the circumference to the centre. The capsule containing it is suspended or held in its place by little bands proceeding from the choroid coat and known as the *ciliary processes*.

324. The part of the eye between the iris and the cornea is called the *anterior chamber* of the eye to distinguish it from the part between the iris and the lens, which is called the *posterior chamber* of the eye.

325. THE AQUEOUS HUMOR (*aqua* "water") is a thin watery fluid which fills the whole of the eye between the cornea and the lens, so that it fills the unoccupied space both before and behind the iris.

326. THE VITREOUS HUMOR (*vitreum* "glass") is a denser fluid, having the appearance and consistence of the white of a raw egg. It fills the large chamber behind the crystalline lens, and consequently constitutes the bulk of the eye.

327. The external appendages of the eye consist of the eyebrow, the eyelids, the eyelashes, and the conjunctiva. The eyebrow serves to protect the eye from falling dust, and hence it becomes very long and bushy in millers and others who are much exposed to dust. It also prevents the perspiration from rolling into the eye. The eyelids and eyelashes serve to partially or completely shade the eye, so as to protect it from the too great or too long continued action of light. The lids also, by rapidly sweeping over the ball of the eye every few moments, keep it freed from impurities and equally moistened. The conjunctiva (so called because it *conjoins* the eye-ball with the lids) is an exceedingly thin, sensitive membrane, which covers the whole front of the eye, and doubles back so as to line the eyelids. It is perfectly transparent where it covers the cornea,

but is white and semi-opaque where it covers the sclerotic proper.

NOTE.—Birds and reptiles have a third eyelid called the *nictitating membrane;* it is frequently swept over the eye to cleanse it, and being semi-transparent, serves when required, to protect the eye from the too powerful rays of light without interfering with the power of vision.

328. The Lachrymal Gland (*láchryma* "a tear") lies beneath the upper eyelid in the upper and outer portion of the orbit. It constantly secretes a watery fluid, which, being diffused over the surface of the eye by the motion of the lids, washes it and keeps it moist. Except during the act of weeping the fluid is drawn off as fast as formed. This is accomplished by the *lachrymal ducts*, two small tubes, one opening on the inner corner of each lid, which collect the moisture and convey it into a reservoir called the *lachrymal sac*, upon the side of the upper part of the nose; from this it is removed by a passage into the interior of the nasal cavity, whence it is carried off by the current of air which passes in respiration.

329. The globe of the eye is moved by six muscles, four straight and two oblique. These are attached to various parts of the orbit and the ball; and, except in certain diseased states, enable us to turn the axis of the eye in any direction.

NOTE.—Strabismus or squinting commonly arises from the permanent contraction of either the muscle whose office it is to turn the eye inward, or that whose duty it is to turn the eye outwards. It is frequently completely cured by a surgical operation which consists in cutting the contracted muscle.

330. The functions of the several parts of the eye proper are as follows:

I. The convex cornea collects the rays of light, emanating from an object, and to some extent converges them through the pupil upon the crystalline lens.

II. The iris instinctively contracts and enlarges so as to regulate the amount of light admitted into the interior of the eye.

III. By the combined action of the crystalline lens and the vitreous humor, the light is converged to a focus on the retina so as to there depict a minute but well defined inverted image.

IV. The pigmentum nigrum absorbs the rays of light as soon as they have passed through the retina, in order to prevent them from being reflected from one part of the interior of the eye to another, as this would cause much indistinctness of vision.

NOTE.—The pupil in man is circular and contracts circularly—varying in diameter from one-tenth to one-fourth of an inch. It cannot contract or enlarge instantly, but requires a certain length of time. Hence if a person comes from a darkened room into one brilliantly illuminated he is at first dazzled by too much light being admitted into the eye. On the other hand when a person goes from a light apartment into the open air at night it is some time before the pupil enlarges so as to allow sufficient light to enter to enable him to see surrounding objects.

In the owl the pupil is so large that during the daytime he cannot contract it sufficiently to protect his eye from the sun's light, and hence he is nearly blind by day.

In the cat, and other beasts of prey that leap up and down in pursuit of food, the opening of the iris is in the form of an ellipse with its long diameter vertical; in herbivorous animals, on the other hand, which require a long horizontal range of vision, the pupil is elliptical with its long diameter horizontal.

331. Spherical aberration is overcome in the eye in part by the difference in curvature of the cornea and crystalline lens—the latter being more convex in front than behind, and in part by the iris, which acts as a *stop* or *diaphragm* so as to allow the admitted rays of light to fall only upon the centre of the crystalline lens.

332. Chromatic aberration is corrected by the different density of the several humors, the increased density of the crystalline lens from its circumference to its centre, and the action of the iris as a diaphragm.

333. We have seen that the distance of the image from the lens which forms it, varies with the distance of the object, and that in the telescope, the microscope, and other optical instruments, some mechanical contrivance is employed to *adjust* the instrument to a proper focus. The healthy eye possesses this power of adjustment, to see near or distant objects in the utmost perfection, but of the mode in which this is accomplished very little is known. It is however, supposed, that either the position or the form, or perhaps both the position and the form of the crystalline

lens are changed so as, under all circumstances, to throw the image on the retina.

334. NEAR SIGHTEDNESS arises commonly from the too great convergent power of the eye. The cornea or the crystalline lens or both are too convex, and hence they bring parallel or slightly divergent rays to a focus before they reach the retina; by bringing the object nearer, however, the rays that proceed to the eye are more divergent, and their focus is therefore removed further back so as to fall upon the retina. The remedy for this defect is the employment of concave spectacles, which neutralize the too great convexity of the eye.

NOTE.—Care should be taken by persons who wear spectacles always to employ lenses whose power is not too great, as such have a tendency to increase rather than remedy the imperfection of the eye.

335. LONG SIGHTEDNESS is for the most part peculiar to old persons, and arises from the partial flattening of the eye, and consequent loss of refractive power. The result is that the divergent rays which proceed from a near object are refracted to a focus behind the retina, and the image on the latter is indistinct. Long sightedness is remedied by the use of convex glasses, which assist the eye in bringing the rays to a focus on the retina.

336. The principal conditions of distinct vision are the following:

I. The object must be situated at such a distance as to form on the retina an image of some appreciable magnitude.

II. The object must be sufficiently illuminated to produce a distinct impression on the retina.

III. Distinct vision is obtained only by rays that are sensibly parallel or very slightly divergent.

NOTE 1.—The minimum limit of distinct vision varies in different eyes—being commonly about 10 inches but in some as low as 3 inches. The maximum distance to which an object may be seen varies with its size, color, and degree of illumination. A white object illuminated by the light of the sun can be seen by a good eye to the distance of 17250 times its own diameter, a red object about half as far, and a blue one somewhere about one-third as far.

The distance to which an eye can penetrate depends, however, very much upon habit and training. As a general rule, dark-colored eyes can see farther than light-colored ones.

NOTE 2.—The *apparent brightness* of the object remains constant whatever may be its distance from the eye. This arises from the fact that although the amount of light received by the eye from the object varies inversely as the square of the distance of the object, the superficial dimensions of the image on the retina also varies inversely as the square of the distance; hence as the amount of light received decreases, the space over which it is spread decreases in the same proportion.

NOTE. 3.—When the eye is adjusted for viewing an object at the distance say of 8 or 10 inches from it, the pupil is contracted to about $\frac{1}{16}$ of an inch, so that the cone of light entering the eye from any point of the object will have an angular divergence of only about half a degree. Hence it is evident that the rays that produce distinct vision are either parallel or very slightly divergent.

337. The mode in which an inverted image gives us the idea of an erect object has long been a matter of much discussion among scientific men. The simple explanation appears to be that *up and down*, with reference to the image formed on the retina, are merely relative terms, up meaning towards the sky, and down towards the earth. When a man stands before the eye, he is seen erect, merely because his feet appear towards the ground and his head towards the sky

338. Ideas of the distance and magnitude of an object are acquired only by experience, by means of which the eye is enabled to appreciate its size and the distance by comparison with neighbouring familiar objects, its dimness or distinctness, the visual angle, &c.

339. Many theories have been advanced to account for the fact that, though an image is cast upon the retina of each eye, only a single object is seen. This blending of the two images, by the mind, into a single perception, is apparently chiefly the effect of habit, since, when the two images do not fall upon parts of the retina which are accustomed to act together, *double vision* results. But it must be remembered that the *mind does not look in upon the retina*, and although there are two images depicted of the same object, the mind instinctively acquires the idea of but one object.

NOTE.—If one eye be forced a little to one side by pressure with the finger, an object examined by both eyes will appear double.

340. An impression on the retina is not instantaneously made, nor does it instantaneously die out. The former is shown by the fact that we cannot see a rifle ball or a cannon ball when we stand at right angles to the course of its flight, but, if the projectile is approaching us or is going from us, it preserves the same direction long enough to produce an impression, and we see it. With regard to the time the impression remains on the retina, it may be remarked that it is well known that winking does not interfere with distinct vision, because the image remains on the retina so as to give the sense of continuous vision. Moreover if a lighted stick be whirled rapidly in a circle its track appears to be a continuous ring of fire. By carefully conducted experiments it has been ascertained that the time an impression remains on the retina varies in different eyes from $\frac{1}{16}$ to $\frac{1}{4}$ of a second.

341. COLOR BLINDNESS is a peculiar affection of the retina, by which the eye is rendered unable to distinguish certain colors of the spectrum. Some can only discern yellow and blue in the spectrum; some mistake orange for green or green for orange; some can only distinguish with certainty yellow, white, and green; some cannot distinguish by color the ripe cherries on a tree from its leaves, &c.

342. THE SIMPLE EYE, of which that of man is the most perfect type, belongs peculiarly to the vertebrate kingdom, but is occasionally found also in invertebrate animals. The snail and kindred creatures have this simple eye, mounted on the tip of a long stalk or pedicle. In spiders the eyes are simple, usually eight in number, and are situated on the top of the head. The larvæ of many insects possess simple eyes only, but the eye of the perfect or fully developed insect is *compound*. These compound eyes have the same general form as simple eyes, and are placed either on the side of the head as in insects, or are supported on pedicles as in crabs. When examined by aid of a magnifying lens, the compound eye is found to consist of many hexagonal facettes or eyes, each being the large end of a cone, which is about six times as long as it is broad, and which receives a single filament of the optic nerve. In one species of beetle the eye

contains 25,000 of these facettes; in the eye of the butterfly 17,000, in that of the dragon-fly 12,500, and in that of the house-fly 4,000 have been counted. The number of facettes is evidently intended to compensate for the immovability of the eye—each facette being a perfect eye in itself, although having, on account of its fixed axis, but little range of vision.

LECTURE XXIV.

OPTICAL PHENOMENA OF THE ATMOSPHERE.

343. The diffused light of the atmosphere is due to the reflection of the rays by its individual particles and by the earth's surface. Were it not for this *scattering* of the rays of light, the atmosphere would not be illuminated at all, and we should, even at mid-day, see the stars shining forth from an intensely black ground.

344. The dark vault of heaven appears, during a fine day, of a fine blue tint. This is due to the *unequal* reflection of light by the particles of air—the blue rays being for the most part reflected, and the yellow and red absorbed. The darkest blue is always in the zenith, the atmosphere near the horizon appearing much lighter in color. And as we ascend into the higher regions, the blue deepens until at length it becomes black.

NOTE.—The evening and morning red depends in all probability upon the vapour contained in the air.

345. TWILIGHT is the partial illumination of the atmosphere that intervenes between sunset or sunrise and total darkness. It is due to the rays of the sun striking the higher regions of the atmosphere and being *refracted* to the earth. In Canada, the twilight continues till the sun is 18° below the horizon, but in equatorial regions the twilight is of much shorter duration.

346. LOOMING is a term applied to the apparent elevation of objects, at sea, above their true level. Thus, islands and vessels seem raised above the water, or very distant vessels

appear above the horizon. In all these cases the appearance is due to extraordinary atmospheric refraction.

NOTE.—Occasionally a vessel appears suspended in the clouds with an inverted image beneath it, producing an appearance known as the *Fata Morgana*.

347. THE MIRAGE, often seen in hot sandy deserts, is an appearance in which distant objects *seem* to be reflected in the waters of a placid and beautiful lake. It is caused by the partial rarefaction of the lower stratum of air, which rests upon the heated surface of sand, causing the rays that emanate from remote objects to pass in a curvilinear path to the eye.

348. Atmospheric refraction causes all the heavenly bodies which are not in the zenith to appear nearer to that point than they really are. In the horizon such bodies are lifted out of their true position about half a degree, so that we actually see the lower limb of the sun or moon before the upper has come to the horizon, and in the evening continue to see the lower limb until the upper has, in fact, sunk beneath the horizon. Similarly the stars all appear to rise before they in reality come above the horizon, and are visible for some time after they have set. Atmospheric refraction also, by acting more upon the lower limb of the sun and moon, when on the horizon, relatively lifts that portion up so as to give these luminaries an apparently oval form.

THE RAINBOW.

349. THE RAINBOW consists of one or more circular arcs of prismatic colors seen when the observer is standing with his back to the sun and rain is falling between him and a cloud, which serves as a screen on which the bow is depicted. When the bow is double, i. e. when two bows are seen, the inner or brightest is called the *primary*, and the outer one, which is not so bright, is termed the *secondary*. In the primary bow the order of colors is, beginning with the innermost or lowest, violet, indigo, blue, green, yellow, orange and red; in the secondary bow this order of colors is reversed. The inner bow is not seen when the sun is more than 42° above the horizon, and the outer one does not appear when the elevation of the sun is more than 64°. When the sun is in the horizon both bows extend to semicircles but become smaller arcs of a circle as he is higher above the horizon.

THE RAINBOW.   141

350. The rainbow is caused by the refractions and reflections of light by the falling drops of rain. In the primary bow there is one reflection and two refractions, and in the secondary there are two reflections and two refractions.

Let $O P$ be a line drawn from the eye of the observer to the centre of the rainbows, and let A, B, C, and D, E, F, be spherical drops of rain in the act of falling. Then of the cones of light that fall upon each of the drops A, B, C, the rays that pass through or near the axis are refracted to a focus

Fig. 43.

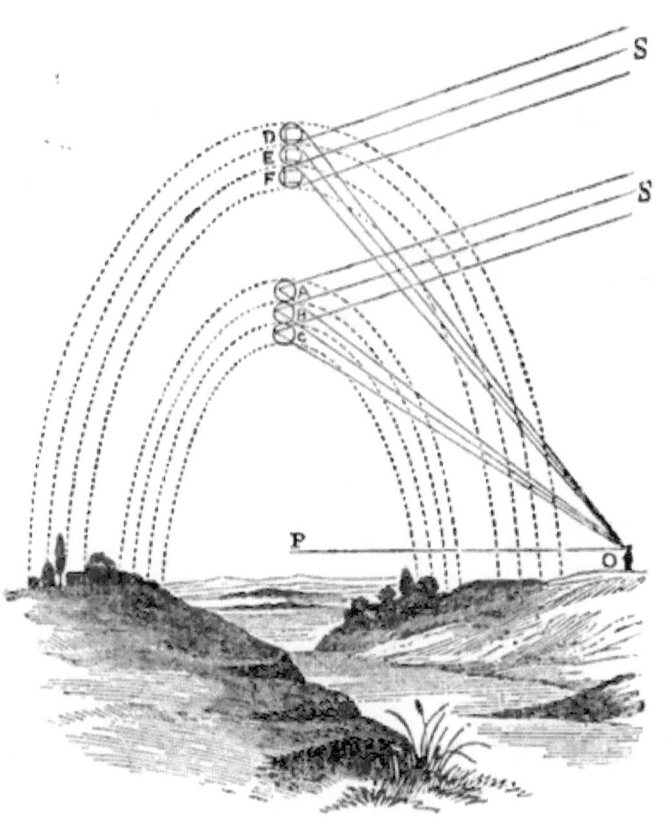

behind the drop, but those that fall upon the upper side of the drop will be refracted, the red least and the violet most, and will fall upon the back of the drop so obliquely that some of them will be reflected as shewn in Fig 43. Upon again passing out of the drop they are refracted in the eye at O, and, since the red is refracted least and the violet most, the red will form the outer color of the spectrum perceived by the eye, and the violet the lower or innermost band. Similarly, by tracing the course of the rays that enter the lower part of the drops D, E, F, it will be found that the rays are refracted twice and reflected twice so as to finally reach the eye, depicting on the retina a spectrum having the violet for the outer band and the red for the inner.

The bows are circular arcs because of the many rain-drops that compose the shower. Those only can reflect red to the eye that make an angle with $P\,O$ equal to the angle $A\,O\,P$ or the angle $F\,O\,P$; those only can reflect violet to the eye that make angles equal to $C\,O\,P$ or $D\,O\,F$, &c., and these drops must necessarily be for the moment in the arc of a circle having P for its centre.

351. HALOES are prismatic rings occasionally seen around the sun and varying from 2° to 45° in diameter. They are caused by reflection from minute crystals of ice floating in the higher regions of the air.

352. CORONAS are rings circling the moon and are said to generally indicate the approach of a storm. They are caused by reflection of light from the external surface of watery vapour floating across the face of the moon.

353. PARHELIA (false suns, sun dogs) are bands of light which are sometimes seen surrounding the sun and sometimes passing through it. They are attributed to reflection from minute crystals of ice in the air.

LECTURE XXV.

POLARIZATION AND DOUBLE REFRACTION OF LIGHT.

POLARIZATION.

354. When a ray of light, ab Fig. 44, is incident upon a plane glass plate $A\,B$ (blackened at the back) at an angle of 54½ degrees, it is, for the most part reflected in the direction bc, according to the usual laws. Now if the ray bc, which has been once reflected at the angle 54½°, fall upon a second

plane glass plate *C D* (also blackened at the back) parallel to *A B*, the ray *bc* will be incident on *C D* at an angle of 54½°. In this position of the plates their planes of reflection are coincident, and the ray *bc* will be reflected like any ray of ordinary light; but if we turn the plate *C D* in such a manner that the ray *bc* forms the axis of rotation, the angle of incidence will remain the same, but the parallelism of the mirrors will cease, and consequently their planes of

Fig. 44.

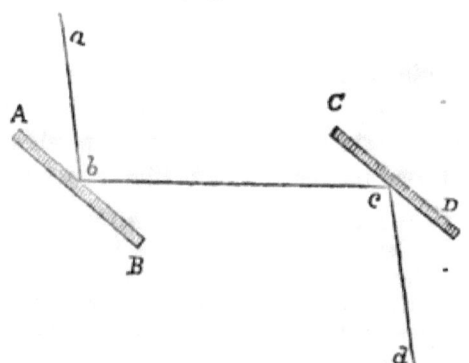

reflection will no longer be coincident. Under these circumstances we shall find that, while revolving the plate *C D*, the brilliancy of the twice reflected light alternately dies out and is renewed. When the plate *C D* is turned 90° or a quarter round, the ray *bc* is no longer reflected from the plate *C D* as it would be were it a ray of ordinary light; when we have revolved the plate *C D*, 180° or half round, the planes of reflection of the plates are again coincident, and the ray *bc* is totally reflected; when the plate *C D* has been revolved 270° or three quarters round, their planes of reflection are once more at right angles to one another, and the ray *bc* is not reflected at all; and so on. Of course at intermediate points of revolution the ray is partially reflected.

355. It appears then that when a ray of common light has suffered **reflection from a glass surface at an angle of 54½°, it has acquired certain remarkable and peculiar** properties. It is reflectable **on one side but not on the other, so** that its opposite **sides have opposite properties.** Under these circumstances the ray of light is said to be *polarized*.

NOTE.—The *Plane of polarization* is the plane in **which the ray can be** *completely* reflected by the second mirror, and is, of course, coincident with the plane of reflection from the first mirror.

356. A POLARISCOPE or *polarizing apparatus* is an arrangement **of mirrors or reflectors, by** means **of which the** effects **of polar**ization can be examined, the **angle of** polarization measured, &c. Polariscopes are of various forms.

357. We have seen that the vibrations in the ether which produce light **are made** transverse to the course of the ray

in all conceivable planes. Now it is supposed that the difference between polarized light and common light consists in the fact that the vibrations producing the former are all made in one single plane.

358. Certain crystals seem to possess the power of polarizing all the light that passes through them in particular directions. This appears to be due to their partly absorbing the light, and causing the remainder to vibrate in a single plane.

Thus, if a transparent tourmaline be cut parallel to its principal axis into plates $\frac{1}{30}$ of an inch in thickness, and two of these be taken and polished, they exhibit with great beauty the property of polarizing light. The light is readily transmitted through either plate separately or through both when they are held lengthwise parallel to one another, but if the second plate is made to cross the first, it totally obstructs the light.

A tourmaline plate therefore affords a means of olarizing light and also of determining whether a ray has already been polarized by other means. When used for the latter purpose, the plate of tourmaline, or other suitable substance is called an *analyzer*.

359. When a ray of light is polarized by reflection from the first or second surface of a transparent body a part of the transmitted light equal to it is also polarized by refraction. The whole amount of light transmitted, however, greatly exceeds the part polarized, so that, in common language, we say that light is only *partially* polarized by a single refraction. When however a ray of light is transmitted obliquely through a number of parallel plates of glass or other transparent medium, a new portion is polarized by each plate, until at length the whole of the transmitted beam is polarized.

360. The kind of polarization we have been hitherto describing is called *Plane Polarization*, to distinguish it from *Elliptical and Circular Polarization*. In order to effect the plane polarization of light by reflection from metallic surfaces, it must be reflected many times at the proper angle of polarization.

361. If a ray of light has been twice reflected from the second surfaces of bodies at their angle of greatest polarization, or if it has been reflected but once at that angle from a metallic surface, it appears to consist of light vibrating in two planes only

at right angles to one another, and the phase of vibration in one is retarded ¼ of a vibration. Under these circumstances the light is said to be *circularly polarized*.

362. ELLIPTICAL POLARIZATION takes place when a ray of light is reflected *once* from a metallic surface at its angle of maximum polarization. It appears as light vibrating in two planes which are not at right angles to one another, and the light vibrating in the one plane is retarded less than ¼ of a vibration behind that vibrating in the other plane.

363. The colored phenomena dependent on polarization, plane, circular and elliptical, are exceedingly beautiful and varied. All of these colors are produced by the interference of rays. The polarization of light has now become a most reliable means of investigation in the hands of the analytical chemist, as it often enables him to detect the slightest adulteration in a solution.

DOUBLE REFRACTION.

364. By Double Refraction, we mean a property possessed by certain crystals, as Iceland spar, of splitting or dividing a single incident ray into two emergent ones.

Thus, when a crystal of Iceland spar is laid upon a dark line on paper, it conveys to the eye the impression of two parallel lines removed from one another by a small intervening space.

365. A crystal of Iceland spar is rhombohedral in form, and a line drawn from an obtuse angle of the crystal through the centre to the opposite obtuse angle is called its *principal axis*. Now the two emergent rays are distinguished as *ordinary* and *extraordinary*; the former in the case of Iceland spar being that which appears most removed from the principal axis, and the latter that nearest the principal axis.

366. Crystals, like Iceland spar, which refract the rays as indicated in Art. 365, are called *Positive Crystals;* while those in which the ordinary ray lies nearer to the principal axis than the extraordinary ray are called *Negative Crystals*.

NOTE.—Some crystals have two axes of **double** refraction, as for example mica, topaz, gypsum, **nitrate of** potash, &c.

367. When the two rays that emerge from a crystal of Iceland spar or other crystal possessing the power of double refraction are examined, they are both found to consist of light totally polarized—the one being polarized at right angles to the other. Hence the various ways by which light may be polarized are *reflection, refraction, absorption,* and *double refraction.*

NOTE 1.—A crystal of Iceland spar, one of tourmaline, is among the most valuable pieces of polarizing apparatus we possess. The former cut into the form of a prism (a *Nicol's prism*) is used for throwing the ordinary image out of the field of view, as it transmits only the extraordinary ray.

NOTE 2.—Thin plates of double refracting crystals exhibit colored rings of exquisite beauty marked by a black cross, when viewed in certain directions by polarized light.

ELECTRICITY.

LECTURE XXVI.

DEFINITIONS, SKETCH OF THE HISTORY OF THE SCIENCE, IDIO-ELECTRICS AND AN-ELECTRICS, CONDUCTORS, NON-CONDUCTORS, INSULATION.

368. Electricity (Greek, *electron* "amber") is the name given to a highly elastic, attenuated and imponderable agent which pervades the material world, and which is visible only in its effects. It is susceptible of a very great degree of intensity, and has a tendency to equilibrium unlike that of any other known agent. The word *"fluid,"* as applied to electricity, must be taken in a conventional sense only.

369. When a rod of glass or of sealing wax is smartly rubbed for a few moments by a piece of warm flannel or silk, it acquires the power of acting upon light bodies, so as to attract and repel them.

While this transient power lasts, the rod is said to be *electrified* or *charged;* the piece of paper or other light body is said to be *attracted* when it approaches the rod, and is said to be

HISTORY OF ELECTRICITY.   147

repelled when it recedes from it. In the dark a faint light is seen to follow the track of the rubber, and this is accompanied by a crackling noise.

These are the fundamental phenomena of electricity.

370. The science of electricity was to some extent known and studied by the ancients. The discoveries were, however, very few, and the science was not systematized until the time of Franklin and Du Fay, between the years 1733 and 1760.

The following is a brief sketch of the history of electrical science:

B. C.	
600	THALES of Miletus discovered that amber, when excited by friction, attracts light substances.
371.	THEOPHRASTUS, a pupil of Aristotle, noticed the electric properties of the mineral called tourmaline.
	PLINY and ARISTOTLE were acquainted with the peculiar effect resulting from the touch of the torpedo, but had no idea that it was referable to the same cause as the properties already observed in amber and in tourmaline.
A. D.	
1600.	DR. W. GILBERT, physician to James I. of England, in an appendix to a valuable work on the magnet, published a variety of electrical experiments on gems, glass, gums, &c.
1670.	MR. ROBT. BOYLE added to the number of electrics, and discovered the electric light emitted by the diamond when rubbed in the dark.
	OTTO GUERICKE, in Germany, contemporary with Mr. Boyle, mounted a globe of sulphur upon an axis, and thus procured electricity in greater quantities. He also discovered electrical repulsion.
	SIR ISAAC NEWTON discovered that glass does not prevent electrical attraction and repulsion.
1709.	MR. HAWKSBEE mounted a glass instead of a sulphur globe.

A.D.	
1729.	MR. STEPHEN GRAY, of the London Charter-House, first observed the fact that some substances are conductors, and others non-conductors, and hence he discovered a method of insulating bodies.
1735.	DU FAY inferred the existence of two fluids to which he gave the names of *Vitreous and Resinous Electricities*.
1742.	PROFESSOR BOZE, of Wurtemberg, added the *Prime Conductor* of the globe machine. It was at first supported by a man standing on a cake of resin, afterwards it was suspended by a cord of silk from the ceiling.
	MR. WINCKLER, of Leipsic, about the same time, substituted a cushion instead of the hand, which had hitherto been used as a rubber to excite the globe.
1746.	PROFESSOR MUSCHENBRŒCK, of Leyden, in conjunction with his associate CUNEUS, by accident discovered that electricity could be collected in a glass vessel containing water.
	VON KLEIST, dean of a cathedral in Germany, made the same discovery simultaneously with Prof. Muschenbrœck.
	SIR W. WATSON, SMEATON, BEVIS, WILSON, and CANTON, all distinguished members of the Royal Society of London, improved and extended the discovery of Muschenbrœck, and gave us the *Leyden Jar* in its present form.
1752.	Dr. B. FRANKLIN discovered the identity of electricity and lightning; introduced points for protection; combined several Leyden jars into a battery; and gave his hypothesis of a single fluid.
1771.	CAVENDISH and ŒPINUS investigated the hypotheses of Du Fay and Franklin.
	WATSON and CANTON fused metals by electricity.
	BECCARIA decomposed water by means of electricity.

ELECTRICS AND NON-ELECTRICS. 149

A. D.
1785. VOLTA invented the *Electrophorus*.

COULOMB, by means of his *torsion electrometer*, reduced electricity, the most subtile of all physical agents, beneath the rigorous sway of mathematics, and thus placed it at once among the Physical Sciences.

PROFESSOR FARADAY and SIR W. SNOW HARRIS are perhaps the most distinguished cultivators of electrical science at the present day.

371. Those substances which, under ordinary circumstances, readily evince electrical properties by friction, are termed *electrics* or *idio-electrics*. They are exhibited in the following:

TABLE OF ELECTRICS, OR NON-CONDUCTORS.

Shellac	Fur
Brimstone	Hair
Amber	Wool
Jet	Feathers
Resin	Paper
Gums	Turpentine
Gun-Cotton	Oils
Glass	All dry Gases
Diamond	Atmospheric Air
Gems	Steam of high elasticity
Bituminous Substances	Ice at 0° Fahr., &c.
Silk	

372. Those substances which do not readily evince electricity under ordinary circumstances by friction, are called *non-electrics* or *an-electrics*. They are shown in the following:

TABLE OF NON-ELECTRICS, OR CONDUCTORS.

All Metals	Steam
Well burned Charcoal	Flame
Plumbago	Smoke
Acids	Animal and vegetable substances containing moisture, &c.
Saline Fluids	
Water	

373. Electrics are also called *non-conductors*, from the fact that they transmit electricity very imperfectly, but non-electrics are generally speaking very good *conductors*. Some substances become conductors or non-conductors by a change of temperature—thus glass, when heated to redness, becomes a conductor; water, when in the state either of steam of high elasticity, or of ice at or below 0° Fahr., becomes a non-conductor.

374. When a metal rod is subjected to friction, electricity is developed upon its surface, but the metal being a good conductor it is conveyed away by the hand as fast as it is generated. If, however, the metal rod be attached to a glass handle, the fluid accumulates upon the rod and becomes visible in its effects. Hence electricity may be developed on any one of the so called non-electrics if it be *insulated*.

375. A body is said to be insulated when it is supported by a non-conducting substance, such as a rod of glass or shellac.

LECTURE XXVII.

SOURCES OF ELECTRICAL EXCITATION AND KINDS OF ELECTRICITY, ELECTROSCOPES AND ELECTROMETERS, THEORIES AS REGARDS THE NATURE OF ELECTRICITY.

SOURCES OF EXCITATION.

376. The principal sources of electrical excitation and the kind of electricity developed by each, are as follows:

I. FRICTION producing Frictional, Statical, Tensional, Common or Machine Electricity.*

II. CHEMICAL ACTION producing Dynamical Electricity, Voltaism or Galvanism.

III. DIFFERENCE OF TEMPERATURE in connected metallic bars—giving rise to Thermo-Electricity.

---

* See Art. 391, NOTE.

ELECTROMETERS.

IV. MAGNETIC ACTION developing Magneto-Electricity.

V. LIVING ANIMAL MATTER—Animal Electricity.

NOTE.—Change of form, mere contact, simple pressure, change of temperature, &c., also give rise to the manifestation of electrical force, but these must be regarded as coming properly under the head of one or other of the above five sources.

ELECTROSCOPES.

377. ELECTROSCOPES are instruments used to detect the presence of *free* electricity. The principal electroscopes in use are the following :

I. THE PITH-BALL ELECTROSCOPE. This consists of two small pith balls insulated by silk threads. When brought into the neighbourhood of an excited body, the balls become similarly electrified, and repel each other.

II. THE GOLD-LEAF ELECTROSCOPE. This consists of two slips of gold-leaf properly insulated and inclosed in a glass jar. When brought into the neighborhood of an electrified body, the leaves diverge and thus indicate the presence of the electric fluid. Fig. 45.

III. BOHNENBERGER'S GOLD-LEAF ELECTROSCOPE. This consists of a small Zamboni's pile* $a\ b$ placed horizontally and having each extremity connected by a wire to perpendicular metallic plates p and m. One of these plates is therefore the positive and the other the negative electrode of the pile. A metallic disc $o\ n$ is connected by a wire $c\ d$ to a slip of gold-leaf $d\ g$ which hangs midway between the two plates p, m, being equally attracted by each. When, however, the slightest trace of electricity is communicated to the disc $o\ n$, the leaf instantly moves towards the plate, which has the opposite polarity.

ELECTROMETERS.

378. ELECTROMETERS are instruments employed to measure the *intensity* of electrical force, and, like electroscopes, they depend for their action upon electrical attraction and repulsion.

Electrometers differ from electroscopes merely in having attached a graduated arc or some other means by which to *compare* the intensities of different accumulations of the fluid. The chief electrometers in common use are the following:

---

* See Art. 437.

I. THE QUADRANT ELECTROMETER. This consists of a light pith ball a attached by an exceedingly thin and light insulating rod f to an upright metallic bar $b\ c$. The rod $m\ f$ moves freely round the pivot f which is the centre of the circle of which the graduated ivory semicircle S is an arc. The number of degrees of the graduated arc through which the rod $f\ m$ is driven when the instrument is placed on a charged conductor, is, in a measure, indicative of the intensity of the accumulated fluid. It is obvious that no amount of electricity, no matter what its intensity, can repel the ball beyond 90°.

Fig. 46.

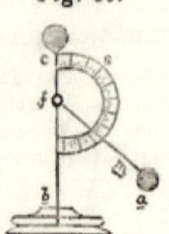

Fig. 47.

II. COULOMB'S TORSION ELECTROMETER consists of a tube, ac, 8 or 10 inches in length, having a flat graduated plate at the top and terminating downwards in a glass jar $c\ d$. Through the tube there passes a fine thread of glass, or of shellac, or of unspun silk, which terminates upward in a button and index on the plate d and downwards in a horizontal bar of gum-lac, b having a small gilt pith ball p at one extremity and a paper vane n, to arrest oscillations, fixed at the other. Through another aperture f in the top of the glass case, a second rod of shellac, called the *carrier rod*, with a gilt pith ball at its extremity, is introduced. On the glass case there is a graduated circle $m\ t\ n$, by which the number of degrees through which the ball p is repelled, may be measured.

Coulomb has demonstrated that the reactive force of an elastic filament or its tendency to return to its previous state is exactly proportional to its torsion. Hence the number of degrees through which the ball p is repelled by the charged ball at the end of the carrier rod is the measure of the electrical force accumulated on the latter.

Suppose the electricity accumulated on the carrier ball repels the ball p through 20°, and it is required to ascertain the torsion force necessary to maintain the ball at a divergence of 10°. If when the balls are 20° apart we begin to turn the button on the plate a backwards we shall gradually bring the ball p nearer to the charged ball at the end of the carrier rod, and upon thus turning the index on a back through 70° we shall have brought the balls within 10° of each other

Now the filament of glass or lac is twisted 10° to the right, and 70° to the left so that its torsion is represented by 80°, and hence we have the numbers 20 and 10 for the relative values of the repulsive forces at the distances of 20° and 80°; and since the numbers 20 and 80 are in the proportion of 1 to 4, we infer that electrical repulsion and attraction vary inversely as the square of the distance.

ELECTRICAL THEORIES.

379. The theories that have been advanced in explanation of electrical phenomena are chiefly two, viz:

I. The one-fluid theory, or theory of Franklin.

II. The two-fluid theory, or theory of Du Fay.

NOTE.—Of these theories that of Franklin is the simpler, but Du Fay's is considered to be the more philosophical.

380. THE ONE-FLUID THEORY, OR THEORY OF FRANKLIN, assumes the existence of a single elementary imponderable fluid of extreme tenuity and elasticity, existing in a state of equable distribution throughout the material world. This fluid is supposed to be repulsive of its own particles, but attractive of the particles of all other matter. Every body has a certain amount of capacity for this fluid, and when it contains its natural share is said to be in a state of electrical quiescence or repose. When, however, by friction or other mechanical or chemical means, we increase or diminish its quantity in a body, there ensues a powerful action arising from the tendency of the body to regain its natural share, if its original quantity has been diminished, or to throw it off to other bodies, if it has been increased.

381. According to Franklin's theory a body having more than its natural share of electricity is said to be *positively* electrified or + electrified; one having less than its natural share is said to be *negatively* electrified, or — electrified.

382. THE TWO-FLUID THEORY, OR THEORY OF DU FAY assumes the existence of an infinitely attenuated fluid, highly elastic and imponderable and pervading all bodies. It is supposed to be compounded of two elementary fluids possessed of distinct and opposite properties, and called *vitreous* and *resinous* electricities. These elementary fluids are further assumed to be each repulsive of its own particles but attractive of the particles of the other, so that when combined in proper proportions they completely condense or neutralize each other, thus producing perfect electrical repose. When, however, by friction or other mechanical or chemical means, we decompose this compound, the vitreous and resinous fluids are separated, one adhering to the surface of the rubber, and the other to the surface of the excited substance, and hence in no case of electrical excitation can we obtain one kind of electricity, without the simultaneous development of the other.

383. The two-fluid theory is the one commonly adopted by scientific men, but instead of using the terms vitreous and negative electricities, the terms positive and negative are employed. It is hence necessary to note carefully that:

Positive or *Vitreous* electricity is that kind of electricity that adheres to the surface of *glass* when it is excited by friction with a *silk* rubber.

Negative or *Resinous* electricity is that kind of electricity that adheres to the surface of *resin* when it is excited by friction with a *silk* rubber.

NOTE.—In the former case the electricity adhering to the rubber is *negative*, in the latter it is *positive*.

384. No general rule can be given as to which kind of electricity will be developed by friction on a given substance, this depending upon the material that forms the rubber, and even then the question can be determined only by experiment. The following table of substances is given by Faraday, and is so arranged that each body becomes excited *positively* by friction with those below it in the list, and *negatively* by those above it.

1. Catskin or Bearskin
2. Flannel
3. Ivory
4. Quill
5. Rock Crystal
6. Flint-glass
7. Cotton
8. Linen Canvas
9. White Silk
10. Black Silk
11. The Hand
12. Shellac
13. Wood
14. Metal
15. Sulphur.

NOTE.—Of all known substances catskin is most susceptible of positive and, perhaps, sulphur of negative, electricity.

LECTURE XXVIII.

DISTRIBUTION OF ELECTRICITY ON CHARGED BODIES, ACTION OF POINTS, THEORY OF INDUCTION, TENSION, INTENSITY AND QUANTITY, LAW OF VARIATION IN FORCE OF ELECTRICAL ATTRACTION AND REPULSION.

DISTRIBUTION OF FREE ELECTRICITY.

385. Electricity, in its natural or compound state, appears to be diffused equally throughout any given mass of matter, but when separated into its component elements, each appears confined to the surface of the body in which it has been set free in the form of an exceedingly thin layer, not penetrating sensibly into the substance of the mass.

386. As free electricity resides on the surface only, of bodies, the quantity that can be accumulated in a given body necessarily depends upon the extent of surface, and when the same quantity of electricity is thrown on surfaces of different magnitudes the force exerted by the charged surfaces will vary inversely as their squares.

387. When a spherical body is charged, the electricity distributes itself equally over every part of the surface; but in a spheroid it becomes accumulated at the extremities, and the more elongated the spheroid, the greater the disproportion between the force exerted at its extremities, and that manifested at its middle part.

388. On a flat disc or plate, with sharp edges, the electric fluid increases in depth or quantity from the centre to the edge, but the increase is not regular, being much more rapid near the edge than towards the middle of the plate.

389. Electricity is always given off rapidly from points. This arises from the fact that the fluid accumulates in such quantities, at the extremities of points, as to acquire sufficient tension to overcome the small amount of atmospheric pressure that can

there be exerted, and accordingly flows off in a continuous stream to the surrounding bodies.

NOTE.—So rapidly is the fluid given off from points, that it is impossible to charge the prime conductor of an electric machine, if a point be attached to it, or if a point be presented to it.

INTENSITY, TENSION AND QUANTITY.

390. By the *intensity* of a charge of electricity, we mean its attractive force upon surrounding bodies as measured by the electrometer. The intensity varies as the square of the quantity accumulated in a given amount of surface.

Thus, if there be three *equal surfaces* so charged that the second shall have accumulated upon it twice as much and the third three times as much as the first, then the intensities of the charges will be as 1, 4 and 9; the squares of the numbers 1, 2 and 3.

NOTE.—The same distinction exists between the terms intensity and quantity in electricity as in heat. The intensity of the latter agent is determined, it will be remembered, by the thermometer, while the quantity in a given body is ascertained by the calorimeter; so the intensity of electricity is measured by the electrometer but its quantity by the amount of chemical decomposition it can effect.

391. The term *tension*, as applied in electricity, is employed to denote the power or ability possessed by an accumulation of the fluid to pass or force its way through any resisting medium.

NOTE.—Electricity as set free by friction is of high tension, but is small in quantity, i. e. its mechanical or disruptive power is immense, but it can but feebly perform such offices as chemical decomposition; hence its name *tensional* electricity. It is called *statical* to distinguish it from *dynamical* electricity, the latter moving constantly in currents, while the former appears to be in a state of rest except at the moment of discharge. The origin of the names *common*, *frictional*, and *machine*, are obvious.

INDUCTION.

392. When an electrified body is placed near a conducting body in its natural state, the whole of the latter becomes *oppositely* electrified unless it be insulated, in which case the extremity next the electrified body becomes *oppositely* and that farthest from it *similarly* electrified. The electricity thus acquired by the second body is called *induced* electricity, or is said to be produced by induction.

393. All non-conductors allow induction to take place through them, and are from this circumstance, called *di-electrics.*

Sir W. S. Harris gives the following list of di-electrics, in which it will be observed that air is the worst and shellac the best.

SUBSTANCE.	SPECIFIC INDUCTIVE CAPACITY.
Air,	1·00
Rosin,	1·77
Pitch,	1·80
Wax,	1·86
Glass,	1·90
Sulphur,	1·93
Shellac,	1·95

394. According to Faraday's theory, induction is essentially physical action, occurring between contiguous particles only, and never taking place at a distance without polarizing the molecules of the intervening di-electric, causing them to assume a peculiar constrained postion, which they retain as long as they are under the influence of the inductive body.

Fig. 48.

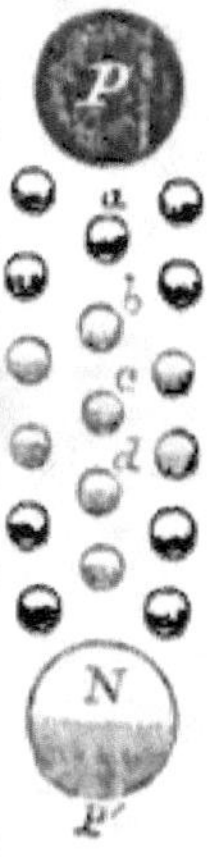

For example, if *P*, Fig. 48, represent a body charged positively, and *a b c d*, &c., intermediate molecules of air or any other di-electric, then the free electricity in *P* acts upon the body *N* by *polarizing* these intermediate particles. Thus, since positive electricity repels positive and attracts negative, the stratum of atoms lying adjacent to *P* is acted upon by the electricity resident in the latter in such a manner that the side of each next *P* becomes negatively and the side remote from *P* positively electrified. This stratum of atoms acts similarly upon the molecules next beyond, and so on until the action is carried to the body *N*.

LAW OF ATTRACTION AND REPULSION.

395. *Bodies similarly electrified repel each other, and those differently electrified attract each other, with a force varying inversely as the square of their distance apart.*

396. Electricity is transferred *silently* from a charged body by the double power of conduction and convection. When a body is carefully insulated upon a resinous support, the rapidity

with which it parts with its charge by exposure to the air, depends principally upon the amount of moisture in the latter. Bodies imperfectly insulated, as by silk or uncoated glass, lose an additional portion by its escape along the imperfectly insulating support.

NOTE.—Particles of dust in the air act as *carriers* in conveying away a charge from an insulated electrified body.

LECTURE XXIX.

ELECTRICAL MACHINES AND GENERAL THEORY OF THEIR ACTION, THE ELECTROPHORUS, THE LEYDEN JAR, DISCHARGES OF ACCUMULATIONS OF FLUID.

397. The two kinds of electrical machines in common use are the *plate* and the *cylinder machines,* of which the former is by far the most powerful and convenient.

The Plate Electrical Machine consists of a circular glass

Fig. 49.

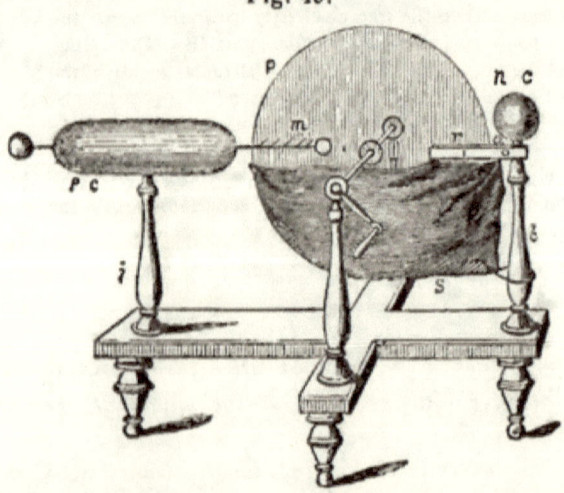

plate p, of any diameter from 10 to 40 or 50 inches, a prime conductor $p\ c$, insulated on a glass pillar i, and furnished with points *m*, to collect the fluid from the revolving plate; a negative conductor *n c*, likewise insulated on a glass pillar *b*, and having a metallic connection with the rubber *r*. A silk bag *s* is made to enclose the lower half of the plate for the purpose of retaining the fluid on its surface till it reaches the points *m*, in connection with the prime conductor.—The rubber *r* is commonly formed of two cushions of buckskin stuffed with horse hair, and the degree of pressure is regulated by a small screw *a*, near the negative conductor. When the machine is in action either the prime or the negative conductor is connected with the ground by a brass chain.

398. The theory of the action of the electrical machine is, according to the one-fluid hypothesis, as follows:

Upon turning the handle of the machine the glass plate becomes positively electrified at the expense of the rubber, and in revolving gives up this surplus fluid to the prime conductor as it passes between the points of the latter. The prime conductor thus becomes charged positively, while the rubber is left negatively electrified. After a few revolutions the process ceases on account of the negative condition of the rubber, but when this latter has a metallic or other proper connection with the earth, it draws the electric fluid from the latter as fast as it is carried to the prime conductor by the plate, and thus the production of free electricity may be continued for any length of time.

NOTE 1.—It is manifestly impossible, according to this view of the nature of electricity, to charge a body positively without at the same time charging some other body (commonly the earth) negatively, because we cannot give one body more than its natural share of the fluid without removing a portion from some other body.

NOTE 2.—Adopting this theory we may liken the action of the electrical machine to the action of a common pump. Thus, we may regard

> The *earth* as the *well*,
> The *chain* as the *lower pipe* of the pump,
> The *rubber* as the *barrel*,
> The *plate* or *cylinder* as the *piston*,
> The *silk* as the *spout*, and
> The *prime conductor* as the pail

399. According to the two-fluid hypothesis, the action of the electrical machine is not so simple, nor are electricians agreed as to its precise rationale. The following is the explanation generally adopted:

On turning the glass plate or cylinder the electricity naturally present in it becomes decomposed—the positive adhering to the surface of the glass and the negative to the rubber. The positively electrified portions of the glass coming, during each revolution, in close proximity to the prime conductor, act powerfully by *induction* upon the electricity naturally present therein—decomposing it into its component elements and attracting the negative, which, being accumulated in a state of tension at the points of the conductor, darts off towards the plate, to meet the positive fluid, and thus re-constitute the neutral compound. The prime conductor is thus left powerfully positive, *not by acquiring electricity from the revolving glass, but by giving up its own negative fluid to the latter.*

400. From this explanation it appears that the negative conductor is connected with the earth in order to afford a route for the escape of the negative fluid from the rubber.

NOTE.—Certain strong objections have been urged against this explanation of the action of the electrical machine. The most important of these objections is that it practically assumes that the amount of combined electricity in the prime conductor, is infinitely great, since there is no limit to the quantity of free positive fluid that can be obtained from it by simply withdrawing its negative electricity. To this it may be answered:

1st. That the term fluid as used in electricity is liable to lead to misapprehension. Electricity is quite as likely to be, like light and heat, a mere motion among the particles of matter; in which case we must regard the waves or undulations produced by negative electricity as tending to neutralize those produced by positive, and hence the withdrawal, i. e. the stoppage of the former must necessarily allow the latter to act with increased vigour.

2nd. That in order to obtain an infinitely great amount of positive electricity, the conducting or containing surface, (i. e. the conductor and the inner surface of Leyden jars,) must be infinitely great, and hence there will be an infinitely great amount of negative fluid to be given up to the revolving plate.

3rd. That the amount of the electric fluid, combined with a very small quantity of matter, is truly inconceivably great. Thus, it has been estimated by Faraday, that the decomposition of *one grain* of water evolves as much electricity as is contained in a vivid flash of lightning, or, to use his own words, a certain electro-chemical arrangement produced "as much electricity in a little more than three seconds of time as a Leyden battery charged by thirty turns of a very large and powerful plate electrical machine in full action. This quantity, though sufficient if passed through the head of a rat or a cat, to have killed it as by a flash of lightning, was evolved by the mutual action of so small a portion of zinc wire and water in contact with it, that the loss of weight sustained by either would be inappreciable by our most delicate instruments. It would appear that 800,000 such charges as I have referred to above, would be necessary to supply electricity sufficient to decompose a single grain of water."

401. During the development of machine electricity a peculiar odour like that of phosphorus is evolved. This odour arises from the formation of a substance called *ozone*, which is considered to be an allotropic form of oxygen. (See Chem., Arts. 93 and 110.)

402. The development of machine electricity is greatly facilitated by the use of an amalgam, applied to the rubbers, consisting of two parts zinc, one of tin, and six of mercury, heated together in a crucible, and afterwards formed into a paste with lard. It is supposed that the oxidation of the amalgam aids the evolution of electricity.

THE ELECTROPHORUS.

403. The ELECTROPHORUS, invented by Volta, consists of a circular metallic dish, *a b*, Fig. 50, having a rim about a third of an inch high. This dish is filled with a mixture of 1 part Venice turpentine, 1 part shellac, and 1 part resin, melted together at a gentle heat, and, after being poured into the dish, allowed to cool gradually, so as to acquire a smooth surface. A second circular conducting disc *c*, called the *cover*, and furnished with an insulating glass handle, *d*, fits upon the upper surface of the resinous plate.

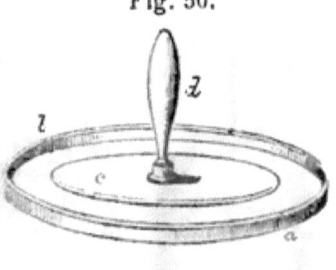

Fig. 50.

404. The resinous plate of the Electrophorus becomes negatively electrified when rubbed with dry flannel or fur. Upon replacing the cover, this being insulated, is acted upon inductively by the charged plate of resin—the positive electricity being attracted to the lower surface, and the negative repelled to the upper. Upon now presenting the knuckle to the cover a spark of positive electricity passes from the hand to the cover, so as to neutralize the free fluid upon its upper surface. If, under these circumstances, the cover is raised beyond the immediate influence of the excited plate of resin, it is found to be charged with free positive fluid; and upon again presenting the knuckle to it a spark passes from it to the hand.

NOTE.—Since no electricity is taken from the plate, it is manifest that one excitation of it is sufficient, under favorable circumstances, for the development of any amount of electricity.

The theory of the action of the electrophorus according to the Franklinian theory is as follows:

When the plate is rubbed with fur it loses electricity and becomes *negatively* charged, and, acting inductively upon the cover, it attracts a portion of its fluid to the under surface, leaving the upper negatively charged. Upon now presenting the hand, electricity passes from it to the cover, but when the cover is subsequently removed beyond the inductive influence of the plate, the fluid which was held to the under surface becomes free, and upon again presenting the knuckle it passes from the cover to the hand.

THE LEYDEN JAR.

405. The LEYDEN JAR consists of a wide mouthed glass vessel coated with tin-foil, both inside and outside, to within two or three inches of the top. It is closed by means of a dry wooden stopper, through which passes a metallic rod terminating upwards in a brass knob, and connecting, by means of a wire or chain at the other end, with the inside coating of the jar. When the jar is charged, the two electricities are held on the opposite sides of the glass by their mutual attraction—the metallic coatings merely serving as good conductors and never accumulating in themselves any electricity. When a jar is discharged under ordinary circumstances, there remains in the jar, after the first dis-

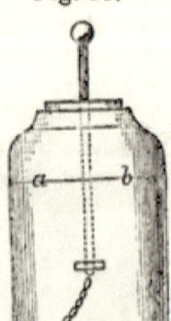

Fig. 51.

charge, a *residual charge* of $\frac{2}{13}$ of the quantity originally accumulated. In passing from one coat to the other of the jar, electricity travels at the rate of 288000 miles a second.

NOTE.—In the above figure of the Leyden jar, the tin-foil on both sides reaches as high as the line $a\ b$. The jar is discharged by making a metallic or other conducting connection between the outside and inside coatings. Two or more Leyden jars having their terminal knobs connected by wires, constitute what is called a battery of Leyden jars.

406. The instrument represented in Fig. 52 is called a *Jointed Discharger*. It consists of a glass handle, b, with two curved metallic wires, $c\ c$, having metallic balls at their extremities. The wires are movable round a joint, a, so as to be set at any required distance apart. When used for discharging a charged jar or battery, it is held by the glass handle, and one knob being placed in connection with the outside coating, the other is brought to one of the terminal balls of the battery.

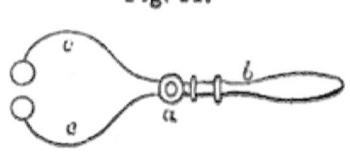

Fig. 52.

LECTURE XXX.

ELECTRICAL DISCHARGES AND THEIR EFFECTS, ELECTRICAL EXPERIMENTS.

ELECTRICAL DISCHARGES.

407. Discharges of accumulated electricity are of three kinds, viz:

        I. The Disruptive Discharge.
       II. The Convective Discharge.
     III. The Conductive Discharge.

Under the term *disruptive* discharge are included all varieties of electric discharge accompanied by the manifestation of light. The *Convective* discharge consists in the accumulated fluid being *conveyed* away silently by small particles of ponderable matter floating in the atmosphere; the *Conductive* discharge, in the conveyance of electricity from particle to particle of matter without any change of place among the particles themselves.

EFFECTS OF ELECTRICAL DISCHARGES.

408. The effects of the electrical discharge may be classed as:

        I. Physiological.
        II. Chemical.
        III. Mechanical.

409. The physiological effects are experienced when the discharge is transmitted through the animal body. It causes the muscles to contract momentarily with convulsive energy, and produces a peculiar *wrenching* sensation in the limbs through which it passes. If sufficiently powerful, it destroys life.

<small>NOTE.—The shock may be transmitted through any number of persons at the same time. The Abbé Nollet sent it through a chain of 600 persons. In a very long chain the effects are slightly stronger at the extremities than at the centre.</small>

410. The chemical effects of statical electricity are very feeble. It produces, however, a slow and feeble decomposition in certain chemical compounds when in the fluid state, such as iodide of potassium, ammonia, sulphuric acid, water, &c., and it causes a mixture of two volumes of hydrogen and one of oxygen to combine instantly with explosive violence.

411. The mechanical effects of the electrical discharge are seen when the passage of the fluid is impeded by meeting with a bad conductor. Under these circumstances the fluid either rends the obstacles asunder, or, in forcing its way through it, developes sufficient heat to ignite it if combustible.

412. A variety of amusing and instructive experiments are commonly exhibited in the lecture room to illustrate the nature of electricity, and the physiological, chemical and mechanical effects of its discharge. A few of the most interesting of these are the following:

    I. A person placed upon an *insulating stool* (a stool with glass legs) can be charged, and sparks can be drawn from any part of his body.

II. If a person with fine soft hair stands upon the insulating stool, upon charging him his hair becomes repelled, and stands out from his head in the most laughable manner.

III. A person charged on the insulating stool can light the gas or ignite some ether by applying his knuckle to it, or by presenting an icicle to it.

IV. A small quantity of gunpowder may be ignited by placing it on a dish or plate so as to cover the ends of two wires, one attached directly to the inside of a Leyden jar and the other connected by means of a wet string with the outside coating of the jar.

V. A mixture of hydrogen and oxygen may be exploded in the hydrogen or electrical pistol. When the pistol is filled with the mixture its mouth is stopped by a tightly fitting cork; upon then passing the spark through the instrument, the gases combine to form water which the heat developed converts into steam of high elasticity, and the cork is forced out with a loud explosion.

VI. If a battery of jars be discharged through a card or several folds of paper, the latter is perforated by a minute hole. A powerful battery will pierce a hole through a pane of common window-glass.

VII. A discharge thrown through an egg illuminates it very brilliantly, and so destroys its vitality that it soon begins to putrefy

VIII. Sparks of different colors are obtained by covering one ball of the discharger with leather gilt with silver or with gold, or with other substances.

IX. The luminous effects of electricity are very beautifully exhibited by *leading* the discharge over the surface of glass by means of small squares of tin foil separated by minute spaces. Letters and various complicated figures can thus be shown as a full blaze of electrical light. Among the pieces of apparatus designed for these purposes are *spiral tubes*, the *diamond jar*, and *magic squares*.

X. Electrical attraction and repulsion are illustrated by a variety of apparatus as the *electric bells*, the *electric swing*, the *electric see-saw*, the *electric spider*, *dancing images*, &c. In all of these a light figure or figures is employed to *carry* the electrical fluid from one of two oppositely electrified bodies or surfaces to the other.

XI. A metallic point is attached to the prime or negative conductor, and the machine set in action. The following facts may then be noticed:

1st. By holding the face an inch or two from the point, a breeze proceeding from it, and called the *electric aura*, is very distinctly felt. At the same time the taste and smell of the electric fluid or of its effects may be experienced.

2nd. In the dark, the electricity as it flows from the point escapes in *brushes* of light of exceeding great beauty when the point is attached to the prime conductor; but appears as a brilliant *star* of light when the point is attached to the negative conductor.

XII. The electrical discharge is sent through an exhausted receiver (in the form of a long tube if possible). The appearance presented is that of flashes of diffused light, bearing a strong resemblance to the *Aurora borealis*.

LECTURE XXXI.
ATMOSPHERIC ELECTRICITY.

413. The chief sources of free atmospheric electricity are —Evaporation, Condensation, Friction of the wind over the ground, especially in frosty weather, Chemical Action, and the Phenomena of Animal and Vegetable Life.

414. It has been found by experiment that the electricity of the air is always positive, and that it varies in quantity several times through the day, being least at mid-day and mid-night, and greatest shortly after sunrise, and just before sunset. It also increases in amount from July to January, from which time it decreases till the following July. The quantity likewise increases as we ascend into the higher regions of the atmosphere.

NOTE.—The earth is always *negatively* electrified, and, acting inductively on the air surrounding it, causes it to assume the positive state.

415. The principal phenomena dependent on aërial electricity, are Thunder-storms and Meteors; Whirlwinds, Water-spouts, and Earthquakes have also, by some, been attributed to electrical agency.

416. THUNDER-STORMS are most common and violent in the torrid zone, and decrease in intensity and in frequency towards the poles—never occurring beyond the 75° N. Lat. They are more frequent in summer than winter, and in the afternoon than in the morning. The free electricity of thunder-storms is developed by the rapid and copious condensation of vapour in the higher regions of the atmosphere. The clouds may become either positively or negatively electrified, and the same cloud sometimes consists of concentric bands or zones alternately positive and negative—the electricity being weakest at the edges and strongest at the centre. When a cloud charged with either electricity floats near the surface of the earth it *induces* the opposite kind in the ground immediately beneath

it. nen two oppositely electrified clouds, or an electrified cloud and the earth, approach within striking distance, a union of the electricities occurs and is accompanied by the phenomena of light (lightning) and sound (thunder).

417. Lightning is of three kinds, distinguished by their form:

Zigzag, Fork, or Chain lightning.
Sheet lightning.
Ball lightning.

418. ZIGZAG LIGHTNING is the most vivid, intense and dangerous, and is said usually to pass between the earth and the clouds, seldom flashing from cloud to cloud. SHEET LIGHTNING is the most common, and is probably owing to the vivid light of zigzag lightning being intercepted by some intervening cloud. BALL or GLOBE LIGHTNING is extremely rare and exceedingly dangerous.

NOTE.—When a highly charged thunder-cloud of great extent approaches the earth, it induces the opposite kind of electricity in the part of the earth beneath it, and repels that of the same kind. Now if the cloud comes within striking distance of the earth, a flash at one extremity is frequently followed immediately by a flash at the other. This second discharge is called the return stroke, and is quite as dangerous as the first or direct discharge.

419. As light travels 192000 miles per second, and sound only 1118 feet in the same space of time, it follows that we may easily determine the distance of a flash of lightning by simply counting the number of seconds that elapse between the occurrence of the flash and the arrival of the report, and allowing 1118 ft. for each second, or about one mile for every five seconds.

420. When a flash of lightning falls upon sand, its path below the surface is often marked by a *Fulgurite*, which is a tube formed of sand vitrified by the action of lightning. The fulgurite is winding in its shape, and often throws out lateral spurs or branches; it contracts towards the lower extremity, and usually terminates in a reservoir of water. The tubes are generally coated internally with a brilliant glass, and vary in diameter, from $\frac{1}{30}$ of an inch to $3\frac{1}{2}$ inches; the thickness of their sides varies from $\frac{1}{50}$ of an inch to $\frac{7}{8}$ of an inch; the branches vary in length from $\frac{1}{3}$ of an inch to 12 inches, and the main tube from $\frac{3}{4}$ of an inch to 40 feet.

ATMOSPHERIC ELECTRICITY.

421. Heat Lightning, or lightning unaccompanied by thunder, is produced by the atmosphere becoming in sultry weather both rarefied and moist, and thus permitting *silent flashes* of electricity to pass between the earth and the clouds. More commonly, however, heat lightning is simply the *reflection from the atmosphere of the lightnings* of storms so remote that their thunders cannot be heard.

422. Lightning Rods if properly constructed afford almost certain protection from electric discharges during thunder-storms. The most perfect lightning rods are made of copper bars, ⅔ of an inch in diameter, extending from a considerable height above the building to the depth of 6 or 8 feet beneath the ground. Commonly, however, they are made of iron or of iron galvanized, i.e. coated with zinc, and ought not to be less than an inch or ¾ of an inch in diameter. The rod should either be *continuous* from top to bottom, or should consist of pieces *screwed* together, not merely attached to one another by hooks; it should be fastened to the building by wooden supports and should have a *metallic* connection with any metal pipes or troughs that may be attached to the building. It should extend upwards to the height of from ten to twenty feet above the house top, and downwards to some *permanently moist stratum* of earth. If not galvanized it should be painted with *lamp black* throughout its entire length, and under all circumstances it should terminate upwards in several points *plated* with *gold* or *platinum*, and downward in three or four branches bent from the building, and well *embedded in charcoal*. The lightning rod *protects* the space around it to a distance equal to *twice* its height above the summit of the house—thus, if it rises twenty feet it will protect a circular space eighty feet in diameter. It is as great an error to suppose that lightning rods *attract* the electric fluid towards the building as it would be to suppose that rain pipes attract the rain which falls on the roof—they do, indeed, frequently disperse, by a *silent* and *gradual* discharge, the electric fluid of a thunder-cloud, and thus considerably diminish the chance of the building being **struck at all**.

423. In a building not protected by a paratonnerre or lightning rod, the safest place is in an underground cellar, or, if not in a cellar, on some non-conducting substance, as a feather bed, &c., and the most dangerous locality is near the fire place, as the smoke forms a conducting medium for the descent of the electric fluid.

424. The most remarkable meteoric phenomenon dependent on aërial electricity is the brilliant jet of fire so frequently seen upon the top-masts of ships, the pointed summits of rocks, &c. It is known by the names of St. Elmo's Fire, or Castor and Pollux, and is produced by the slow discharge of the electrical fluid from points.

425. The AURORA BOREALIS, or northern lights, has been supposed to be produced by the passage of electricity through the highly rarefied medium which exists in the higher regions of the atmosphere—the different colors being caused by the current passing through strata of different densities. Its real origin, however, is involved in great obscurity, and very little is satisfactorily known about it. The aurora appears to be intimately connected, in some unexplained manner, with terrestrial magnetic electricity, and this is about all we can say with respect to the nature of the phenomenon.

NOTE.—The aurora is by no means a mere local appearance, as the same aurora has been seen simultaneously in Europe and America, and in other places separated by several thousand miles. Their height has been variously estimated at from 100 to 200 miles. During the continuance of a brilliant aurora, great magnetic disturbances are noticed, and the aurora *induces* sufficient magnetic electricity in telegraph lines to work them for hours together.

DYNAMICAL ELECTRICITY.

LECTURE XXXII.
DYNAMICAL ELECTRICITY, ITS NATURE, HISTORY, ETC.

426. Dynamical electricity is the same in *kind* as common or statical electricity, differing from the latter only in its source and its degree of tension.

NOTE I.—It is developed exclusively by chemical action, and possesses so little tensional power that it is unable to force its way through the thinnest possible stratum of a non-conductor.

NOTE 2.—The term *Dynamical* as applied in electrical science is used in a peculiar sense—merely implying the fact that the fluid travels or moves in currents. This must be distinctly understood, because the variety of electricity in question possesses, in itself, little or no mechanical force, i.e. disruptive power.

427. The principal distinctions between dynamical and common electricity are the following:

I. Common electricity is developed exclusively by friction.
Dynamical electricity is produced only by chemical action.
II. Common electricity is evolved in small quantities, but possesses high tensional power.
Dynamical electricity is developed in considerable quantities, but evinces low tensional power.
III. Common electricity manifests itself only when the circuit is open.
Dynamical electricity manifests itself only when the circuit is closed.

Thus, if the chain from the negative conductor of an electrical machine be attached to the prime conductor, the circuit is closed, and although the machine may be in action there appears to be no electrical disturbance; but if an inch or so of atmospheric air, or other non-conducting body breaks the circuit, the fluid manifests itself. In the voltaic battery on the other hand, all evidence of the existence of the electrical fluid ceases unless the wires from the poles are in contact, or are connected by some conducting body.

428. The chief points of resemblance between the two varieties of electricity are the following:

I. Both are powerful decomposing agents, but, as the *quantity* of electrical fluid determines the amount of chemical decomposition, dynamical electricity is a much more efficient agent in this respect than common electricity.
II. Both exhibit the phenomena of attraction and repulsion.
III. Both possess the power of disturbing the electrical condition of neighboring bodies by *induction*.
IV. Bodies that are conductors or non-conductors of one are likewise conductors or non-conductors of the other.
V. Both possess the same or highly analogous physiological effects.

VI. Both manifest themselves in passing through the **air or other imperfect conductor** by the phenomena of **light and** heat. The light manifested by common electricity is instantaneous only, while that produced by dynamical electricity is continuous on account **of the continuous** stream or current **of** the fluid that passes **in the circuit.**

VII. Both are explicable upon the assumption **of either Franklin's** or DuFay's electric theory.

---

429. The science of dynamical electricity had its origin in the discovery by Galvani, professor of anatomy at Pavia, of the convulsive contractions produced in the legs of a frog by making metallic connection **between the muscles and the nerves.**

NOTE 1.—If two metals be employed, one to touch the nerve and the other the muscle, upon bringing the metals themselves in contact the convulsive movements are much more violent. But metallic contact is not essential to the production of **these** contractions, for **Galvani** found that they are also produced by the contact of the interior nervous matter with the exterior mucus. So also if some recently skinned legs be thrown **into** a mixture of salt and water, they exhibit repeated convulsive **jerks and** contractions.

NOTE 2.—The story of the accidental discovery in 1790 of these movements in frogs' legs prepared as a delicate morsel for Madame Galvani's repast, is known to have been a pure fabrication. **The professor** had then been many years using frogs' legs as delicate electroscopes **in his experiments** upon animal electricity.

430. Galvani conceived the muscular system of an animal to be positively electrified, and the nervous system negatively, and **that** the contractions above spoken **of were produced** by the shock **arising** from the reunion of the fluids through the **metallic conductor.**

431. Volta, another Italian professor, **continuing the experiments** of Galvani, **arrived at** the conclusion **that the** effect produced on the frogs' legs was due not to animal electricity but to the contact of two dissimilar metals; and, although electricians have subsequently satisfactorily shown that it is attributable solely to chemical action, this *contact theory* of **Volta** has still many advocates on the continent of Europe.

432. The following sketch contains a few of the more important points in the history of dynamical electricity:

1762 SULZER, in his work on "the Theory of Agreeable and Disagreeable Sensations," mentions that when the tongue is placed between two discs of dissimilar metals, and the edges are brought in contact, a peculiar metallic taste is experienced. He was not aware that this had any connection with electricity, but accounted for it by supposing that the metals combine, and thus produce a trembling motion in their respective particles which excites the nerves of the tongue.

1786 SUIGI GALVANI, of the University of Bologna, discovered the convulsive movements set up in frogs' legs by contact with metals.

1796 VOLTA, of the University of Pavia, discovered the fact that electricity is apparently produced by mere contact, and was hence led to the invention of his "Pile" and "Couronne des tasses," which are the types of all the arrangements at present used for the production of dynamical electricity. Volta did not communicate his invention of the "Pile" or "Couronne des tasses" to the world till the year 1800.

1800 NICHOLSON and CARLISLE, of London, decomposed water and other compounds, by the agency of the voltaic battery or pile.

1807 SIR H. DAVY succeeded in decomposing potassa and proving it to be the oxide of the metal potassium. He subsequently decomposed other oxides, and thus discovered several new metals.

1807 PROFESSOR ŒRSTED, of Copenhagen, called attention to the analogy between magnetism and voltaic electricity, and thus laid the foundation of the science of electro-magnetism.

1807 M. ARAGO discovered that the electrical current possesses the power of imparting magnetism to steel and iron; and M. Ampère announced his theory that magnetism is induced by circular currents around the magnetized body.

1830	M. Ampère suggested the application of deflected needles for telegraphic purposes.
1831	Faraday laid the foundations of the science of magneto-electricity.
1837	M. Alexander, of Edinburgh, exhibited in London an electric telegraph on Ampère's principle, but his instrument was so complicated as to be useless, a separate needle and insulated wire being required for each letter of the alphabet.

[Since 1837 between two and three hundred patents have been granted for different methods of telegraphic correspondence, nearly all depending upon electricity.]

LECTURE XXXIII.
ARRANGEMENTS EMPLOYED FOR THE PRODUCTION OF DYNAMIC ELECTRICITY.

VOLTAIC PILES.

433. The arrangements employed for the development of dynamical electricity are of two kinds, viz. :
   I. Voltaic Piles : and
   II. Voltaic Batteries.

434. Voltaic or Galvanic Piles consist, essentially, of an arrangement of metallic discs separated by discs of paper or of cloth. The two metals commonly used are either silver and zinc, copper and zinc, or zinc and binoxide of manganese, and the pile is composed of an alternation of several hundred of these discs bound together by screws, or packed in a glass tube. Voltaic piles are either :
   I. Moist Piles : or
   II. Dry Piles.

435. The MOIST PILE, originally invented by Volta, is formed by taking discs of silver, zinc, and cloth or paper, about one and a half inches in diameter, and alternating them, always observing the order—zinc, cloth, silver, zinc, cloth, silver,—so as to have the bottom plate zinc and the top one silver. The outside discs

are each supplied with a conducting wire; and the intermediate cloth or paper discs are kept moist by brine or weakly acidulated water.

Note.—The paper or cloth discs are made somewhat smaller than the others, and the whole arrangement is placed between three or four glass rods and held together by binding screws.

436. De Luc's DRY PILE is formed by soaking sheets of thick writing paper in milk or honey, or other analogous animal fluid, and then gumming on one side of it a sheet of tin-foil or zinc-foil, and a coating of black oxide of manganese on the other. The sheets are now cut into discs about the size of shilling pieces, and these are packed in a glass tube so that all the zinc or tin-foils face the same way. Two or three hundred, or even thousands, are placed in the same tube and are pressed together by metallic caps and screws.

Note.—One end of the pile is positive and the other negative, and this disturbance is exhibited for a great length of time; but, if the paper discs are artificially dried before being packed, no electrical excitement is produced, thus proving that here, as elsewhere, the evolution of the fluid is due to chemical action.

437. Zamboni's DRY PILE consists of several thousand discs of metallic paper, having one side coated with zinc and the other with gold-leaf, packed in a tube as in the case of De Luc's dry pile.

BATTERIES.

438. A VOLTAIC BATTERY properly consists of a combination of two or more simple voltaic circles, but the term is also applied to the simple circle itself when capable of producing any considerable effects.

439. The essential elements of a simple voltaic circle are:

I. An elementary body (zinc) and a compound body (dilute acid), which act chemically upon one another in such a manner that the elementary substance (zinc) is substituted for a constitutent (hydrogen) of the compound, which constituent is expelled; and

II. A conducting substance (platinum, copper, silver, charcoal, &c.), which is not chemically acted upon, but merely furnishes a route for the passage of the electrical fluids, to recombine with one another continually.

SINGLE FLUID BATTERIES.

440. Voltaic batteries may, for the most part, be divided into the following classes; viz.:

I. Those formed of two different metals and one fluid.
II. Those formed of two different metals and two dissimilar liquids.
III. Those formed of two different fluids and one metal.

SINGLE-FLUID BATTERIES.

441. The principal single-fluid batteries are the following:

I. Cruickshank's trough.
II. Wollaston's battery.
III. Œrsted's trough.
IV. Hare's spiral or calorimotor.
V. The sulphate of copper battery.
VI. Smee's battery.

442. CRUICKSHANK'S TROUGH, the first improvement on Volta's couronne des tasses, consists of zinc and copper plates cemented water-tight into grooves in the sides of a porcelain trough so as to be parallel to one another and a short distance apart.

NOTE.—One of the chief objections to this battery is the tediousness of filling the separate cells with the exciting liquid. It was improved by Davy and Nicholson, who soldered the metallic plates to a rod of metal so as to immerse the arrangement with ease.

443. WOLLASTON'S BATTERY resembles Cruickshank's as improved by Davy and Nicholson, the essential difference being that each zinc plate is placed between two copper plates. The active surface is thus doubled, and the battery rendered more effective in the same proportion.

NOTE.—The battery employed by Davy in his immortal discovery of the metals of the alkalies (October, 1807) was of this kind, and was made in 1803. It consisted of a combination of 24 plates twelve inches square, 100 plates six inches, and 150 plates four inches, the whole being equivalent to 274 plates four inches square.

The celebrated battery of the London Royal Institution, made in 1810, was also of this construction, and consisted of 2000 couples arranged in 200 glass troughs, each trough containing 10 couples, and each plate having an effective surface of 22 square inches.

SINGLE-FLUID BATTERIES.

444. Œrsted's Trough consists of copper compartments, which contain the exciting fluid, and in which the zinc is placed so as not to touch the other metal in any part.

445. Hare's Spiral, or **Calorimotor,** is formed by rolling zinc and copper sheets into a spiral or coil, so that the plates are everywhere about half an inch asunder. Several of these arrangements are placed in cells containing dilute acid.

Note.—The original calorimotor of Dr. Hare consisted of 20 zinc and 30 copper plates each 10 inches square, rolled into a coil and combined in a box in such a manner as to form but *two* large elements of 50 square feet each, or 200 square feet of active surface in both members. The enormous battery of Mr. Children was also of this construction, being formed of 16 pairs of plates, each 6 feet wide and 23 feet long.

Pepys' spiral at the London Institution was formed of sheets of copper and zinc each 50 feet long and 2 feet wide. These were coiled upon one another with horse-hair ropes between them. Each bucket contained 55 gallons of the exciting fluid.

446. The Sulphate of Copper Battery consists of an outer and an inner cylinder of copper, the intermediate space containing a solution of sulphate of copper in very dilute sulphuric acid. A zinc cylinder is plunged between the coppers into this exciting liquid, and is kept from contact with the copper by wooden rings.

447. Smee's Battery is the most efficient of all single fluid batteries. It consists of two plates of zinc, z, z, clamped to a piece of wood w by means of the clamp b. Between the zinc plates there is a plate of platinum foil, p, or of platinized silver, the exciting fluid is formed by diluting sulphuric acid with from seven to sixteen times its bulk of water.

Fig. 53.

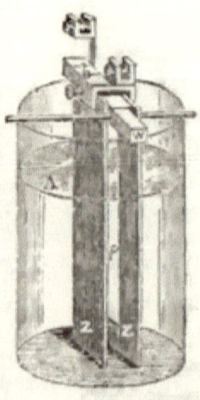

TWO-FLUID BATTERIES.

448. The principal two-fluid batteries involving the use of two dissimilar metals or their substitutes are:

I. Daniell's Constant Battery.
II. Grove's Nitric Acid Battery.
III. Bunsen's Carbon Battery.

449. DANIELL'S CONSTANT BATTERY consists of a copper vessel, C, Fig. 54, in which is placed a porous earthenware cell, *p*, containing a cylinder of zinc. The copper vessel is filled with a saturated solution of sulphate of copper, and the earthenware cell with dilute sulphuric acid. Finally, as in all other compound batteries, the zincs and coppers are alternately connected by copper wires.

Fig. 54.

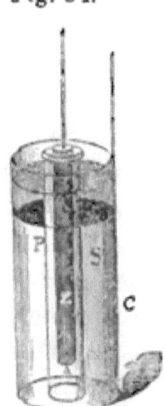

NOTE.—In order to keep the solution in the outer vessel saturated, some crystals of sulphate of copper are placed on a perforated shelf at the top of the jar—extending from the porous cell to the copper vessel. This is necessary, because as the zinc oxidizes in the inner cell, the sulphate of copper in the outer cell is decomposed.

450. This battery is called the constant battery on account of the permanence of its action, and this permanence is to be accounted for as follows:

In all other forms of voltaic battery the particles of hydrogen, and ultimately those of oxide of zinc, as they are liberated or formed, are deposited on the copper, and thus mar its conducting capacity: the action of the battery becoming weaker and weaker, from this cause, till it finally ceases entirely. In Daniell's battery this is obviated as follows: The hydrogen of the decomposed water is not given off in bubbles at the copper surface, as in other batteries; but the sulphate of copper in the outer cell being decomposed atom for atom with the decomposed water, the hydrogen takes the oxygen of the oxide of copper, and metallic copper is deposited on the inner surface of the outer cell. Thus the metallic copper surface is constantly renewed; and if the zinc be well amalgamated, and means be taken for renewing the strength of the acid solution, the battery remains in unimpaired action for many hours.

451. GROVE'S BATTERY consists of a cylinder of zinc open at both ends, and containing a porous earthenware cup, in which

is immersed a slip of platinum foil. The arrangement is plunged in an outer glass or porcelain vessel containing dilute sulphuric acid. The porous earthenware cup is filled with strong nitric acid, and the zinc and platinum elements are properly connected by conducting wires.

452. GROVE'S BATTERY is the most powerful and energetic voltaic arrangement in use, the platinum in it being estimated to be equivalent to 18 times as much copper surface in Daniell's battery. Four cells with platinum foil 3 inches long and half-an inch wide decompose water rapidly; and an arrangement of from 20 to 50 such cells forms a battery of amazing power.

453. In Grove's Battery there is a double decomposition, and consequently an increased evolution of electricity. The water is decomposed, as in other batteries; but the hydrogen, in place of being evolved, decomposes the nitric acid in the porous cell, and combines with part of its oxygen. Copious fumes of peroxide of nitrogen are given off, and so vitiate the surrounding air as to render it important to keep the battery while in action in a good draught of air. A part of the peroxide of nitrogen being absorbed by the nitric acid, colors it green.

454. BUNSEN'S CARBON BATTERY is the same in principle as Grove's nitric acid battery, the same fluids and porous cups being used in each. The essential difference is that Bunsen substitutes a cylinder of baked coke in the porous cup in place of a slip of platinum foil.

BATTERIES OF ONE METAL AND TWO FLUIDS.

455. The third class of batteries, or that comprehending the arrangement in which two dissimilar fluids and but one metal are used, includes:

       I. Becquerel's Battery.
      II. Reinsch's Charcoal Battery.
     III. Grove's Gas Battery.

456. BECQUEREL'S BATTERY consists of a U-shaped tube of glass, one arm of which contains a solution of caustic potash or any other powerful base, and the other arm sulphuric acid or any other strong acid,—the two fluids being separated by a plug

of clay or some other porous substance. A strip of platinum having a wire attached is immersed in each arm, and upon bringing these wires into contact an electrical current passes.

457. REINSCH'S CHARCOAL BATTERY is formed of a glass jar containing a porous earthenware cell—both the outer vessel and the inner cell being filled with coarsely powdered charcoal. The charcoal in the outer vessel is saturated with sulphuric acid, and that in the porous cell with nitric acid. Finally a rod of coke or charcoal, having a wire attached, is placed in each compartment.

458. GROVE'S GAS BATTERY consists of a glass tube, AC, having a series of legs attached at right angles to it, and a series of glass jars $Z B$, each, except Z, having fixed in it two platinum plates, one long and narrow and the other shorter and wider. The wide plate of each cell is placed higher than the narrow one, and is connected to the narrow plate of the next cell by a platinum wire. The glasses are filled to the top of the narrow

Fig. 55.

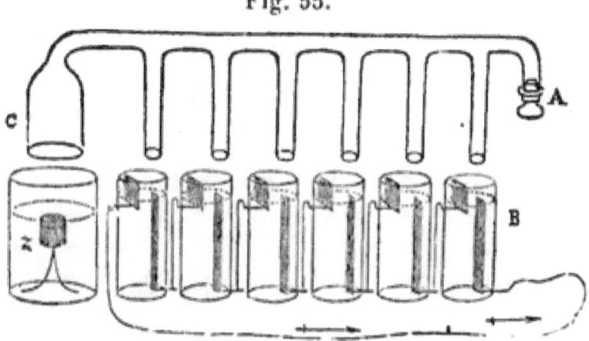

plates with acidulated water. In the vessel Z is a piece of zinc supported on a little tripod, and surrounded by dilute sulphuric acid. The stopper being removed from the tube, $A C$, the legs are immersed in the cells so that each narrow platinum plate may be inclosed in a leg, the wide ones being excluded and exposed to the air: the hydrogen evolved in the vessel Z will rise and fill AC, expelling the atmospheric air. The glass stopper is then to be inserted into A, and the generation of hydrogen will continue until the piece of zinc becomes uncovered with acid : then the narrow slips of platinum will be exposed to an atmosphere of hydrogen in the legs of the tube, the wide ones being exposed to the oxygen of the air. A current of electricity will thus be generated, the wire connected with the narrow plate conveying negative, and that connected with the wide plate positive electricity.

459. Although the *electrometers*, as they are termed, are commonly zinc, copper, and dilute sulphuric acid, or zinc, platinum, and dilute sulphuric acid, many other substances may be employed for the production of a current of electricity.

460. In the following table the most positive metals are placed first in the list, and the least positive or those less oxidizible last. The generating plate of the battery is, therefore, made of one of the plates first in the list, and the conducting plate of one of the last; and the more remote the two metals stand from each other in the scale, the more decidedly will the electrical current be produced.

TABLE OF TENSION.

Positive.	
1. Zinc.	8. Brass.
2. Lead.	9. Copper.
3. Cadmium.	10. Silver.
4. Tin.	11. Gold.
5. Antimony.	12. Platinum.
6. Bismuth.	13. Graphite.
7. Iron.	14. Charcoal.
	Negative.

NOTE.—A second zinc plate of the same kind as the first can never act as a conducting plate, because it generates a current opposed in direction to the first. But if the generating plate be of rough cast zinc, a plate of rolled zinc, made perfectly smooth, will act as a conducting plate, and cause the evolution of a weak current.

461. The exciting liquid may be any acid, but that commonly employed is either dilute sulphuric acid or hydrochloric acid. Nitric acid is objectionable on account of the production of

fumes of peroxide. The acid may be used of any degree of strength, but usually, if sulphuric acid, it is diluted with from 8 to 16 times its weight of water.

LECTURE XXXIV.
CONDUCTORS AND NON-CONDUCTORS, OHM'S FORMULÆ FOR COMPARATIVE STRENGTH OF VOLTAIC CURRENTS, MEANS OF INCREASING THE INTENSITY OR THE QUANTITY OF THE FLUID IN THE CURRENT.

CONDUCTORS.

462. We have seen that bodies may be divided into the two classes of conductors and non-conductors of statical electricity, and the same division holds with respect to voltaic—the same bodies being good or imperfect conductors of both. Faraday has shown that it is a general law that the so-called solid non-conductors "assume the conducting power during liquefaction and lose it during congelation."

Thus, water is a tolerably good conductor, ice is a very imperfect conductor; liquid chloride of lead is a good conductor, solid chloride of lead a very imperfect conductor.

463. As a class the metals are excellent conductors, but they differ among themselves very much in this respect—copper being among the best and potassium among the worst metallic conductors. In the following table the conducting power of copper is expressed by 100.

TABLE OF CONDUCTING POWERS.

Copper	100	Iron	15
Gold	93	Lead	8
Silver	73	Mercury	3
Zinc	28	Potassium	1
Platinum	16		

464. Since all metals are more or less imperfect conductors, it follows that:

I. The resistance offered by a metallic conducting wire increases with its length.

II. The resistance afforded by a metallic conducting wire decreases as its sectional area increases, and hence

III. The resistance of a conductor, of the same substance throughout, varies directly as its length, and inversely as its sectional area, or

$$r \propto \frac{l}{s}$$

where $r =$ resistance, $l =$ length, and $s =$ sectional area of the conducting wire.

NOTE.—From this it appears if we have a conducting wire of uniform thickness—doubling its length halves the quantity conducted, &c. On the contrary, if the length remains unchanged, doubling the sectional area doubles the quantity conducted, &c.

465. If $l\ s\ c$ respectively represent the length, the sectional area, and the conducting power of a wire of any given metal, and $l'\ s'\ c'$ the same elements of a wire of a different metal: their resisting effects will be equal when:

$$\frac{l}{sc} = \frac{l'}{s'c'}.$$

466. From the expression in the last article we may easily determine the *reduced length* of any wire, i. e. the length of a wire of any substance which shall produce the same retarding effects in a given length of a given wire.

For since $\dfrac{l}{s\,c} = \dfrac{l'}{s'c'}$. $l's\,c = l\,s'c'$ or $l' = \dfrac{ls'c'}{sc}$; i. e. the

reduced length, l', of the second wire, is found by multiplying its sectional area by the relative conducting power of the metal of which it is formed, and this product by the length of the first wire, and dividing by the product of the sectional area of the first wire, and the relative conducting power of the metal composing it.

OHM'S FORMULÆ OF RESISTANCE.

467. The amount of electrical or chemical power possessed by a voltaic circle, simple or compound, is determined by the *quantity* which passes through a transverse section of the arrangement, in a unit of time, and depends upon two circumstances.

OHM'S FORMULÆ OF RESISTANCE.

I. The power or electromotive force of the battery.

II. The resistance offered to the passage of the current, by the liquid and solid conductors through which it has to pass.

From this it directly follows that:

I. The electromotive force remaining the same, doubling the resistance reduces the strength of the current to one-half, trebling the resistance reduces the strength of the current to one-third, &c.

II. The resistance remaining the same, doubling the electromotive force doubles the power of the battery, trebling the electromotive force trebles the strength of the current, &c., and hence

III. If E = electromotive force, R = total resistance, and Q = quantity in circuit:

$$Q \propto \frac{E}{R};$$

That is, *the quantity of the fluid that passes in a unit of time through a transverse section of the conducting wire or any other part of the circuit varies directly as the electromotive force and inversely as the total resistance.*

NOTE 1.—This and the following formulæ are known as Ohm's Formulæ, and were first investigated in 1827 by the distinguished mathematician whose name they bear. That given above must be regarded as a definition of what we mean by electromotive force and what we mean by resistance, rather than as the expression of a theorem or law.

NOTE 2.—It must be distinctly understood that in the following formulas we merely compare the strength of electrical currents *with one another*, and not with any unit of mechanical force or even of electrical or magnetic attraction or repulsion.

468. The following formulæ are useful chiefly as enabling us to determine the effect produced on the strength of the current by

I. Increasing the number of plates or cells.
II. Increasing the size of each plate or cell.
III. Increasing the length of the conducting wire, &c.

469. The total resistance experienced by a voltaic current consists of two parts, viz:

I. The external resistance, or that offered by the conductor joining the poles, and this, as we have seen, depends upon the length, conductibility, and sectional area of the wire.

II. The internal resistance or resistance of the cell, and this depends upon the nature, size, and distance apart of the metallic plates, and the conductibility of the exciting fluid.

470. If $l =$ external resistance, $I =$ intensity, and $r =$ internal resistance, then for a single cell,

$$I \propto \frac{E}{l+r}.$$

NOTE.—If the external resistance consists in part of that afforded by a metallic conducting wire, and in part of that afforded by an electrolyzable liquid r', then:

$$I \propto \frac{E}{l+r'+r}.$$

471. If we now regard the battery as being composed of n cells, perfectly similar, the electromotive force becomes nE, the internal resistance nr, and l, remaining the same

$$I \propto \frac{nE}{l+nr}$$

Dividing both numerator and denominator of this expression by n we find that

$$I \propto \frac{E}{\frac{l}{n}+r}.$$

It is evident that the value of the last expression increases with n, or in other words the intensity increases with the number of cells in the battery.

NOTE 1.—This increase of intensity by increasing the number of cells is most evident when the external resistance is great in proportion to the internal, while on the contrary if l is very small, $\frac{l}{n}$ is very small, and the intensity changes but little with any increase in the number of cells in the battery.

NOTE 2.—If $l = 0$, $I \propto \frac{nE}{0+nr}$ or $I \propto \frac{nE}{nr}$ or $I \propto \frac{E}{r}$.

NOTE 3.—If each added cell is accompanied by an external resistance equal to l, the intensity is not increased by increasing the number of couples, for in that case, $I \propto \frac{nE}{nl+nr}$ or $I \propto \frac{E}{l+r}$.

472. If the external resistance, l, is very great, I is very

small unless n is also very great; for if l is very great compared with n, $\frac{l}{n}$ is very great, and therefore $\dfrac{E}{\frac{l}{n}+r}$ is very small.

Hence it is necessary to employ a very large number of cells in a compound battery when a considerable amount of resistance is to be overcome, as in the electrolysis of imperfect conductors, the production of the voltaic arch, the transmission of a message through a long telegraphic circuit, &c.

473. In connecting the metallic elements of the cells together we commonly unite the zinc of one cell with the copper of the next, and so on. By this arrangement, we form a compound battery of many cells. If on the contrary we take a number of cells and connect all the zincs together, and also all the coppers together, the arrangement will constitute but a simple circle, and will be, in effect, equal to that produced by two plates each possessing a surface equal to the aggregate surface of the several plates of the coresponding metal.

In this case if there be m cells the internal resistance will necessarily be only the m part of what it would be in a compound battery of the same number of cells. Hence in m cells having all the zincs connected together and also all the coppers,

$$I \propto \frac{E}{l+\frac{r}{m}}$$

Hence if l be very great compared with r the intensity will be but little increased by enlarging the size of the plates.

NOTE.—If l be very small in proportion to m the intensity is much increased by this method, and if $l = o$ or be infinitely small $I \propto \frac{mE}{r}$, i. e. the intensity will be proportional to the extent of surface acting as a single couple.

474. Since the *quantity* of electricity developed is in direct proportion to the amount of metallic surface chemically acted upon, we have the quantity of electric fluid that passes in a unit of time through any part of the circuit equal to the electromotive force divided by the sum of all the resistances, i. e.,

$$q \propto \frac{E}{l+r}$$

and hence in the case referred to in Art. 471,

$$q \propto \frac{E}{\frac{l}{n}+r}$$

and in that alluded to in Art. 473,

$$q \propto \frac{E}{l+\frac{r}{m}}$$

When the external resistance l becomes so small as to be neglected these formulæ severally become

$$q \propto \frac{E}{r} \quad \text{and} \quad q \propto \frac{mE}{r}$$

It hence appears that:

I. Increasing the number of cells in a battery, when the external resistance is not great, does not increase the quantity of electricity in current.

II. When the external resistance is not great, increasing the size of the plates increases in the same proportion the quantity of fluid in the current.

475. If, at the same time, we increase both the number of cells, and also the size of the plates,

$$I \text{ or } q \propto \frac{E}{\frac{l}{n}+\frac{r}{m}}$$

From which we learn that:

If, l, the external resistance, is great, as in the electrolysis of imperfectly conducting fluids, it is most advantageous to unite many cells into a compound battery; but if the external resistance be small, as in electro-magnetic experiments, greater advantage may be obtained by uniting all the zincs together and all the coppers together so as to form a couple of large extent of surface.

LECTURE XXXV.

EFFECTS OF THE VOLTAIC CURRENT, HEATING EFFECTS, LUMINOUS EFFECTS, PHYSIOLOGICAL EFFECTS, CHEMICAL EFFECTS, ELECTROTYPE PROCESS, THEORIES AS REGARDS VOLTAIC ELECTRICITY.

CALORIFIC EFFECTS.

476. Heat is evolved whenever a current of electricity is sent through an imperfectly conducting body; and, since the intensity of the heat developed is greatest when large plates are employed, we may infer that the calorific effects of the battery are due rather to the quantity than to the intensity of the current.

477. The heat of the current has been carefully measured by Becquerel and others, by means of a close spiral inclosed in a glass calorimotor. It has thus been determined that when a current traverses a homogeneous wire the heat evolved in a unit of time is proportional.

I. To the resisting power of the metal forming the wire.

II. To the square of the quantity which passes in the current.

Thus, if we link together platinum, silver, iron, and copper, and pass a current of electricity through them, the platinum, being the worst conductor, becomes most heated, and the copper least.

478. When a fine wire of platinum is made to connect the poles of a battery, it becomes, if sufficiently short, incandescent, and finally melts. If such a wire be immersed in water contained in any small vessel it causes it to boil, if in alcohol or ether it ignites it, or if we carry it through phosphorus or gunpowder it inflames it.

NOTE.—An arrangement of this kind has been employed for blasting in mines, and in submarine blasting. In England it has been extensively adopted for blasting the chalk cliffs. A number of holes are bored and filled with powder, each having a strip of platinum wire placed in it. These platinum wires are connected to one another by means of copper wire, and the whole properly connected with the battery. The instant the battery is set in action the pieces of platinum become sufficiently hot to explode, at the same moment, the gunpowder in every hole.

479. The principal experiments illustrative of the calorific agency of the battery are the following:

I. When the positive electrode is formed of carbon, and is fashioned into a small crucible, gold, silver, platinum and other substances are rapidly melted, deflagrated and volatilized. Under these circumstances it is found that gold burns with a blue light; silica with a fine green; sodium, yellow; potassium, violet; strontium, red; calcium, violet-red; barium, reddish-yellow, &c.

II. Sapphire, quartz, lime, slate, &c., are readily fused, and the earths reduced to their metallic bases.

III. A piece of diamond placed *in* the charcoal cup, when the other pole is brought over it so as to bring the voltaic arch over the gem, melts, boils up, and presently spreading open is converted into coke, thus showing that diamond and coke or charcoal are but different modifications of one and the same body.

LUMINOUS EFFECTS.

480. The luminous effects of the battery follow directly from its heating power, for all solid bodies become incandescent when heated to about 1000° F. (Draper.)

481. The luminous effects of the battery are seen on a small scale whenever the circuit, even of a very weak arrangement, is closed or opened. In using the very powerful battery of the Royal Institution (2000 couples), Sir H. Davy discovered, in 1809, that when charcoal points are attached to the poles they may be separated to the distance of two or three inches, and that the intermediate space becomes occupied by an ovoid of light of the most dazzling brilliancy. To the light thus produced he gave the name *voltaic arch*.

482. Although other substances may be employed as the terminal poles of the battery for developing the voltaic arch—graphite or well-burned charcoal is by far the most effective. The arch may be produced equally well in atmospheric air, a vacuum, in nitrogen, in carbonic acid, under water, &c, and therefore cannot be connected with the combustion of the charcoal.

483. When charcoal or other points are employed, it is always found that the charcoal on the positive electrode becomes *cupped* or *hollowed out*, while that on the negative electrode becomes *elongated* by a small cone which exactly fits into the opposite depression. It is hence inferred that the electrical light is due to the transference of highly incandescent particles from the positive to the negative electrode. The rushing and hissing noise which accompanies the voltaic arch is due to this mechanical removal and passage of the particles of carbon or other body forming the points.

484. In order to develop the arch under water or in air, or in any other gas, it is necessary to first approach the points into contact, and then gradually remove them to the maximum distance (two, three, or even four inches). This appears to be owing to the fact that the energy or intensity of the current is not sufficiently powerful to enable it to penetrate the intervening stratum of air or other non-conductor; but when the points are brought into contact and then separated, the projection of material atoms commences, and the flow of the current is established.

NOTE.—Herschel has shown that when the points are approached within an inch or two of one another, and a charge from a Leyden jar transmitted through them, it at once determines the formation of the voltaic arch—doubtless by commencing the transportation of atoms.

NOTE 2.—In a vacuum it is not necessary to approach the points into actual contact in order to commence the flow. This is owing to the fact that a vacuum does not offer so much resistance to the passage of the electric fluid. The voltaic arch is extinguished by a strong wind.

485. The electric light is, like solar light, unpolarised. It explodes a mixture of hydrogen and chlorine, and acts upon chloride of silver and other photographic agents like the sun. Like the solar light it imparts phosphorescence to the diamond, fluor-spar, and other bodies. Fraunhofer has shown that the spectrum formed by electric light differs from the solar spectrum in having a very bright line in the green and another rather bright one in the red.

NOTE.—By means of an arrangement called "Duboscq's photo-electric lantern" the electric light may be used to replace the sun in all experiments requiring simply a strong white light. It is preferred to solar light for taking microscopic photographs. Fizeau and Foucault have, in comparing the photographic power of the voltaic arch with that of the sun, found that a double series of 92 carbon couples gave an effect $\frac{2}{8}$ of that produced by the sun two hours above the meridian on a clear August day. In the same series of experiments they found that the Drummond light is only equal in effect to $\frac{1}{146}$ that of the sun. Bunsen found the voltaic arch produced by 48 carbon couples equal in intensity to that of 572 candles.

PHYSIOLOGICAL EFFECTS.

486. A shock of voltaic electricity transmitted through the animal frame produces effects which differ from those resulting from machine electricity in being less violent and sudden but more continued, and accompanied by a peculiar sensation of prickly heat on the surface.

NOTE 1.—It requires a battery containing a large number of elements to exhibit marked physiological effects. The shock from a battery of 300 or more couples is capable of producing dangerous or even fatal results. When the shock is sent through a chain of many persons their hands should be moistened with salt and water, and even then the effects are sensibly less in the centre than near the poles.

NOTE 2.—A voltaic current sent through the ear produces a roaring sound; thrown upon the tongue it gives rise to a metallic taste; transmitted through the eye it is accompanied by a flash of light.

NOTE 3.—In all cases the peculiar physiological effects are *only experienced when the contact is in the act of being broken or renewed.*

CHEMICAL EFFECTS.

487. In describing the chemical effects of the voltaic battery it has become customary to employ certain technical terms that were first suggested by Faraday. These terms, with their derivations and accepted significations, are as follows:

I. ELECTRODE (*electron,* "electricity," and *hodos,* "a way,") corresponds to the old term *pole* or *terminal wire.* The *negative electrode* is the way or direction in which the current enters the battery, the *positive electrode,* the way or direction in which it leaves the battery.

II. ANODE (*ana* "upwards," "as the sun rises," and *hodos*) is the side of a substance or decomposing cell by which the current enters.

III. CATHOD (*kata* "downwards," "as the sun sets," and *hodos,* is the side of the body or decomposing cell by which the current flows out.

OF VOLTAIC CURRENT. 191

Note.—Let a person suppose himself to be standing with his face towards the north, fronting a battery placed on the ground with its positive end to the east, and the wires bent in the form of an arch in the direction which the sun takes in his daily motion; let him further suppose that the terminal wires instead of joining, pass into a decomposing cell; then the current will pass out at the eastern side, will flow over to the west end, and again enter the battery.

The positive electrode is the eastern or right-hand side of the battery, and of course the western or left-hand side is the negative electrode.

The *anode* is the eastern or receiving side of the decomposing cell, and the western side is the cathode.

IV. Electrolysis (*electron* "electricity," and *luo* "I loosen,") is the term applied to the chemical decomposition of a body by means of electrical agency.

V. Electrolytes (same derivation) are bodies susceptible of decomposition by electricity.

VI. Ions (*iŏn* neuter of *eimi* "to go,") are the chemical constituents of the electrolyte.

VII. Anions (*ana* and *ion*) are the ions that go to the anode, and consequently correspond to what are otherwise called *electro-negative bodies*.

VIII. Cations (*kata* and *ion*) are the ions that go to the cathod, and hence correspond to electro-positive bodies.

488. No electrical current, or only a very weak one, can pass through a compound fluid without effecting, to a certain extent, its decomposition.

One of the simplest and most striking examples of this decomposing power of the electrical current is seen in the electrolysis of water. The apparatus commonly employed to exhibit this analysis is exhibited in Fig. 56, which consists of two tubes filled with water and inverted in a glass jar. The terminal wires of the battery (marked + and —, in the figure) are attached to two platinum plates, one in the lower end of each of the tubes. The water is slightly acidulated with sulphuric acid in order to render it a better conductor. Upon transmitting the current from a battery of several cells through this arrangement, bubbles of hydrogen gas are evolved at the negative pole, and of oxygen at the positive pole, and the gases are collected in the tubes by displacing the water. After continuing the experiment for a short time it will be seen that twice as much gas is evolved at the — electrode as at the + electrode, hence proving that water is a compound of two volumes hydrogen and one volume oxygen.

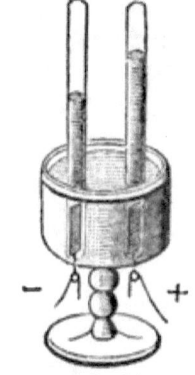

Fig. 56.

489. The electrolysis of salts may be exhibited by filling a U-shaped tube with a solution of the salt, colored purple by the infusion of red cabbage, and then immersing in each end of it a platinum plate connected with the poles of a battery. When the connection is complete and the battery set in action the solution becomes red at the positive electrode from the liberation of the acid, and green at the negative from the alkali set free. If a haloid salt (see Chem. Art. 288) be employed, the chlorine or other halogen appears at the positive pole, and bleaches or discharges the color of the cabbage infusion, and the metal appears as a basic oxide at the negative pole producing the same green tint as before.

NOTE 1.—On account of oppositely electrified bodies attracting one another, the constituent which goes to the positive pole is called the electro-negative body, and *vice versâ*.

NOTE 2.—Bodies differ very much in the degree of facility with which they suffer decomposition by the agency of electricity. Thus:

Iodide of Potassium in solution.......
Fused Chloride of Silver .... } are very easily decomposed.
Fused Proto-chloride of Tin..........

Chloride of Lead fused ....
Iodide of Lead fused.................. } are electrolyzed with more
Hydrochloric acid.....................   difficulty.
Dilute Sulphuric Acid................

NOTE 3.—No body is electrolyzable except when fluid, i. e. either dissolved or melted. The same element or constituent is not invariably electro-negative or electro-positive. Thus, hydrogen is highly electro-positive when compared with oxygen or chlorine, but it is uniformly electro-negative in connection with the metals. Oxygen however is electro-negative in every combination, and potassium electro-positive.

490. The principal laws of electrolysis are known under the title of *Faraday's Laws of Definite Action*. They are as follows:

I. The quantity of a given electrolyte, resolvable into its ions by electrolysis, depends solely upon the *quantity* of the electric fluid which passes into it—being quite independent of the form of apparatus used, the dimensions of the electrodes, the strength of the solution, &c.

II. In every case of electrolysis the ions are separated in atomic proportions, and when the current is made to traverse several electrolytes in succession in the same circuit the whole series of ions are set free in atomic proportions to each other.

III. The oxidation of an atom of zinc in the battery generates exactly as much electricity as is required to decompose one atom of water, or of any other electrolyzable protoxide.

491. The principal sequences or corollaries to this theory re:

1st. The source of voltaic electricity is chemical action exlusively.

2nd. The forces termed chemical affinity and electricity, if ιot absolutely one and the same, are at least very intimately elated to one another.

492. The VOLTAMETER is an instrument designed to measure he quantity of electricity evolved by any arrangement. It conists of a graduated tube into which the combined gases set free .s in Fig. 56 are collected and measured, and depends upon the principle above stated, viz: that the quantity of electrical fluid hat passes into an electrolyte determines the amount of chemical lecomposition.

493. The ELECTRO-CHEMICAL THEORY of Sir H. Davy assumes hat every body has a kind of natural appetency for the assumpion of either the positive or the negative electrical fluid, and that)odies thus naturally possessed of these opposite kinds of elec:ricity attract one another so as to unite and form a compound. ;t thus reduces chemical affinity to a mere case of electrical ιttraction, and of course regards all compounds as binary in their 1ature.

ELECTROTYPE PROCESS.

494. One of the most interesting and important applications of the decomposing power of the voltaic circuit is seen in the process of *electro-metallurgy*, or the precipitation of metals from their salts in solution.

495. The most simple form of electrotype apparatus is shown in Fig. 57. In a glass jar, as for example a tumbler, is placed a saturated solution of a metallic salt, as sulphate of copper. Within this is a porous earthenware cylinder P (or a lamp-glass with a piece of bladder tied firmly over the lower end) filled with dilute sulphuric acid.

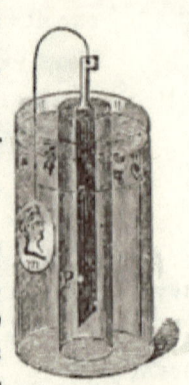

The medal to be copied, or the substance to be coated with the deposited metal, is suspended in the metallic solution by a wire attached to a zinc plate which is immersed in the dilute acid in the inner vessel. The whole thus forms a compound cell resembling that of Daniell. When the arrangement is complete, the chemical action excited on the zinc disengages electricity, which passes over the wire to the suspended medal, and thence escaping into the metallic solution decomposes it. The precipitated metal is deposited upon the surface of the metal, and of course (Art. 490) for every equivalent of zinc dissolved, an equivalent of copper, or other metal used, is deposited, or for every 32·5 grains of zinc combined 32 grains of copper are precipitated.

NOTE 1.—In practice, when medals or engraved plates are to be copied, reversed casts of the objects to be copied are made in wax or fusible metal, and these are subjected to the electrotype process; the back being protected by varnish to prevent the deposition and consequent adhesion of the metal to it.

NOTE 2.—In the electro-plating process by silver or gold, the metallic solution employed is alkaline instead of acid. Even alloys, as brass, bronze, German silver, &c., may be precipitated from solution by the process of electro-metallurgy.

THEORIES OF VOLTAISM.

496. With regard to the theory of the voltaic battery three views have been advanced and are known respectively as:

       I. VOLTA'S CONTACT THEORY.
      II. THE CHEMICAL THEORY.
     III. THE MOLECULAR THEORY.

497. VOLTA'S CONTACT THEORY attributes the effects of the battery to the simple contact of unlike metals—each decomposing the neutral electricity resident in the other, so that one becomes positive and the other negative. It assumes that the chemical action set up merely furnishes conductors for the passage of the unlike electricities from one metal to the other so as to recombine and again form the neutral compound.

NOTE.—The contact theory of Volta is strongly advocated by most of the continental philosophers of Europe, and especially by those of Germany. It seems, however, to be disproved by the simple fact that Faraday has obtained the evolution of copious currents of Voltaic electricity without the use of dissimilar metals.

498. The CHEMICAL THEORY, supported by Fabbroni, Davy, Wollaston, Faraday, Becquerel, De la Rive, &c., supposes that chemical action is the exclusive source of the electric current, and that indeed voltaic excitement and chemical action are the reciprocals of each other.

NOTE.—It appears to be proved by the researches of Faraday and others that chemical action is requisite to the production of the electric current, and that the energy of the former is in exact proportion to the power of the latter.

499. THE MOLECULAR THEORY of Peschell takes a sort of middle ground between the contact theory and the chemical theory. It assumes that when electricity is generated in any Voltaic arrangement, it results from a molecular change, brought about in the touching bodies by the adhesive force which subsists between them.

MAGNETISM.

LECTURE XXXVI.

DEFINITIONS, NATURAL AND ARTIFICIAL MAGNETS, PROPERTIES OF A MAGNET, THEORIES OF MAGNETISM, DIAMAGNETISM.

500. MAGNETISM is the name applied to that peculiar power of attracting iron, which is possessed by the lodestone.

The phenomenon of magnetic attraction was noticed by some of the earliest writers of antiquity—thus Thales, Pythagoras, Plato, Aristotle, Pliny, Cicero, Lucretius, and others, make mention of it in their works.

501. The name *magnet* or *magnetism* is by many supposed to be derived from Magnesia, in Asia Minor, in which locality the lodestone was first discovered.

Others derive the term, "magnot" from "Magnes" a shepherd who first noticed its attractive force for his iron crook when tending his flocks on Mount Ida.

Plato and Euripides call it the *Herculean Stone*, because it commands iron, the strongest of the metals.

The Jews in their Talmud, call it "the stone which attracts."

The Chinese call it *thsu-chy*, "the love stone," i. e. the stone loving towards iron. They also term it "*hy-thy-chy*," or "the stone which snatches up iron."

In the Sanscrit it is named *ayaskanta* "the stone loving towards iron."

The Hungarians call it *magnet kö* "the love stone."

The French term it *l'aimant* "the loving stone."

All the above terms are derived from its attractive force; others are descriptive of its directive power, thus,

The Burmese call it *d'anamtchüm* or "the stone which shows the south."

The Swedes term it *segel-sten* "the seeing stone."

The Icelanders give it the name *leiderstein* "the leading stone."

The English know it as the *lodestone* or "the leading-stone," from the Saxon *lædan* "to lead" (compare the terms *lodestar* "the guiding star" and *lode* "the leading vein" of the mine.)

NATURAL AND ARTIFICIAL MAGNETS.

502. All magnets are either natural or artificial.

503. The NATURAL MAGNET or the lodestone is a valuable iron ore, having a composition represented by the symbol $Fe_3 O_4$ $= FeO + Fe_2 O_3$, i. e. a mixture of the protoxide or black oxide, and the red oxide or sesquioxide of iron. It varies in color from a deep grey to a reddish brown or even black, and it has a specific gravity of about 4·500. When worked, it affords an excellent iron—good specimens giving as much as 73 per cent. of the pure metal. Magnetic iron ore is found massive in iron mines, and also in grains as *magnetic iron sand* in various parts of the world. It occurs massive abundantly in the Laurentian rocks of Canada, and is common in the form of little black granular masses in the boulders derived from these rocks. The massive variety is found in quantity in several places in Canada, as Madoc, Hull, Bedford, South Sherbrooke, Marmora, &c., and in the form of magnetic iron sand on the peninsula opposite

PROPERTIES OF A MAGNET. 197

Toronto, where an abundance may be gathered by passing a horse-shoe magnet through the sand.

504. ARTIFICIAL MAGNETS are formed out of steel or iron bars by contact, or by certain movements, or by induction with another by magnet, or by a current of electricity conveyed through the steel or iron bar.

NOTE.—The mode of magnetizing steel and iron bars will be more fully described hereafter.

505. ARTIFICIAL MAGNETS are either *bar magnets* or *horse-shoe magnets*, and are further either *simple* or *compound*.

A BAR MAGNET consists of a straight rectangular bar of magnetized steel or iron.
A HORSE-SHOE MAGNET is formed by bending such a bar till its extremities approach each other.
A SIMPLE MAGNET is formed of a single magnetized bar.
A COMPOUND MAGNET is composed of two or more simple magnets, riveted together.
Of course simple and compound magnets may be either bar or horse-shoe in shape.
A magnetic needle is a long needle or other light rod of steel suspended on its central axis so as to rotate easily.

506. A NATURAL MAGNET cannot commonly sustain a weight equal to itself; and, although artificial magnets have been formed so as to be capable of lifting from 25 to 30 times their weight, yet their power is usually much less than this.

Sir Isaac Newton is said to have had a small natural magnet, weighing 3 grains, which was capable of sustaining 750 grains, or 250 times its own weight. Cavallo tells us that he saw a natural magnet of 6½ grains that could sustain 300 grains. The Emperor of China gave John V of Portugal a natural magnet weighing 38 lbs., which was found in 1781 to be able to raise 200 lbs., or 5 times its own weight.

Logeman of Haerlem, by an unpublished process, makes artificial magnets capable of lifting 26 times their own weight, but they do not long retain this power; and commonly an artificial magnet is limited in its lifting power to two or three times its own weight.

PROPERTIES OF A MAGNET.

507. The most important properties of a magnet are :
    I. Its attractive force.
    II. Its communicative force.
    III. Its polarity.

508. The attractive power of the magnet is chiefly exerted on iron. Other metals are, however, but in less degree, susceptible of attraction by the magnet, and of these Faraday gives the following list arranged in the order of their magnetic power:

MAGNETIC METALS.

Iron.	Cerium.
Nickel.	Titanium.
Cobalt.	Palladium.
Manganese.	Platinum.
Chromium.	Osmium.

NOTE.—Hammered brass has also been found to be slightly magnetic.

509. By the polarity of a magnet is implied its *directive* force, or in other words the property in virtue of which a magnetic needle or straight bar, when balanced freely on its centre, arranges itself in a direction from north to south. The *north pole* of the magnet is that directed towards the north, the *south pole* is that directed towards the south. (See Note, Art. 510.)

510. In a carefully magnetized bar, it is found that the attractive force is accumulated at the extremities, and that it decreases in intensity towards the centre, where it becomes extinct. The centre of magnitude of such a bar is termed the *magnetic centre*, the extremities of the bar, the *magnetic poles*.

NOTE.—The *north* or *austral* pole is that extremity which, when the bar is suspended horizontally, points towards the north; the *south* or *boreal* pole is that which points towards the south.

This distribution of magnetic force in a bar magnet may be illustrated by rolling the magnet in iron filings or magnetic sand, upon doing which it is found that the particles of iron cluster about the ends of the magnet, but none of them adhere to the middle portion.

511. When a bar magnet is broken into several pieces, each of these becomes a complete magnet in itself, possessing a north and a south pole, and all the other properties of the original magnetic bar.

512. Magnetic attraction is **exerted** through plates of all substances except those enumerated in Art. 508.—And bodies

which thus allow magnetic force to take place *through* their substance are termed *dia-magnetic bodies*.

This may be conveniently shown by scattering some iron filings on a sheet of paper, or on a pane of glass, or on a slate, and passing a horse-shoe magnet, to and fro, underneath it; the iron filings follow the motion of the magnet, although the paper, or slate, or glass intervenes.

513. Every magnet is surrounded by a more or less extended sphere of magnetic influence, which is called its magnetic atmosphere. When a magnetic body, such as iron, is brought within this influence, it becomes, without actual contact, magnetic also, the portion of the second body next the magnet acquiring the opposite kind of polarity to that of the pole to which it is opposed. This separation of the latent magnetism of iron, or other magnetic body, into its constituent elements, is termed *magnetic induction*.

In the case of statical electricity, we have seen that we can, at pleasure, develop over the entire surface of a conductor either positive or negative fluid. We cannot, however, have an exclusively austral or boreal magnet, for in every magnet we have the three parts, a south pole, a north pole, and an intermediate neutral part.

514. All bodies exert more or less resistance to the induction of magnetism. This resistance is termed *coercitive force*, and is at a minimum in soft iron, and at a maximum in the dia-magnetic bodies generally.

515. The phenomenon of magnetism may be accounted for either by the one-fluid or the two-fluid hypothesis, as follows:

By the one-fluid theory, all bodies are supposed to have resident in them a certain or natural share of magnetic fluid. By induction or other means, the equilibrium of this fluid in the so called magnetic bodies may be disturbed, so that it shall accumulate in abnormal quantity at one extremity, and thus leave the remote extremity or pole deficient in amount. According to this theory, then, one pole of the magnet has less than its natural share, or is —, the middle of the magnet retains its normal quantity and is neutral, and the other extremity has more than its proper quantity, or is +, and the so called dia-magnetic bodies are those in which no disturbance of the equilibrium of the magnetic fluid takes place by induction, contact, &c.

The two-fluid theory assumes that there are in existence two magnetic fluids, the *austral* or negative, and the *boreal* or positive, corresponding to the resinous and vitreous fluids of statical electricity, which are contained in non-magnetised bodies, so as to exactly neutralize each other. By induction of the earth, or of another magnet, this compound is broken up and its constituents permanently separated accumulate at either extremity. Dia-magnetic bodies are, according to this hypothesis, those in which this decomposition is not effected by induction, contact, &c.

DIA-MAGNETISM.

516. We have already remarked that substances such as glass, which allow magnetic attraction and repulsion to take place through them, are called *dia-magnetic* bodies to distinguish them from magnetic bodies. When suspended freely between the poles of a powerful horse-shoe magnet, or between the unlike poles of two bar magnets, both magnetic and dia-magnetic bodies are affected, but with this difference, the former arrange themselves in what is termed the *axial line*, i. e., longitudinally or from pole to pole, the latter arrange themselves in the *equatorial* line or at right angles to the axial line. It follows that magnetic bodies are such as are attracted by both poles of a magnet, dia-magnetic bodies such as are repelled by both poles.

517. In Art. 508 a list of magnetic bodies is given. All other bodies whatever are dia-magnetic, and among those that exhibit this property in the most striking manner are the following:

1. Bismuth,
2. Phosphorus,
3. Antimony,
4. Glass,
5. Zinc,
6. Tin,
7. Mercury,
8. Water,
9. Silver,
10. Copper,
11. Gold,
12. Alcohol,
13. Ether,
14. Arsenic.

NOTE.—In the above list of dia-magnetics, bismuth is the best and arsenic the worst.

LECTURE XXXVII.

FORMATION OF ARTIFICIAL MAGNETS

518. ARTIFICIAL MAGNETS may be produced by either of the following processes:

    I. By keeping the iron or steel bar for a time in a certain position.
    II. By hammering, filing, or drilling it.
    III. By suddenly changing its temperature from hot to cold.
    IV. By touch or friction with another magnet.
    V. By induction.
    VI. By electrical currents.

NOTE.—Soft iron acquires magnetism with more facility than steel or any other body, but it parts with it equally readily. Bars of steel on the other hand exert more coercitive force, but once they are saturated with the magnetic fluid, they remain, under proper circumstances, permanently magnetic. On this account all good magnets are made out of hard steel.

519. Magnetism by position is produced when a steel or iron bar is kept for a length of time in the direction of the magnetic dip, or even in a vertical position, or in a position pointing north and south.

NOTE.—The vertical iron bars of windows, iron palisades, &c., are commonly found to be magnetic.

520. If a rod of steel or iron, as for instance the kitchen poker, be placed with one end on the ground, slightly inclining towards the north, and, while in that position, smartly struck two or three times with a hammer upon the upper end, it acquires polarity, and the power of magnetic attraction and repulsion.

521. The modes of magnetizing a steel bar by contact may all be reduced to two, which are technically known as the *single touch* and *double touch*.

522. In magnetizing by *single touch* we place one pole of the magnet in the centre of the steel bar, and draw it, inclined at an angle of about 45°, to the extremity. We then raise the magnet off the bar, carry it back to the middle, place it on the bar,

and as before draw it to the end. This we repeat several times. Next we place the other end of the magnet on the middle of the bar, and inclining it at about the same angle draw it to the other extremity of the bar, and as before we repeat this process several times. The bar thus becomes a magnet, each extremity having the opposite polarity to that by which it was touched.

In place of using a single magnet, we may use two. We then place the north pole of one, and the south pole of the other, together in the middle of the bar, and inclining them in opposite directions, draw to the extremities; raising and returning to the middle, we again draw to the ends, and repeat several times, being careful always to draw the same pole to the same extremity.

523. To magnetize by the *double touch*, two bar magnets are tied together so as to be parallel to one another with their opposite poles only a short distance apart. The north and south poles of the upper extremity are connected by a piece of soft iron, and those of the other separated by a piece of wood or brass, and the combination thus arranged is placed upright in the middle of the bar to be magnetized, so that the centre of the bar shall be between the two free poles of the connected magnets. The whole is now carefully drawn to one end of the bar but not over it, and without turning the combination at all, it is drawn over the bar to the remote extremity. It is thus carefully moved backward and forward several times, and finally having been drawn an equal number of times to each end of the bar, it is drawn to the middle, and slipped off side-ways.

NOTE.—A curved or a horse-shoe shaped bar may be saturated with magnetism either by the single or the double touch as described above for straight bars. In all cases after performing the operation on one side, the bar should be turned over and the process repeated in the same manner.

524. If a soft iron bar be placed within the inductive influence of a powerful magnet, and while in that position hardened by hammering, twisting, or other means, it remains more or less saturated with magnetic fluid.

525. The most powerful means, however, of magnetizing a

FORMATION OF ARTIFICIAL MAGNETS. 203

steel bar, is by placing it within the coils of an electro-magnetic spiral, as in Fig. 58. If the helix is direct (see Art. 555), the north pole of the magnet is next the zinc plate, but with a left handed helix the north pole is next the copper plate. With a spiral of sufficient magnitude, any steel bar may at once be magnetized to saturation. A bar of the horse-shoe form may be magnetized by winding copper wire about it from end to end, and then connecting the extremities of the wire with the zinc and copper plates of a voltaic battery.

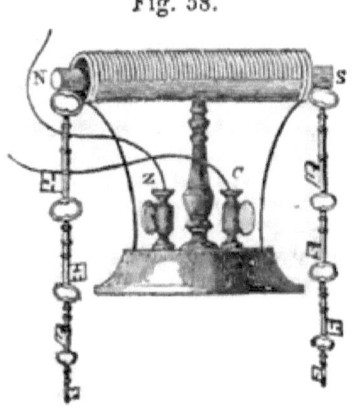

Fig. 58.

NOTE.—When a steel bar is brought to the tempering heat and then placed in an electro-magnetic helix connected with a voltaic battery, and after remaining within the spiral for a few moments, plunged into cold water, or, brine, or oil, or better still a cold solution of yellow prussiate of potassa, it becomes permanently and very powerfully magnetic.

526. The circumstances affecting the value of magnets are chiefly the following, viz:

    I. The mode of keeping;
    II. The form and proportion of its parts; and
    III. The nature and hardness of the steel composing it.

527. To preserve the power of a magnet (horse-shoe) it is essential that it should be suspended, having an armature or bar of soft iron connecting its poles and attached to a weight nearly or quite as great as the magnet can sustain. Thus kept, the magnet gains power, but if left unarmed its magnetism is rapidly dissipated.

Bar magnets should be arranged in pairs parallel to one another and with reversed poles, and having their extremities connected by means of armatures or transverse bars of soft iron.

528. The dimension of a bar magnet should be in the proportion of about 60, 3, and 1, i. e., its width should be three times its

thickness, and its length about twenty times its width. In a horse-shoe magnet the distance between the poles should not be greater than the width of one of the poles, the faces should be smooth and even, and the whole surface highly polished.

NOTE 1.—If a magnet is loaded with the full weight it is able to support, and the weight is suddenly broken off, it will be found that the power of the magnet is very much impaired. On the other hand the power of a magnet may be very much increased by loading it with a small weight and gradually increasing the load.

NOTE 2.—The power of a compound magnet is less than the sum of the powers of its separate bars. Assuming that each of the bars that compose the compound magnet is magnetized to saturation, and that each bar is then able to sustain a weight represented by 82, then, according to Coulomb:

The power of a single bar is equal to 82
"   two bars combined 125
"   four "   "   150
"   six   "   "   172
"   eight "   "   182

NOTE 3.—The power of a magnet is lost or destroyed by allowing it to remain a length of time without its keeper, by allowing it to fall, or giving it any sudden jar or check, by heating it much above the ordinary temperature, by suddenly wrenching the keeper or its load from it, &c.

LECTURE XXXVIII.

TERRESTRIAL MAGNETISM.

DEFINITIONS, VARIATIONS, DIP OF THE NEEDLE, &c.

DEFINITIONS.

529. A magnetic needle suspended so as to move in a horizontal plane is called the *horizontal needle*. The *plane of the magnetic meridian* is a plane perpendicular to the horizon, and passing through the north and south poles of the magnetic needle while in its directive position. The *direction of the magnetic meridian* is a straight line passing through the poles of the suspended needle. The *declination or variation of the magnet* is the angle made between the magnetic meridian and the geographical meridian of the place in which the magnetic needle is suspended.

Note.—The horizontal needle is loaded at one extremity so as to overcome, in a measure, its tendency to dip or incline towards the north or south pole.

530. The horizontal needle does not point towards the north pole except at isolated localities on the earth's surface. At all other places it is directed to a point more or less east or west of the true north, and at each place the amount of this declination varies from time to time.

VARIATION.

531. At each place the declination undergoes periodic changes depending on the hour of the day, and called *diurnal variations*, by which it increases from its minimum to its maximum value, and returns to its minimum again in the course of 24 hours, thus oscillating about a certain middle value called the *mean declination of the day*. At Toronto the hours at which the needle occupies its extreme and mean positions are not exactly the same throughout the year, but taking one month with another, it is at its most easterly limit about 8 A.M., it passes through its mean between 10 A.M. and 11 A.M., reaches its westerly limit about 1 P.M., returns again to its mean position about 10 P.M., and attains its most easterly limit as before at 8 A.M.

532. The *amplitude* of the diurnal variations or the angle between the greatest eastern and western positions of the needle in the course of the day is about 10′ on the average of the year, but it is not the same in all the months, being more than 12′ on the average of the six months from April to September inclusive, and less than 7′ on the average for the rest of the year.

533. The declination proper to any hour, as well as the daily mean declination, undergoes periodic changes depending on the time of year, and called *annual variations*, and it oscillates in the twelve months about a certain middle value called the *mean declination of the year* relative to each hour and to the mean of all hours.

534. At Toronto the months in which the needle occupies its extreme positions are not the same for all hours, but taking one hour with another it is in its most easterly position in January, and in its most westerly position in September.

535. The *amplitude* of the annual variations on the average of all hours is small, amounting to less than 3'. It is generally greater for the hours of the day and less for those of the night, being about 6' for 2 P.M., and less than 2' for 1 A.M.

The mean annual declination is not the same in consecutive years, but undergoes changes from year to year, called *secular variations*.

536. At Toronto the mean declination increased from 1° 29' W. in 1845 to 1° 41' W. in 1851. The westerly movement has been subsequently more rapid, the mean value of the declination being at present (1861) about 2° 20' W.

NOTE.—The amount of this secular variation and its gradual change in direction may be seen by the following table of its amount in London between the years 1580 and 1850. The *plus* sign indicates western declination, and the *minus* sign eastern.

Years,	1580.	1622.	1660.	1692.	1730.	1765.	1818.	1850.
Declination,	−11°15'	−6°	0	+6°	+13°	+20°	+24°11'	+22°30
Rate per year,	7'	8'	10'	11'	11'	9'	6'	5'

It will be observed that the yearly increase or decrease differs—being greatest near the minimum of variation.

At Washington the variation was +0·6° in 1800 and had increased to +2·9° in 1860. At Burlington, Vermont, the variation was +7·8° in 1790, +8°30 in 1830, +9°7 in 1840, and +10°30 in 1860.

537. As regards other parts of Canada while the periodic variations are in their general character approximately the same probably as at Toronto, the mean value about which the periodic oscillation takes place, differs much in different parts of the Province. Lines of equal declination, i. e. lines through places having the same mean annual declination, are inclined at an angle of about 30° to the west of north, this inclination being greater on the lines that are situated more and more to the eastward. On proceeding eastward the declination becomes more and more westerly.

538. As before remarked there are certain places on the earth's surface where there is no variation. These places are connected to one another by two lines called *Agones* or *lines of no variation*, and distinguished as the eastern and western agones. The western agone commences in Hudson's Bay, lat. 60°, runs through Lake Erie about its centre, thence in a southerly direction through Virginia, the Great Antilles, touches Cape St. Roque, and cuts the meridian of Greenwich at lat. 65° S. The principal eastern agone (for there are two) begins in the White Sea and descending in a great semicircle, southward and eastward, to the Sea of Japan; it then goes westward and southward through China, and India, to Bombay; thence southward and eastward to the northern coast of Australia; and thence directly southward along the meridian 130° E. of Greenwich.

NOTE.—These lines and the isogonal lines seem to indicate the existence of two north and two south magnetic poles of the earth. Hansteen has concluded, from a great number of observations made at long intervals and at places widely separated, that these poles have a regular revolution around the earth, the two northern ones from west to east in an oblique direction, and the two southern ones from east to west—their periods of revolution being as follows:

>The strongest north pole, 1740 years.
>The strongest south pole, 4609 years.
>The weakest north pole, 860 years.
>The weakest south pole, 1304 years.

Hansteen has also pointed out a curious connection between these periods and the precession of the equinoxes. The shortest time in which all the four poles can accomplish a cycle and return to the same state as at present coincides exactly with the period in which the precession of the equinoxes amounts to a complete circle at the rate of 1° in 72 years.

539. The more recent hypothesis with regard to the magnetism of the earth, assumes that the crust or surface, and not the interior of the earth, is the seat of magnetic force. The surface of the earth being magnetized, the two fluids are separated, and this separation, though not regular or equal in all latitudes, is most complete at the poles, and least so at the equator. It supposes that this inequality in the degree of separation is due to the difference of temperature, which regulates the coercitive force of the materials of the earth's crust. This view regards the daily and annual variations of temperature and declination as cause and effect, and accounts for the very close relation between the isoclinal lines, and the isothermal lines or lines of equal temperature.

540. ISOGONAL LINES, or lines of equal variation, are lines joining those places on the earth's surface where the declination of the magnetic needle is equal in amount and direction. The

isogonal lines do not by any means coincide with either the meridians or the parallels of latitude, but run in an irregular manner—often crossing one another.

541. Irregular Variations in the magnetic needle are produced by magnetic storms which are simultaneously observed by means of the needle in widely separated countries. They are supposed to be produced by auroras and other natural electrical phenomena.

MAGNETIC DIP.

542. If a bar of non-magnetized steel or iron be carefully balanced by its centre it remains horizontal and takes any direction indifferently. Now, if the bar be magnetized, it points towards the north and is no longer horizontal, but one end *dips* or inclines towards the earth.

543. The dip of the Needle, or, as it is termed, its *inclination*, is greatest near the poles and decreases towards the equator; but the magnetic equator or line of no inclination does not exactly coincide with the terrestrial equator. Of course in the northern magnetic hemisphere the north **pole dips, and in** the southern, the south pole.

544. Isoclinal Lines, or lines of equal inclination, are those that join such places on the earth's surface as exhibit the same degree dip. Of these the most prominent is the magnetic equator, which in one place departs from the terrestrial equator as much as 20° N., and in another as much as 13° S. Isoclinal lines very nearly, if they do not exactly, coincide with the isothermal lines.

545. Isodynamic Lines, or lines of equal power, are lines joining those localities in which the needle *oscillates* with equal energy. They are very nearly coincident with the isoclinal lines.

ELECTRO-MAGNETISM.

LECTURE XXXIX.

ELECTRO-MAGNETS, GALVANOMETERS, ELECTRO-DYNAMIC HELLICES, ELECTRIC TELEGRAPH.

ELECTRO-MAGNETISM.

546. ELECTRO-MAGNETISM is that branch of electrical science which treats of the magnetism produced in dia-magnetic bodies during the passage of a current of **electricity** through them.

547. When a magnetic needle, having freedom of motion around its centre, is brought near a wire of copper, **or** other conducting medium through which a current of electricity is flowing, it is instantly deflected and places itself at right angles to the conducting wire, or *conjunctive wire* as it is called. From this it appears that **the** conjunctive wire becomes itself a magnet, or rather an infinite number of small magnets arranged transversely to the course of the wire, while the current **is passing along it.**

NOTE.—Iron filings adhere to the conjunctive wire while the **current is** traversing it.

548. If a current of positive electricity is transmitted from south **to north through** a conducting wire arranged horizontally in the **magnetic meridian, then a** free magnetic needle would have its **north end deflected to the** *west* **when it is** placed *below* the conjunctive wire, and **to the** *east* when it is placed *above* the wire; **the north** end is *depressed* when the needle is placed on the *west* **side, and** *points upward* when it is on the *east* side. If the current is sent along the **wire from** north to south all these **movements are reversed.**

NOTE.—In order to impress on the memory the direction in which the needle is thus deflected by the conjunctive wire, the following formula has been devised by Ampère:

Let any one identify himself with the current or suppose himself to be lying in the direction of the positive current so that it enters his feet and passes **out** *through* **his head.** *Then, his face being turned to the needle, the north pole of the latter is always deflected to the right hand.*

GALVANOMETERS.

549. The Galvanometer is an instrument used for measuring the intensity of the electric current. It was constructed by Schweigger, and depends in its action upon the deviation of a magnetic needle across the line of the electric current.

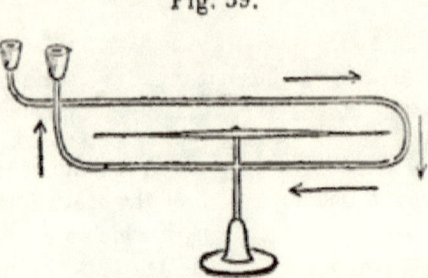

Fig. 59.

The principle on which the galvanometer acts may be understood by a reference to the accompanying figure, in which the conjunctive wire is bent in the form of a rectangle within which the needle is supported on a pivot. The current circulating through the wire in the direction of the arrows, all parts of the wire tend to increase the deflection of the wire in the same direction: and the amount of that deflection depends upon the intensity of the current, being very small for weak currents and approaching 90° for very strong ones.

550. In galvanometers employed in very delicate investigations two improvements are made on the form represented in Fig. 59. The first consists in causing the conjunctive wire instead of making only one convolution or turn, to bend several hundred times on itself so that the current may act again and again on the needle and render a very feeble force perceptible; the second consists in using the so called *astatic needle* in place of a simple needle.

551. The astatic needle is made by fixing two magnetic needles of equal power parallel to one another on the same axis, with their poles reversed. The effect of the arrangement is to neutralize the directive power of the earth, which, in the case of a simple needle, interferes with the indications of the galvanometer, since it acts in opposition to the deflecting power of the current. In the astatic galvanometer one of the needles is placed within the rectangle and the other above it, so that they are both moved in the same direction by the current which circulates through the conjunctive wire.

Fig. 60.

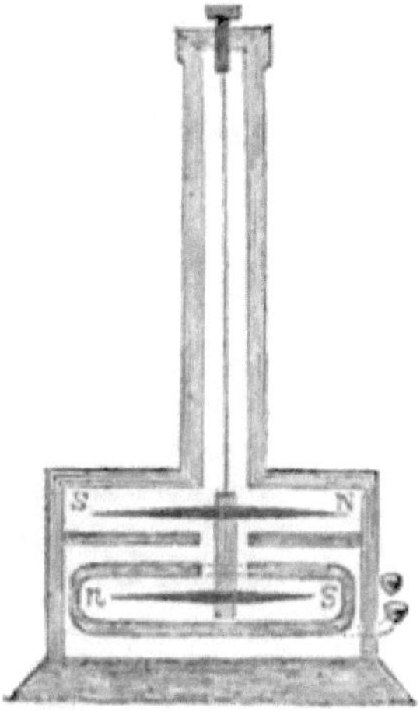

This arrangement will become clear by a reference to Fig. 60, which represents the form of the *astatic galvanometer* in common use. The astatic needle is suspended, it will be observed, by a fine thread, so as to have perfect freedom of motion.

552. When electric currents flow in two parallel wires which have freedom of motion, the wires are attracted or repelled according to the following law:

Parallel currents repel one another when their directions are opposite, but attract one another when they are both moving in the same direction.

553. A conjunctive wire may be made in all respects to simulate a magnet. We have seen that it possesses the power of attraction and repulsion, and we have now to remark that it possesses polarity and the power of induction.

554. If a conjunctive wire be coiled into a spiral form, and its ends carried back through its axis as shown in Fig. 61, it constitutes what is called an *electro-dynamic helix*. Now if this be suspended so as to move freely, horizontally, or vertically, it acts precisely as a magnetized needle, i. e., it points north and south, and exhibits the magnetic dip. Of course it does this only while the electric current is passing along it.

Fig. 61.

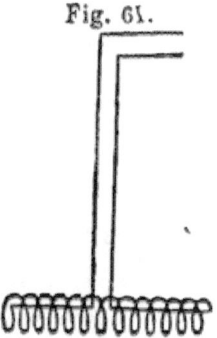

555. It has been already stated that when a copper wire, insulated by being covered with silk, is coiled into a helix and a current of electricity sent through it, a bar of iron placed within the helix becomes powerfully magnetized. This magnetism is *induced* in the bar of iron or steel, by the circular and parallel currents which pass along the several volutes of the

helix, and is temporary in the case of soft iron, but permanent in the case of steel.

If the conjunctive wire which constitutes the helix is coiled to the right, as in a common cork-screw, it forms what is called a *right-handed helix*, and if in the reverse direction, a *left-handed helix*. In a right-handed helix, the north pole of the bar is that towards the zinc plate of the battery, in a left-handed helix that towards the copper plate.

Faraday has given the following rule to enable the student to understand the polarity of the helix. " *Imagine that you are looking down upon the dipping needle or the north magnetic pole of the earth, and think upon the direction in which the hands of a watch move, or of the motion of a direct screw, then currents in that direction would produce such a magnet as the dipping needle.*"

556. Electro-magnets are masses of soft iron wound with coils of closely packed insulated copper wire, the size and length of which varies according to the power required in the electro-magnet. They have been constructed capable of raising several tons, and from their enormous power and the complete and instantaneous paralysis and reversal of that power by reversing the poles of the battery, it has by many been thought possible to apply them economically to the working of machinery.

NOTE.—From a series of experiments made by Hunt, with respect to the applicability of electro-magnetism as a motive power, it appears that:

A grain of coals burnt beneath the boiler of a Cornish engine, lifted .... 143 lbs. 1 foot high.
A grain of zinc consumed in a battery to move an electro-magnetic engine, lifted but .... 80 lbs. 1 foot high.
A cwt. of coal cost .... 9d.
A cwt. of zinc cost .... 216d.

Hence to do an equal amount of work, the electro-magnetic engine is more expensive than the steam engine in the proportion of 50 to 1.

ELECTRIC TELEGRAPH.

557. Of all the practical applications of electro-magnetism, by far the most important is the electric telegraph. All the varieties of electro-telegraphic communications may be reduced to one or other of two methods, viz: the *electro-mechanical* and the *electro-chemical*.

558. Electro-mechanical telegraphic apparatus includes:

I. THE NEEDLE TELEGRAPH, as that of Wheatstone and Cooke, in which the message is indicated by the deflections of a needle by a galvanometer coil.

II. THE DIAL TELEGRAPH, of which that of Ronald's is the type. This was worked by having the letters of the alphabet painted on the circumference of a disk or dial which revolved by clock-work. One of these was at each station, and before it a delicate electrometer was placed, the apparatus being worked by statical electricity. Upon the explosion of some gas, by a preconcerted arrangement, the clocks were started at the same letter, and each time the transmitting operator closed the circuit, the electrometer at the distant station became instantly disturbed, the receiving operator noted the letter then visible, and thus the message was spelled off.

NOTE.—The chief objection to *needle* and *dial* telegraphs is that two operators are required, and that they do not record more than ten or twelve words per minute.

III. ELECTRO-MAGNETIC OR RECORDING TELEGRAPHS, such as that of Morse, in which the message is recorded in cipher; and that of House, in which the message is printed in common characters. The essential parts of these telegraphs are a battery at the transmitting station, to generate power, an insulated wire to convey it to the receiving station, and a recording instrument at the latter to register the indications of that power.

The recording instrument of Morse is represented in Fig. 62.

M, m are the poles of a horse-shoe magnet, wound round with wire; at *a* is a keeper fastened to a lever, *a l*, which works on a fulcrum, at *d*; the other end of the lever bears a steel point, *s*, which serves as a pen. At *c* is a clock work arrangement for the purpose of drawing a narrow strip of paper, *p p*, in the direction of the arrows. W W are the wires which communicate with the distant station. As soon as a voltaic current is made to pass through these wires, the soft iron becomes magnetic and draws the keeper

ELECTRIC TELEGRAPH.

Fig. 62.

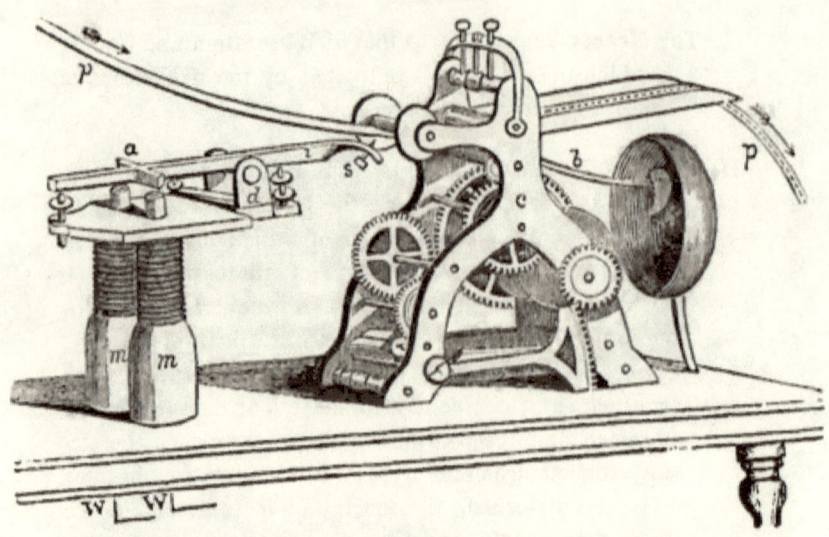

a, to its poles; and the other end of the lever, l, rising up, the point s is pressed against the moving paper and makes a mark. When the lever first moves it sets the clock machinery in motion, and the bell, b, rings to give notice to the observer. The movements of the lever $a\,l$ are the exact repetitions of those made by the transmitting operator on the lever of a finger board at the remote end of the circuit. When the distant operator stops the current, the magnetism of $m\,m$ ceases, and the keeper a the magnet for a short or a longer time a dot or a line is made upon the paper—and all the letters of the alphabet are represented by a combination of these dots and lines. Only one wire is employed, the circuit being completed by the earth.

NOTE.—The following is the alphabet used by Morse.

```
A - --        O - -         1 - -- -- --
B -- - - -    P - -- -- -   2 - - -- - -
C - - -       Q -- -- - --  3 - - - -- --
D -- - -      R - - -       4 - - - - --
E -           S - - -        5 -- -- --
F - -- -      T --           6 - - - - - -
G -- -- -     U - - --       7 -- -- - -
H - - - -     V - - - --     8 -- - - - -
I - -         W - -- --      9 - - - --
J - -- -- -   X - -- - -     0 ⌒
K - -- -      Y - - - -
L ——          Z -- - - -
M -- --       & - - -- -
N -- -
```

559. ELECTRO-CHEMICAL TELEGRAPHS depend upon the production of visible and permanent marks or characters by electro-chemical decompositions. In the best form a paper ribbon, saturated in ferrocyanide of potassium or other salt of iron, is carried by a clock-work movement, similar to that of Morse, over a cylinder of metal which constitutes one pole of the circuit. The other pole terminates in a steel or copper pen which is in contact with the paper. The least passage of electricity produces a stain on the moistened paper, which is red if the pen is copper, and blue if the pen is steel.

MAGNETO-ELECTRICITY.

LECTURE XL.

MAGNETO-ELECTRICITY, THERMO-ELECTRICITY, ANIMAL ELECTRICITY.

MAGNETO-ELECTRICITY.

560. When a current of electricity is transmitted through the wire of a helix it induces magnetism in a bar of iron or steel placed within it. Now the converse of this is equally true; when a permanent magnet is alternately thrust into and removed from a helix, it induces currents of electricity in the wire composing the latter, as is easily evidenced by connection with a galvanometer. The peculiarity of these currents is their momentary duration, and hence their name *momentary currents*, or, from their discoverer, *Faradian-currents*.

561. THE MAGNETO-ELECTRIC MACHINE, Fig. 63, is an instrument by means of which magneto-electricity, induced in the manner alluded to, may be obtained in sufficient intensity and quantity to decompose acidulated water, give powerful physiological shocks, and exhibit the electric spark and other effects of ordinary electricity. It consists of two horse-shoe magnets, $C\ D$, placed one over the other, with an armature on which a double inducing coil is wound. This is made to revolve between the poles of the magnets by means of the multiplying wheel W. The two ends

of the copper wire forming the coils are soldered to a ferrule or break-piece on each side of the axis, and against this two metallic springs press, having also a metallic connection with the two cups a, b. As the armature revolves, the iron centre-pieces

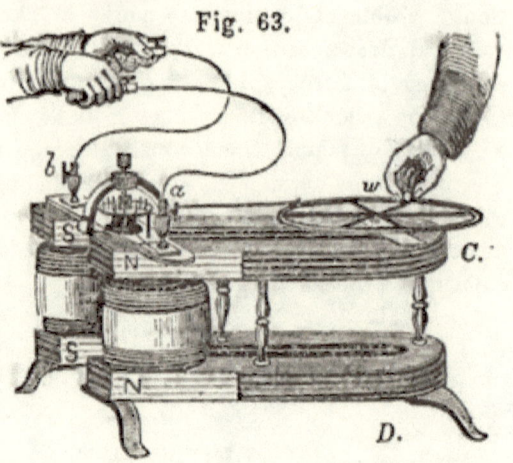

Fig. 63.

are brought between the poles of the horse-shoe magnets, and are rendered magnetic by induction; and this polarity is alternately made, annihilated, reversed, and so on. At each change of polarity a current of electricity is induced in the wire, and flows through it to the cups in a continuous stream, if the wheel revolves with sufficient rapidity.

The physiological effects are experienced, and the spark seen, only when the current is interrupted. In order to break the current, an elastic steel spring, connected with one of the cups, a or b, presses against the pins of a little crown wheel attached to the axis. When the spring presses against the pin the circuit is closed, and the current is unbroken; but while it passes from one pin to another the current is broken, and a secondary current of still greater power induced.

562. The production of induced currents is not exclusively confined to magnetic agency. A current of voltaic electricity from any source whatever, while flowing through a coil of insulated wire, induces a secondary current in a contiguous coil. The most powerful of all artificial means of producing electricity of high tension (*the induction coil*), depends in its action upon the secondary current induced in a very long insulated wire (60,000 or 70,000 feet), by which means voltaic electricity is

THERMO-ELECTRICITY.

563. If a bar of bismuth and one of antimony be soldered together, as in Fig. 64, and a weak current of electricity transmitted through the arrangement from the antimony to the bismuth, the temperature of the junction c will be raised considerably; but if the current be sent from the bismuth to the antimony, the temperature of the junction c is so much lowered that a small quantity of water, placed there, may be frozen.

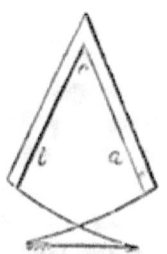

Fig. 64.

Now if, in place of transmitting a current of electricity through the combination, we change the temperature of the part where the bars are soldered together, we shall by that means produce a current of electricity, which flows from the antimony to the bismuth, if we cool the junction, but from the bismuth to the antimony, if we heat it. These currents are termed *thermo-electric* currents.

NOTE 1.—Thermo-electric currents are exceedingly weak, probably owing to their originating in good conductors. The thinnest film of oxide is sufficient to prevent the passage of the current into a wire.

NOTE 2.—Melloni's thermo-multiplier consists of a number of bars of bismuth and antimony soldered together at their alternate ends, and having the opposite members connected, by means of wires, to a galvanometer. The least difference of temperature between the opposite faces of the arrangement produces a thermo-electric current which deflects the needle of the galvanometer.

NOTE 3.—Although bismuth and antimony are the metals employed in thermo-electric batteries, other metals and even non-metallic bodies may be substituted. In the following list the combination of the metals at the two extremes produces the most powerful thermo-electrical arrangement —the effects of the intermediate metals diminishing as they approach.

1. Galena.	5. Manganese.	9. Gold.	13. Iron.
2. Bismuth.	6. Tin.	10. Copper.	14. Arsenic.
3. Mercury.	7. Lead.	11. Silver.	15. Antimony.
4. Platinum.	8. Brass.	12. Zinc.	

ANIMAL ELECTRICITY.

564. It has been shown by Matteucci, of Pisa, that electricity is, in some mysterious manner, intimately connected with vital power. He has demonstrated that a current of positive electricity is always flowing from the interior to the exterior of a muscle. By using delicate galvanometers, Du Bois Raymond, of Vienna, has proved the existence of electric currents in his own person.

NOTE.—The irritable muscles of the frog's leg form an electroscope about 60,000 times more sensitive than the most delicate gold-leaf electroscope.

565. Certain marine and fresh-water fish (about eight genera) possess a special apparatus by means of which they can produce, at pleasure, powerful discharges of statical electricity. This power is doubtless designed either as a means of defence or for the purpose of securing their prey. The special apparatus consists of an alternate arrangement of cellular tissue and nervous matter, the latter being contained in hexagonal cells, and the whole constituting a perpetually charged electric battery, which is discharged, and a violent shock produced, by touching the opposite extremities of the animal. The most remarkable of these electrical animals are:

I. The Gymnotus, or Electric Eel of Surinam; and
II. The Torpedo, or Cramp-Fish of the North American coast.

NOTE.—The shock received from an electric eel is sufficient to disable a man or even a horse. Faraday has estimated the discharge to be equal to that from a fully charged Leyden battery of 15 jars containing a coated surface of 3500 square inches. The same philosopher succeeded in deflecting the galvanometer, evolving light and heat, magnetising steel bars and effecting chemical decompositions by the electricity obtained from the gymnotus.

MISCELLANEOUS PROBLEMS.

1. How many degrees Reaumur are equivalent to $14.6°$ F.? How many F. are equivalent to $- 6.8°$ C.?

2. What time is required for light to come from the moon to the earth, the distance being 240000 miles?

3. How many images will be seen in a kaleidoscope when the two mirrors forming it are placed at an angle of $18°$?

MISCELLANEOUS PROBLEMS.

4. Two similar balls are charged with electricity, and it is found that one repels the needle of Coulomb's torsion electrometer through 30°, while the other repels it through 70°. Compare the intensity of the charges.

5. A concave mirror collects the rays of solar light to a focus 8 inches in front of it. What will be the distance of the image cast by an object 12 feet before the mirror?

6. The north star is estimated to be 281295000000000 miles from the earth—suppose that by the fiat of Omnipotence it were destroyed, what length of time would elapse after its annihilation before we should lose sight of it?—in other words, how long would the last rays that leave it occupy in reaching our earth?

7. If 10 lbs. of lead at the temperature 490° F. melt $1\frac{3}{4}$ lbs. of ice; what is the specific heat of the lead?

8. A railroad is constructed in winter when the average temperature is 30° F.—how far apart must the ends of the iron rails be laid in order to allow sufficient room for expansion at the temperature of 110° F., assuming each rail to be 20 feet long?

9. The speculum of a Gregorian telescope is 30 inches in diameter, taking the diameter of the pupil of the eye as $\frac{1}{4}$ of an inch; compare the relative amounts of light received by each.

10. An incipient red heat is equal to 977° F., a cherry-red heat 1832° F., and a dazzling white heat 9732° F. Express these temperatures in degrees Reaumur and degrees Centigrade.

11. What temperature will be produced by mixing together equal weights of water at 212° F., and mercury at 32° F.? What temperature, by mixing equal volumes of mercury at 212° F., and of water at 32° F.?

12. Calculate the illuminating powers of Herschel's great telescope and also of Rosse's telescope—assuming in each case that $\frac{8}{9}$ of the incident light is reflected by the speculum.

13. Allowing gases to decrease in volume $\frac{1}{491}$ of their bulk at 32° F. for every degree their temperature is lowered—at what temperature would all gases cease to exist, and hence what may we regard as the absolute zero?

14. To what height above the centre of the roof should a single lightning-rod extend in order to protect the whole building—taking its dimensions as 40 feet by 30 feet?

15. How many units of heat are absorbed by 11 lbs. of tin in passing from the solid to the liquid form—the unit of heat being the amount of heat required to raise 1 lb. of water from $32°$ F. to $33°$ F.?

16. The radius of a concave reflector is 9 inches, the focus of incident rays 24 inches—what is the focus for reflected rays?

17. An object 7 inches in diameter, is placed 40 inches before a convex mirror, whose radius of curvature is 60 inches—the upper edge of the object being in the principal axis of the mirror, determine the position, distance, and size of the image.

18. The temperature of a common fire is equal to $616.1°$ C., of human blood $36\frac{2}{3}°$ C., and the estimated temperature of planetary space is $50°$ C. Express these temperatures in degrees F. and R.

19. The greatest degree of cold ever measured, is, according to Faraday, $88°$ R., and according to Natterer $112°$ R. Reduce these temperatures to degrees F. and C.

20. How must an object be placed before a double equi-convex lens so that the image shall be double the size of the object, and erect?

21. Equal weights of water at $32°$ F. and ice at $32°$ F. are mixed together. What is the resulting temperature? What is the temperature produced by placing together equal parts of boiling water and melting mercury?

22. What is the focal length, for solar rays, of a meniscus whose radii are 19 and 21 inches?

23. What is the focal length of a double convex lens whose radii of curvature are 11 and 7 inches, for rays of light emanating from a point 30 inches before the lens?

24. In order to determine the melting point of lead, 100 ounces of the melted metal were poured into 900 ounces of water at $27°$ R., and the resulting temperature was $20.7°$ C. Required the heat of fusion of lead in degrees F.

MISCELLANEOUS PROBLEMS.

25. What are the linear and superficial magnifying powers of a convex lens whose focal length is $\frac{2}{3}$ of an inch—taking the limit of distinct vision as 6 inches? What taking the limit of distinct vision as 8 inches or 4 inches?

26. How long would electricity, light, and sound respectively require to travel from the sun to the earth?

27. Compare together the retarding powers of two copper wires for a current of electricity—one being 100 feet in length, and $\frac{1}{100}$ of an inch in diameter, the other 250 feet in length and $\frac{1}{250}$ of an inch in diameter.

28. In a magic lantern the object has a diameter of 2 inches and is placed 2 inches behind the magnifying lens, the screen being 10 feet before the same lens. What is the diameter of the image?

29. The eye-piece of a microscope has a focal length of $\frac{2}{3}$ of an inch—the object being placed $\frac{2}{3}$ of an inch from the objective, and the distance between the latter and the focus of the eye-glass being 12 inches—what are the linear and superficial magnifying powers of the instrument to a person whose limit of distinct vision is $4\frac{1}{2}$ inches? What to a person whose limit of distinct vision is 9 inches?

30. How much latent heat is there in the vapour of water at the temperature of 350° F? How much at the temperature of 96° F.? How much at 200° C.?

31. The mean annual temperature of Canada is about 44° F. At what depths beneath the surface of the earth would the thermometer severally indicate a temperature of 70° F.; of 100° F.; of 212° F.; of 400° F.?

32. Two lights are compared with one another in Ritchie's Photometer, and it is found that in order to equally illuminate the different sides of the wedge one has to be placed at the distance of 6 inches, and the other at the distance of 10 inches. What are their comparative illuminating powers?

33. Compare together the brightness of the picture cast by a magic lantern on a screen at the several distances of 4 feet, 7 feet, and 12 feet, from the magnifying lens?

MISCELLANEOUS PROBLEMS.

34. In a refracting telescope the focal length of the object glass is 100 feet, the focal length of the eye-piece is 10 inches, the object glass has a diameter of 4 inches, and the total number of lenses employed is four—assuming the pupil of the eye to be $\frac{1}{10}$ of an inch in diameter—what is the magnifying power, the illuminating power, the penetrating power, and the visual power of the instrument?

35. What are the illuminating and penetrating powers of a night-glass having a convex lens of 12 inches in diameter—the pupil of the eye being $\frac{1}{5}$ of an inch in diameter?

36. A Pouillet's pyrometer holds 20 cubic inches of air at 32° F., and it was placed in a furnace, by which means $\frac{7}{10}$ of the air is expelled. Express in degrees F., C., and R. the temperature to which it was exposed.

37. In a refracting telescope the object glass is 11 inches in diameter and has a focal length of 200 feet, the eye glass has a focal length of 4 inches, the whole number of lenses through which the light has to pass before entering the eye, is five. Required the penetrating, illuminating, visual, and magnifying powers of the instrument.

38. A mass of platinum weighing 5 lbs. is exposed to the full heat of a furnace, and then plunged into 13 lbs. of water of the temperature of 65° F., when it is observed that the temperature of the water is raised to 65° R. Required the temperature of the furnace in degrees F. and C.

39. How many units of heat are absorbed by 17 lbs. of sulphur in passing from the solid to the liquid state? (See Problem 15).

40. A dealer purchases 1000 gallons of alcohol in mid-winter, how much may he expect it to measure in mid-summer, the temperature of the former being 40° F., and of the latter 80° F.?

THE END OF PART II.

www.ingramcontent.com/pod-product-compliance
Lightning Source LLC
Chambersburg PA
CBHW021835230426
43669CB00008B/977